JEWISH BEDTIME STORIES & SONGS FOR FAMILIES

www.pjlibrary.org

GETTING OUR GR∞VE BACK

How to Energize American Jewry

Scott A. Shay

DEVORA
PUBLISHING
JERUSALEM ◆ NEW YORK

Getting Our Groove Back – How to Energize American Jewry
Published by Devora Publishing Company
Text Copyright © 2007 by Scott Shay

COVER DESIGN: David Yaphe
TYPESETTING: Jerusalem Typesetting
EDITOR: Ari Goldman

Hard Cover ISBN: 1-932687-85-8

E-mail: publisher@devorapublishing.com
Web Site: www.devorapublishing.com

Extraordinary Reviews

GETTING OUR GROOVE BACK
How to Energize American Jewry

It has been said that the only way to make a dream come true is to wake up. Scott Shay offers a wake-up call to the Jewish community, but goes beyond. In this remarkable work, the author concretizes the thinking of much of today's Jewish leadership. While many either focus on the diagnosis of Jewry's ills, or offer partial prescriptions to address partial cures, Shay takes a global approach to diagnosis and prescription. While one can differ with particular planks in his platform, his serious contribution is to teach us that the House of Israel cannot be rebuilt piecemeal, but commands total architecture.

Both his descriptions and his solutions are thoughtful, some more controversial than others, but, at the very least, frame an important conversation.

RICHARD M. JOEL
President, Yeshiva University

Scott Shay offers a refreshingly candid discussion of major challenges facing American Jewry coupled with a bold, if controversial, set of prescriptions.

His unconventional book is sure to arouse much needed debate. There is plenty here to provoke all kinds of American Jews – and maybe energize them too.

JACK WERTHEIMER
Provost and Professor of American Jewish History
at the Jewish Theological Seminary

In *Getting Our Groove Back: How to Energize American Jewry*, Scott Shay has written a remarkably comprehensive portrait of the state of American Judaism and Jews, and has defined the overarching challenges that confront the American Jewish community today while at the same time delineating practical programs of action designed to meet those challenges. He has done so with intelligence and passion in a captivating and engaging style. Anyone – lay or professional – concerned with the future of Judaism and Jews in the United States will profit greatly from this provocative and sensible book.

RABBI DAVID ELLENSON
President, Hebrew Union College-Jewish Institute of Religion

*This book is dedicated
to my wife*

SUSAN

and our wonderful children

BENJAMIN

ARIEL

ALISON

&

ABIGAIL

Contents

INTRODUCTION 1

CHAPTER I
The Physics of the Jewish Future 11

CHAPTER II
The Demographic Decline of American Jewry Today 31

CHAPTER III
Hebrew School and More 49

CHAPTER IV
Day Schools for More Jews 67

CHAPTER V
Israel Trips for all American Jews 87

CHAPTER VI
Three Needs to be the New Two 101

CHAPTER VII
Funding the Platform 121

CHAPTER VIII
Intermarriage and Patrilineal Descent 145

CHAPTER IX
A New American Minhag to Promote
Jewish Identity and Learning 165

CHAPTER X
Reimagining the Conservative Movement 185

CHAPTER XI
Combating External Threats   205

CHAPTER XII
Social Action, Ethical Behavior and Tzedakah   229

CHAPTER XIII
The "To Do List" for American Jewry   255

CHAPTER XIV
Putting it All Together – A Theory of Everything   267

CHAPTER XV
The Future Can Be Bright   273

ACKNOWLEDGMENTS   279

BIBLIOGRAPHY   283

INDEX   301

Introduction

American Jewry is facing its most significant crisis in the 350 years since the first Jews arrived in New Amsterdam. The crisis is community-wide and is caused by failures at the movement, congregational, institutional, family and individual levels and is therefore relentlessly progressive. Initiatives to correct these problems piecemeal are doomed to failure. What is needed is a comprehensible community-wide solution. This book presents a comprehensive, positive, practical and self-reinforcing platform to revitalize American Jewry as a leading force for good in America and the world.

The most visible symptom of the crisis in American Jewry today is its current demographic decline. The number of Americans who identify as Jews has already dropped significantly. In 1980 there were 5.9 million American Jews, today; there are a reported 5.2 million, a loss of *700,000* Jews. Yet, only 2.6 million of today's 5.2 million American Jews are even somewhat committed to their Jewish identities, and at least 1 million non-committed Jews are on the permanent exit lane from the Jewish people.[1] If current demographic trends continue, the American Jewish population will drop to as low as 2.5 million in 2030. In other words,

1

we will have lost more than 3 million American Jews in 50 years and within the lifetime of most people reading this book. If we don't take action, American Jewry will lose its critical mass and its numbers will decline irreversibly. As dark as this assessment might appear, other once-proud Jewish communities, unaffected by anti-Semitism, entered an irreversible spiral of decline as a result of community-wide forces which led to a loss of critical mass. Two examples are presented in Chapter 11, namely, the Jewish communities of India and China. If we do not take drastic action to maintain our current population, American Jewry will soon lack the critical mass to have a substantial impact on American society, which would undermine Judaism's fundamental purpose of positively impacting humanity.

Part of the danger of the current demographic decline of American Jewry is its silent nature. Few American Jews are fully aware of the extent of our demographic decline and many continue to hold common misconceptions about American Jewry. Some readers probably still believe that there are more Jews in America than there are in Israel, however, this is no longer the case. In 2006, the number of Jews in Israel exceeds the number in America and there will likely be far fewer American Jews than Israelis in the next 25 years if American Jewry does not renew itself.

The principal cause of American Jewry's decline is its loss of a sense of wholeness and purpose. For a large number of American Jews, the future of American Jewry as a whole community is irrelevant. So what if the forces of assimilation, high intermarriage rates, low fertility rates and inadequate Jewish education cause the majority of American Jewry to dissolve into the American melting pot? So what if Orthodox, Conservative, Reform and secular Jews each create their own exclusive enclaves? Some Jews believe that losing uncommitted Jews simply cannot be helped and have given up trying. Others feel that every individual Jew should choose the life that best suits him or her. Some argue that although Jews have been a positive influence on the world up to now, in the modern era there is no longer a need for Jews as a distinct group. There are Jews today who question expending significant time, effort, and money to energize American Jewry.

Although innumerable Jews believe that a Jewish existence is more than justified by the desire not to hand victory to anti-Semites, this book is for those who believe in the positive reasons for renewing American Jewry. Certainly, anti-Semites from the President of Iran to rank and file members of the Aryan Nation and Islamic Jihad would be all too happy to see an end to American and world Jewry. As Emil Fackenheim famously put it, "Since Auschwitz, I will boldly term a 614th commandment: the authentic Jew of today is forbidden to hand Hitler yet another posthumous victory."[2] Unfortunately, this jarring rhetoric has proven to be insufficient. Since Fackenheim uttered his charge in the 1970s, intermarriage has more than doubled from 20% to 47% and the Jewish population has shrunk by at least 700,000 souls. We clearly cannot continue for generations simply out of spite for anti-Semites.

This book is for those people who believe in the positive reasons for renewing American Jewry. It is for those people who share the conviction that the Jewish people have a particularistic and universalistic mission that must be reconciled in order to make our contribution to the world; that the renewal of American Jewry will advance the Jewish people, America and the world; and that American Jewry possesses unprecedented wealth and opportunities to help others. Although a full exploration of the Jewish mission in the world is beyond the scope of this book, Chapters XI and XII will explore ways that American Jews can contribute to the community and society as a whole in complementary ways. Other books deal extensively with this issue.[3]

American Jewry needs to survive for its own sake. Never before has there been as wealthy a Diaspora Jewish community as in America, and not since ancient times has so much of the Jewish Diaspora been contained in one country. It is probably conservative to estimate that over 85% of the economic resources of the Jewish Diaspora are in the U.S. and that almost 70% of the Jewish population outside of Israel is in the United States.[4] Likewise, Jews in the Diaspora have never enjoyed such freedom, opportunity, influence and good relations with the surrounding society as in America today. Jews are represented in every major professional field and also hold prominent political posts at the local, state and federal level. American Jewry also has a proud 350-year history of helping to shape American society. From the American Revolution to the Civil Rights Movement, American Jews have made an important contribution to the fabric of American society. America would also be a lesser place without the contributions of Jonas Salk, Saul Bellow, Aaron Copland, Henry Kissinger, Louis Brandeis, Betty Friedan, Isaac Stern, Barbra Streisand, Steven Spielberg, Benny Goodman, Samuel Gompers, Benjamin Cardozo, Maurice Sendak, Edna Ferber, Dorothy Parker, Isaac Bashevis Singer, Bob Dylan, William Paley, George and Ira Gershwin, Richard Rodgers and Oscar Hammerstein, Paul Simon and Art Garfunkel, Ben Cohen and Jerry Greenfield, Roy Lichtenstein, Emma Lazarus, Gloria Steinem and Ruth Westheimer – and the list goes on and on. Losing American Jewry would be an unprecedented loss for the Jewish people and American society.

American Jewry must also survive for the sake of Diaspora Jewry as a whole. Indeed, many other major Diaspora communities are shrinking at an alarming rate and may already be falling below critical mass. The intermarriage rate in the former Soviet Union exceeds 80%.[5] Only 613 Jewish children were born in all of Russia in 2001.[6] Over the past fifty years, American Jews – often in partnership with Israel – have been instrumental in saving other Diaspora communities. Operation Magic Carpet (which brought the Jews from Northern Africa to Israel), Operations Moses and Solomon (which brought the Jews from Ethiopia to Israel) and Operation Exodus (which brought the great Russian aliyah) were all heavily financed by the American Jewish community. Other smaller and in some cases more secret (at the time) evacuations of Jewish communities from troubled lands were financed by American Jews. Every day the American Jewish community supports needy Jews throughout the world on an ongoing basis. When the Argentinean economy collapsed, the American Jewish community provided a safety-net, albeit a limited one. The State of Israel itself received a perhaps essential boost when Golda Meir returned from the U.S. with the money Israel needed to turn the tide of Israel's War of Independence. Each year, the American Jewish community contributes in the range of $1 billion to Israel. This contribution is leveraged by the $3 billion in aid that the U.S. Government grants to the State of Israel.[7] The continuing strength of American Jewry is crucial for the survival of other Diaspora communities and for many Jews around the world.

American Jewry must also save itself for moral reasons. We have already failed to save Jews once before, and we cannot afford to fail again. The biggest stain on American Jewish history is when we did not act with enough vigor to stop the Shoah (the Holocaust of European Jewry). It can be debated how much American Jews knew, whether the truth was so abominable that it was simply un-believable to the Jews of that era and whether American govern-ment officials would have acted any differently if American Jews had protested more vociferously. It can also be understood that American Jews at the time felt vulnerable themselves.[8] However, the uncharacteristic lack of sustained widespread protest by the American Jewish community cannot be ignored. It is a mistake American Jews have instinctively taken to heart. The finest hour of particularistic American Jewish protest was the movement to save Soviet Jews, which was ultimately successful in enabling ap-proximately 1 million Jews to emigrate from the lands of the Soviet Union.[9] It is now time for American Jewry to help itself.

The core purpose of this book is to present a practical pro-gram not only to reverse the current demographic tide but also to reinvigorate American Jewry by renewing our sense of whole-ness and purpose. The platform will have ten major planks that are specific and practical. The word practical here does not mean cheap, easy, or politically correct; rather it means that it can be successful if implemented and is not beyond the resources of the

Jewish community to do so. A revitalized American Jewry can emerge if we make it so. H.L. Mencken said "there is always a well known solution to every human problem – neat, plausible and wrong."[10] Similarly, for us there are no magic, quick, or simple solutions. It took us a long time to get into our present fix and it will take a long time and a lot of money to reverse. When the 1990 national Jewish population study was published, it headlined a 52% intermarriage rate; and American Jewish leaders looked for single-initiative solutions that could provide a fast reversal (the correct rate was later revised downward to 43%). No single-initiative solutions have been a panacea. However, as a result of some of those efforts and of much follow-up research, fifteen years later we have a lot of directional data. It is now possible to take this disjointed data and reformulate it to provide a coherent, comprehensive and self-reinforcing plan for action.

Luckily we still have the resources to renew American Jewry. Of the initiatives for renewal that are in place; we simply need a comprehensive plan that can be embraced by all movements, local communities, congregations, and institutions for the whole of American Jewry. Chapters I and II analyze the current demographic crisis facing American Jewry in detail and demonstrate why we must devote urgent attention to this problem. Chapters III–XII detail ten planks that comprise a comprehensive program for change. By making each plank both internally consistent and consistent with all other nine planks, American Jewry can begin to be mindful of the frictions and negative complications that all too often accompany sometimes wonderful and necessary programs. Let me just offer a few examples that will later be discussed in more detail: birthright israel has come to compete with longer Israel travel programs; Hebrew schools and day schools sometimes compete and rarely cooperate, and the Reform Movement's patrilineal descent decision, which began as an outreach initiative, has had divisive consequences for all of world Jewry. The friction is particularly intense in the fundraising arena where worthwhile projects that will promote a Jewish future compete with Jewish white elephant projects. This book offers a platform for productive solutions to renew American Jewry.

As soon will be clear, I passionately believe in the feasibility of the renewal of American Jewry. I am writing as a concerned citizen of American Jewry. As a volunteer, I have been actively involved with or lead Jewish organizations concerned with Hebrew schools, day schools, Hillels, synagogues, Israel experiences, Federations, culture, and fundraising. I have also had the privilege of meeting a lot of Americans and Israelis at the forefront of the Jewish renewal movement. And although my business career has been focused primarily in the United States, I have also served on the board of Israel's largest bank and as a partner of a prominent Israel venture capital fund. As a result of these experiences and a lot of research, I have become convinced that American Jewry desperately needs to get out of its present rut. We must urgently identify and rise to our present challenges, as we have throughout our history. Complacency means defeat.

Each and every one of us must follow the example of great Jewish figures of the past. Consider the famous story of Purim in which Mordechai delivered the news to Esther that all of the Jews in Persia will shortly be destroyed by Haman. Although Esther's first response was to deny the truth of this report as she feared that any action she took would be both futile and dangerous, Mordechai explained to her that if she were to keep "silent in this crisis, relief and deliverance will come to the Jews from another quarter and who knows – perhaps you have attained [this] position for just such a crisis." We American Jews are part of the richest and most well-educated Jewish community in the history of the world. It is up to each and every one of us to act in a way that provides "relief and deliverance" to American Jewry. In the Book of Esther, God is not mentioned once; instead, the book's Jewish heroes utilize their own individual assets and execute a careful strategy. The result was nothing short of the survival of an entire community. Yet, after Mordechai and Esther save the Jews, Esther still has to send out her proclamation twice to get the Jews to pay attention to observing Purim and Mordechai only receives the support of most, but not all, Jews. In the Jewish community, no one person and no one program is ever unanimously acclaimed: controversy is a given, but success is within our reach.

In the spirit of the Book of Esther, this book is part plea, part polemic and most important a practical plan. This is a platform that every synagogue leader, every federation contributor and every Jew who is proud to be a Jew must consider. It will require major disruptions to current Jewish communal organizations and major upheaval in the current pattern of charitable contributions and philanthropy among American Jews. We will consider issues of family formation and size frankly and we will talk candidly about the external threats facing Jews today. I hope that no one finishes this book feeling content and self-satisfied. If you are disconcerted by what you have read then I have succeeded, since confronting the brutal truth, however uncomfortable, is perhaps the greatest gift the Torah has given to us. The Hebrew prophets never hesitated to criticize an Israelite king or the entire Jewish people, while maintaining the deepest love for the Jewish people; we must do the same.

We will, however, only succeed if we approach the renewal of American Jewry with a sense of optimism. The Torah teaches that without faith and perseverance we will fail. Bamidbar/Numbers Chapters 13–14 tells the story of the twelve leaders from the twelve tribes who are sent on an intelligence gathering mission in preparation for conquering the region that was slated to be the land of Israel. The twelve leaders return from their spy mission, all having witnessed the same facts, "a land flowing with milk and honey," powerful cities with strong inhabitants, and luscious fruits. Yet, ten of the spies give their factual report and then shrivel in fear at the thought of conquering the land, whereas two of the leaders. Caleb and Joshua, acknowledge all the same facts but urge the people to have courage, faith and the will to move forward. For the ten frightened leaders, managing the status quo was preferable to taking a calculated risk to move forward emboldened by faith, despite having witnessed the plagues upon Egypt, the splitting of the sea, the receipt of the Ten Commandments at Mt. Sinai and other numerous miracles only weeks prior to their reconnaissance mission. These ten spies frightened people so much that the people began to speak of returning to Egypt. By not being prepared to lead the people forward, these ten leaders were ready to let the people waste away in the wilderness or return in self-defeat to Egypt. These leaders' lack of vision led directly to forty years of wandering in the wilderness and the death of a generation.

Our generation needs to combine the Hebrew prophets' tradition of recognizing the brutal truth with Caleb and Joshua's faith, optimism, courage and willingness to implement a difficult plan – a spirit not unlike the optimism of the American dream. It is in this spirit that we begin our journey with our own reconnaissance of our surrounding environment and the American Jewish demographic landscape and then move to develop practical plans to improve the current situation. This book is therefore meant to be informative and practical. It is written for everyone concerned about the future of American Jewry. We all have important roles to play. Even those who disagree with the prescriptions offered herein should use this platform as a challenge to create their own platforms that advance the whole of American Jewry. We can not return to the status quo or shrivel in fear. My hope is that this platform will inspire each synagogue, movement, Jewish organization and individual Jew to take action to improve our collective Jewish future. With realism, faith and a lot of hard work we will succeed.

Notes

1. 2001 United Jewish Communities in cooperation with The Mandell L. Berman Institute – North American Jewish Data Bank, *The National Jewish Population Survey 2000–2001:* Strength, Challenge, and Diversity in the American Jewish Population, (New York: United Jewish Communities, 2002), p. 10, http://www.ujc.org/content_display.html?ArticleID=60346, accessed June 2006. Jewish professionals I have spoken with on the topic corroborate the estimate. The 2000–01 National Jewish Population Survey

(NJPS) also counts 900,000 people as Jews even though these individuals no longer consider themselves to be Jewish anymore, if they ever did. The figure of 1 million Jews on the permanent exit lane from American Jewry is derived from the addition of the 900, 000 individuals who do not consider themselves as Jews and the estimated 100,000 Jews in institutional settings

2. Emil L. Fackenheim, *The Jewish Return into History: Reflection in the Age of Auschwitz and a New Jerusalem* (New York: Schoken Books, 1978), p. 22.

3. Three books I would highly recommend are: Daniel Gordis, *Does the World Need the Jews?: Rethinking Chosenness and American Jewish Identity* (New York: Scribner, 1997), Jonathan Sacks, *A Letter in the Scroll: Understanding Our Jewish Identity and Exploring the Legacy of the World's Oldest Religion* (New York: The Free Press, 2000) and Thomas Cahill, *The Gifts of the Jews: How a Tribe of Desert Nomads Changed The Way Everyone Thinks and Feels* (New York: Nan A. Talese, 1998).

4. Sergio DellaPergola and Brig. Gen (Res) Amos Gilboa, *The Jewish People Policy Planning Institute Annual Assessment 2004–2005: Between Thriving and Decline* (Jerusalem: The Jewish People Policy Planning Institute, 2005), pp. 35 and 153.

5. *JPPPI Annual Assessment 2004–2005*, p. 35.

6. Sergio DellaPergola, *Jewish Demography: Facts, Outlooks, Challenges, Alert Paper No. 3* (Jerusalem: The Jewish Population Policy Planning Institute, June 2003), http://www.jpppi.org.il/JPPPI/SendFile.asp?TID=68&FID=2264, accessed June 2006. 2222002006.2006.http:/www.jpppi.org.il/JPPPI/SendFile. asp?TID=68&FID=2264.

7. Clyde Mark, *Israel: US Foreign Assistance* (Washington DC: Congressional Research Service, 1997–2003); JTA, (February 27, 2003), www. jewishvirtuallibrary.org/ jsource/US-Israel/foreign_aid.html, accessed June 2006.

8. For a discussion of American Jewish responses to the Holocaust see: Haskel Lookstein, *Were We Our Brothers' Keepers?: The Public Response of American Jews to the Holocaust, 1938–1944* (New York: Hartmore House, 1985).

9. *JPPPI Annual Assessment 2004–2005*, p. 181.

10. H.L. Mencken,"The Divine Afflatus," in *A Mencken Chrestomathy* (New York: Knopf, 1949), p. 158.

Chapter 1

The Physics of the
Jewish Future

"The community is Israel's rampart."
Talmud: Babba Bathra 7a.

Discussions about the Jewish demographic challenge often
sound as though they are taking place at an advertising
agency. We hear countless times that "Jews are losing market
share," or that "the Jewish brand is being crowded out by all the
other attractions of modern culture." Another popular refrain is
that "the Jewish message is not being communicated well enough."[1]
Listening to these conversations and at conferences, one would
conclude that the core problem of American Jewry is either bad
"P.R." or poor brand management.[2] According to many the solution
is simple: with better marketing, Jews would return to the fold.

Unfortunately, speaking about the Jewish demographic challenge as a marketing failure understates the urgency of the current
demographic devastation of American Jewry and badly misdirects
us from responding constructively. We are not failing to promote current Jewish educational initiatives and Jewish identity

programs effectively. Rather, the issue is that current programs are simply not working. The marketing model is misguided; spiffing up the "Jewish brand" is not enough.

A more compelling model for understanding and treating American Jewry's demographic challenges comes from physics. This approach is not as unusual it might seem. In his book *Critical Mass: How One Thing Leads to Another*,[3] Philip Ball uses models from physics to describe social phenomena such as traffic patterns, walking paths, financial markets and friendships. Other social scientists have applied quantitative methods to human behavior with remarkable success. These scholars turned to the hard sciences for methods and models to describe human behavior because of their conceptual advantage: they clarify the multiple dynamics of current social phenomena and predict future outcomes; as a result, they are an excellent basis for developing workable solutions to social problems. The conceptual advantage of models from physics is a powerful reason to apply them to the Jewish community. By imagining Jewish commitment as a physical substance susceptible to changing physical states and subject to physical laws, we can identify the key dynamics of Jewish assimilation within the American environment and predict their almost inevitable consequences.

Change in Jewish Commitment: Change in Physical State

Consider Jewish commitment to be a physical state. A fully committed Jew is a solid, a moderate to marginally committed Jew is a liquid, while an uncommitted Jew is akin to a gas. Each type of Jew can move from one state to another, but such movement, as with matter, constitutes a dramatic change. The state change of matter is a complex and energy-consuming reaction to changes in the physical environment and is subject to certain physical laws. These laws govern when the changes occur and their consequences. Similarly, when the Jewish community does not take action, but simply observes changes in the commitment of its members as they react to their environment, the consequences of these changes will also follow certain rules and have predictable consequences.

Let us then pretend to do two experiments together using water. Imagine a room separated by a thick glass window. On one side we will place an observer, and on the other, a transparent container of water. During the experiments, the temperature of the container will be altered. The observer will be asked to look at the water in the container across the window, but he/she will not be forewarned of any temperature changes to the container or be able to touch the window to determine if any change of temperature had taken place on the other side of the room as a result of the heat from the container. Therefore, the observer will not be able to tell if the water is in the process of being heated or cooled.

Experiment #1

In the first experiment the temperature of the water in the container is 100° below Fahrenheit. As the observer watches, the container is warmed to 31° Fahrenheit, a change of 131° Fahrenheit. This is a dramatically new environment. Yet to the observer nothing has happened because the water has remained in ice solid form. Next, the container is heated just one more degree to 32° Fahrenheit. At first, the observer thinks it is just more of the same boring scene. But soon, parts of the ice will liquefy. Just like on the first warm day after a snow storm, there can be plenty of snow on the ground, but at 32° Fahrenheit it is only a question of time before it all melts.

Let us imagine that the same observer had entered the room slightly later, when the container had already been heated to 32° and the ice had partially melted. Since the observer did not know the original physical state of the water, or whether the temperature was going up or down, he/she might think that the water was on its way to becoming ice. Alternatively, if our observer did not understand the critical nature of melting points he/she might think that the part ice, part liquid water solution in front of him/her was in equilibrium. Only in the fullness of time would our observer learn that the final state of the ice was to become liquid as soon as the temperature went above the critical point.

An Ice Cube at 32° Fahrenheit

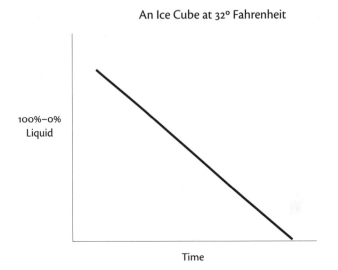

100%–0%
Liquid

Time

Percentage of Jews in Total U.S. Population, Partially Projected

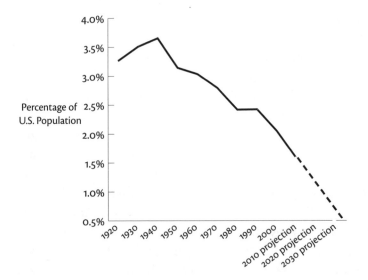

Percentage of
U.S. Population

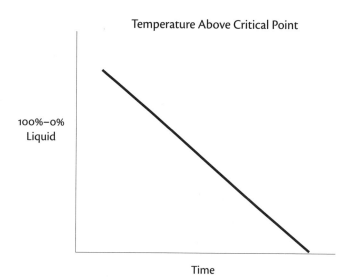

Temperature Above Critical Point

100%–0%
Liquid

Time

Thankfully, the changes in the composition of our community, like the state changes of water, are reversible; however, returning to a previous state requires considerable energy, a phenomenon scientists explain through the Second Law of Thermodynamics. The Second Law of Thermodynamics states that every action leads to increased entropy. Because entropy is a measure of disorder, it follows that the process of transferring any kind of energy always leads to some wasted heat. This wasted energy enlarges the entropy of the universe, however minutely, and cannot be effectively harnessed to do anything useful. Living organisms, the epitome of efficiency, struggle mightily and successfully to cope with the Second Law, yet no matter how efficient they are, they too must discharge substantial excess energy – much of which is released as waste product – simply to maintain biological order. Recreating a lost state, however, requires much more. With the Second Law of Thermodynamics in mind, let us turn to our second experiment.

Experiment #2

In the second experiment the water is quickly heated to 211° Fahrenheit. At first, it appears to the observer that nothing has happened since the water remains a liquid. However, once the temperature is raised to 212° Fahrenheit the water will begin to boil and vaporize. Thus, the observer is in fact witnessing two states – liquid and gas (water vapor) – coexisting. Once again the water is not in a state of equilibrium. As soon as the temperature exceeds 212° Fahrenheit, the final state of the water molecules is certain: the water will become gas. Once the water is entirely vaporized, it is invisible to the observer. The water now seems irrelevant to the environment.

Unless the containers are precisely designed, the Second Law dictates that condensing vapor requires more energy and leads to more entropy than would be the case had the water never evaporated in the first place. It would also be a messy job requiring a lot of energy, to gather up all of the now scattered vapor molecules, for if we were to cool the environment, the liquid water would condense all over the container. And, if the container were only slightly open, most of the vapor would also have disappeared into the room. Thus, transforming vapor back into water requires a lot of wasted energy and likely would not transform all of the vapor back into water.

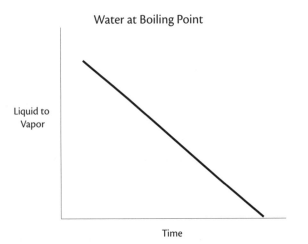

Water at Boiling Point

Liquid to Vapor

Time

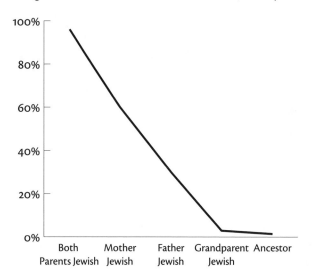
Percentage of Children who Consider Themselves Jewish (see note 4)

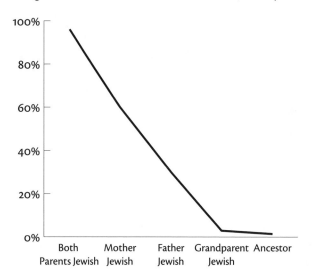

State Change in Matter and Intermarriage: Predictable Results

The result of intermarriage or extreme assimilation among Jews can be compared to water evaporating in an open container.[4] Although on an individual basis, the decision to intermarry may make perfect and compelling sense, it threatens the future of the system as a whole since the destiny of the individual's progeny is cast within a high degree of probability. The likelihood that a child of an intermarried couple will consider him or herself Jewish is 33%.[5] The likelihood of the grandchild of this Jewish person being Jewish is under 10%. The 2000 National Jewish Population Survey (NJPS) noted that 10 million Americans had some Jewish ancestry.[6] Reversing this trend requires a lot of energy and creates a great deal of entropy. Later we will discuss the merits of expending energy, funds, and resources on intermarried couples in comparison with other segments of the Jewish spectrum, since these are loved members of our families not just physical particles. In contrast to restoring vapor to its previous liquid form, it is less difficult to return liquid water in a vessel to its solid form. Less excess energy is needed and we can be sure that all of the substance has remained in the container.[7] Likewise, when we allocate our resources/energy we need to be mindful of the liquid and gas analogy.

Thankfully, as observers of American Jewry we are neither ignorant nor passive like the observer in the experiment. We have an array of measuring devices at our disposal. Using these we have witnessed a lot of boiling, melting, and some solidifying and condensation in the Jewish community in recent years. And although we cannot be sure of precise boiling and freezing temperatures, we have developed strong hypotheses to help us determine when to adjust the heat. The physics model also reveals other factors we need to take into consideration to keep Jewish commitment strong.

Safeguarding Jewish Commitment: Exposed Surface Area

Exposed surface area is another physical factor that affects matter and our American Jewish environment. We can think of exposed surface area as analogous to the population density of a given Jewish community in the Diaspora: in a densely populated Jewish community such as Boro Park, a Jew is surrounded predominantly, if not totally, by other Jews; alternatively, in a sparsely populated Jewish community, such as Anchorage, a Jew is surrounded predominantly by non-Jews. The exposed surface area of a substance greatly affects the time it takes for a physical state change to take place. For example, a compact pound block of ice will take much longer to melt than that same one pound of ice spread in a flat plate over 50 feet. Similarly, the more compact the Jewish community in a given location, the smaller and slower their rate of assimilation. The diagram below aggregates the density of zip codes where there are a significant number of Jews into three categories – high, medium, and low density. Judith Veinstein took these three categories of Jewish density and compared them to intermarriage rates within those zip codes.[8] The results closely correlate with our model.

Relationship between Density of Jewish Population and Intermarriage Rate

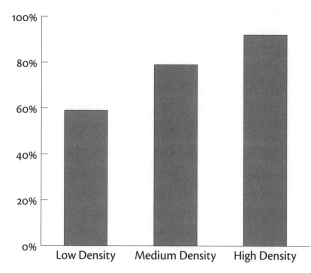

The more Jews there are in a community and the larger the percentage of Jews in the total population, the less likely it is that future generations of Jews will melt away. Unlike a gas, the molecules in solids and liquid are tightly bound together, giving the substance shape and strength. However, a thinly spread solid or liquid is quicker to change state than a compact amount of the same matter. As we shall see, taking multiple and self-reinforcing initiatives to augment the spiritual, communal and educational, if not residential, density of Jews and to unite Jews in knowledge and purpose will reinvigorate American Jewry into a solid and compact community that can fulfill our mission in this world.

External and Internal Forces Affecting Jewish Commitment: Pressure and Nucleation

Internal and external pressure can also create a physical state change. Unusually intense pressure can force molecules that are heated above their boiling point to remain together in a plasma state. These molecules are "coerced" into acting together. However, as soon as the pressure is reduced, the plasma quickly becomes gaseous. Internal peer or family pressure to conform has had a similar effect on the Jewish community. It is not uncommon today for increasingly secular Jews to continue to observe Jewish holidays simply to please their parents.[9] In America, children of recent immigrants often felt such pressure most strongly, but by the second and third generation this influence has dissipated, loosening community bonds.[10] An exogenous pressure such as anti-Semitism also forces Jews to act as a group even if some members would prefer to disassociate themselves from the Jewish community. In America, for example, intermarriage rates remained low earlier in the century, despite increasing acculturation, due in some part to anti-Semitism.[11] Pressure can thus have a positive short-term effect, though it is rarely a longer-term solution for safeguarding Jewish identity or making Jews fundamentally solid as a people. We should not rely on pressure to preserve Jewish continuity.

Nucleation can also hasten solidification. Snow forms around dust particles. An ice cube will form faster if the crystallization process can be seeded. In the world of living organisms, an oyster needs a speck of dirt to start forming a pearl. So, nucleation, i.e. throwing an impurity into a substance, or in human terms, being a pain, can make solidification occur much more quickly. Historically, agents of change in the Jewish community were outsiders and often viewed as irritators. Prominent examples are most of the Prophets, Hillel, Yohanan ben Zakkai, and Rabbi Akiva. Many positive changes in American Jewish life were also initiated by outsiders.[12] However, the overall environment must still be right. Neither pressure nor nucleation alone can keep the Jewish people solid. The solidity of the Jewish people depends on the combination of the right state and nucleation (read leadership).

The physics model of state change in matter, which incorporates temperature change, pressure and nucleation works unnervingly well to describe the changes that most segments of American Jewry have undergone over the last hundred years. During this time the temperature has risen steadily, pressure has diminished and irritation has been reduced, and as a result, the number of American Jews changing from the solid to the liquid state and then from the liquid to the gas has increased. Yet, this model seems to break down when applied to the "ultra-Orthodox" or Chareidi[13] community, whom we shall refer to collectively as the "fervently Orthodox," "Chareidi" or "Chareidim." This group includes Chassidim (Satmar, Bobov, Pupe, Belz et al.), Chabad, Yeshiva-centered communities (sometimes referred to as "black hat") and some Sephardim, especially the community from Syria, who have formed dense communities upon relocating to America, often in specific neighborhoods such as Williamsburg (Satmar), Lakewood (Yeshiva-centered), Crown Heights (Chabad) and Flatbush (Syrian). The historical experience of these Chareidim, who are growing in number, seems to contradict our model of American Jewish life.

Ultra-Orthodoxy: Permanently Solid?

There is no question that the fervently Orthodox community is not only sustaining itself, but growing rapidly. One indicator of the dynamic growth of Chareidim is that elementary and high school enrollment in their affiliated schools in the U.S. grew by over 17,000 between the 1998–99 and 2003–04 academic years.[14] This growth was on a base of 111,000,[15] an impressive 15% growth rate over these five years. Given past trends, some within the fervently Orthodox community argue that while the non-Orthodox Jewish population might disappear over the next 50 years, the fervently Orthodox will continue to grow in size and in devotion as they become the new dominant center of American Jewry. There are, however, three main objections to this claim.

The first objection to this notion comes from the American Jewish experience: the historical record in America shows that Orthodox communities do not necessarily remain Orthodox. In 1952 a survey of one American city indicated that 81% of the grandparents of these families were, or had been, Orthodox. Only 16% of the parents were Orthodox. Among the then Orthodox, only a fifth intended to remain Orthodox.[16] Among current Jewish adults raised Orthodox, only 41% are presently Orthodox.[17] There is, however, a major difference between the situation of Orthodox Jews today and that of Orthodox Jews in 1952, or adult Jews raised since then; namely, Chareidim have actively sought to "cool" their environment through education and relocation.

The energy that has been put into Jewish education among the Orthodox has been both astounding and the single greatest guarantor of the strength and growth of their communities. In 1958, approximately 43,000 students were enrolled in day schools and Yeshivas, virtually all Orthodox.[18] In 2003, all Orthodox and fervently Orthodox schools counted over 163,000 students, nearly a four-fold increase.[19] This massive amount of energy is akin to the cooling or refrigerating energy we spoke of before. The fervently Orthodox have focused almost all of their energy on education and have succeeded in becoming a more solid and compact community than just decades ago.

The Chareidim have also instinctively tried to change their exposed surface area/density simply by moving into tight-knit communities where they separate as much as possible from the overall environment of American society. The communities of Lakewood, New Jersey and Monsey, New York come to mind, but there are also Orthodox enclaves in Brooklyn and Queens. Compact community structure, like the focus on intensive Jewish education, is an effective strategy for coping with the entropy that American society exerts on every ethnic group. For just as on mountains some snow is visible when the temperature has been above 32° Fahrenheit for months, snow can also fall into deep ditches and survive there into the next winter if conditions are right. Similarly, isolation can help to keep Jewish identity solid against the odds. Both education and isolation make the near-term and intermediate term outlook for the fervently Orthodox quite good. However, further reflection suggests that the current state of affairs would not ensure the survival of the presently flourishing Chareidi community.

The second objection to the claim that the fervently Orthodox are permanently solid is that isolation from the wider world and particularly the more secular Jewish community is not a sustainable solution for Chareidim. Truly, the current community structure and choices of the fervently Orthodox community have depended on secular Jews for representation in American politics, on services provided by secular Jews and most importantly on their financial support. The integration of Jews into the fabric of American life, where Jews spoke out for civil rights and pluralism, has assisted and perhaps enabled the fervently orthodox community to establish itself.[20] Furthermore, the social welfare measures that non-Orthodox Jews in America promoted also benefited the pride of Chareidi Torah education, the kollel system.[21] The Chareidi Jewish infrastructure continues to be heavily, though unevenly, supported by modern Orthodox and non-Orthodox Jews.

Among the Chareidim, Chabad is the most dependent on outside funds. Because it does the most outreach work, it is also the most geared towards fundraising, though other groups benefit from outside help as well. No exact breakdown exists between the quantity of funds Chabad receives from Chareidi and from non-Chareidi Jews, but it is safe to say that a substantial amount of money comes from donors who do not live a Chareidi lifestyle, or call themselves Chareidi.[22] Other communities, such as Satmar, Bobov and Syrian Jews are financially more self-sufficient, but depend on a wide variety of free or discounted Jewish professional services from Jewish doctors and from Jewish institutions such as hospitals and social welfare agencies that are staffed by more liberal Orthodox or non-Orthodox Jews and usually funded by Federations. Therefore, it is questionable that isolation will enable Chareidim to continue to live the current lifestyle they enjoy and invest the kind of resources they currently have at their disposal to maintain their day schools and vibrant neighborhoods, the cornerstone of their solid communities were there is no non-Chareidi Jewish community. Though many Chareidim believe that Jewish men should learn fulltime – and a large number today do – they do so thanks to the funds of working, and often more liberal, Jews. As the Talmud states regarding the debate between Shimon bar Yochai who advocated Torah learning fulltime and Rabbi Ishmael who advocated leaning Torah and engaging in a worldly occupations to earn a livelihood: "Many followed the advice of Rabbi Ishmael and it has worked well; other have followed Rabbi Shimon bar Yochai, and it has not been successful." (Talmud, Berachot 35b).[23]

The third objection is historical. In our two millennia-long history in the diaspora we have no precedent for any sizable Diaspora Jewish community in which the less fervent assimilated away, while the fervently Orthodox community remained vibrant. In the final analysis, once assimilation reached the critical point, the question was pace, not ultimate outcome. Witness the Jewish communities of China and India in which the Jews assimilated by choice and lack of communal strength, not through persecution or threat.

In India, the home of six different Jewish communities for over two thousand years, assimilation has increased dramatically in the Modern era as a result of a lack of education and communal infrastructure, though most Indian Jews are traditional. The much shrunken remnant of Indian Jewry, the 5000 Bene Israel Jews currently living in India, are assimilating at a rate of 50%. This development cannot be attributed to anti-Semitism, lack of will or commitment to Jewish identity; rather once the community fell below the critical mass their education and communal infrastructure deteriorated and their purpose for being was lost. Over the last two hundred years, the Bene Israel had been dependent on two other Indian Jewish communities, the Cochin Jews and the Iraqi Jews, for their teachers, shochtim (kosher butchers) and chazanim (cantors). Since most of these two groups have departed for Israel, the remaining Bene Israel cannot sustain and promote Jewish life, which they had hitherto welded so effectively with participation in Indian society. Thus, the Indian example demonstrates that only education, communal infrastructure and a critical mass of Jews can stave off assimilation *even among traditional Jews*, a process which once begun is very hard to reverse.[24]

In China, a lack of leadership also precipitated the disappearance of the Jewish community through assimilation over one hundred and fifty years. As in India, Chinese Jews faced little to no anti-Semitism and lived by melding traditional Jewish practices with local customs. However, assimilation began to occur because of the opportunities Jews had to ascend in the Chinese bureaucracy. As these Jews studied the Confucian classics to enter the civil service, they neglected traditional Jewish learning. Moreover, because the Chinese government also required them to serve far from their home communities, the bonds of Jewish family life were loosened. Thus, young would-be leaders of the Jewish community had – to use the analogy from physics – an increased exposed surface area and assimilated rapidly. As a result, though its members were committed to Jewish life, without leadership the Jews of China were not able to perpetuate it alone. The assimilation of the Chinese Jewish elite precipitated the assimilation of the entire community.[25]

In both India and China the survival of these two highly acculturated communities who combined Jewish identity practices and traditions with an active involvement in the wider Indian and Chinese culture depended on their commitment to Jewish education and community life. Once this was threatened assimilation took its natural course. There are no Jews left in China and though the remaining Indian Jews wish to stay faithful to tradition, their dwindling numbers and lack of knowledge is having a dispiriting effect on the community as a whole. These two examples teach us that without Jewish leadership and knowledge, successful acculturation becomes assimilation. Likewise it demonstrates that without a vibrant community, even traditional Jews would likely become dispirited. As Benjamin Franklin put it in another context, "We must all hang together or we will all hang separately."

Finally, if despite all the objections, we assumed that American Jewry were to evolve to become purely Chareidi, the separation that would be necessary to sustain that community would make American Jewry largely irrelevant to American society and the body politic. The legacy of Jewish influence on American life has been overwhelmingly positive: Jews have contributed to all aspects of American culture and society from the professions to the arts, from sports to government. The historical experience of Jews in America has been both as a center of tradition for the Jewish community and a glowing example of the positive influence of Jewish culture in the diaspora. Without re-invigorating the Jewish identity of so many non-Chareidi Jews, we will not be able to continue this balance.

The Potential Effects of Jewish Culture

In recent years there has been an efflorescence of Jewish cultural activity in America. Jewish art, music, theatre and literature have the potential to act on the state of current Jews. However, these experiences must be supported by other positive initiatives at the individual and community level; otherwise the positive effects of culture are ephemeral. At its simplest level, cultural experiences are like a momentary cooling. The passion and intensity of a concert or the beauty of a work of art can temporarily "solidify" a "liquid" Jew, or "liquefy" a "gaseous" Jew. Unfortunately, if the positive Jewish environment that a cultural event creates is not sustained in other parts of an individual's life, the effect of the experience will wane. Thus, cultural experiences have the potential to be powerful, because they can facilitate state change. They are not, however, a solution in themselves.

Jewish art, music, literature and theatre have the potential to facilitate state change because they bring Jews of all different stripes together. A concert or art exhibit is often a uniquely positive space of encounter between different types of Jews. It is also a place where Jews can imagine themselves in a different physical state. Just as part of Jewish culture has always been a creative tension with the "other," in the environment of modern American Jewry we also have a tension – sometimes creative, sometimes not – with other conceptions of Jewishness. For individuals with no conception of Jewishness, Jewish culture makes everything momentarily possible. We should therefore foster the potential of Jewish culture, as well as work to ensure that its positive effect is lasting by connecting cultural initiatives to broader changes in the community. At a practical level, this means that Jewish cultural events can be places where we share ideas and connect with people, as well as places to spark our imaginations.

Re-solidifying American Jewry

While we will not be slavish in utilizing the physics model metaphor for re-solidifying Jewish life in America, it is an excellent guide for developing effective solutions. It underscores that any solutions we undertake must be multiple, comprehensive and embrace all segments of the Jewish community. We will not solidify the Jewish community through programs that only target certain Jewish groups. The model also makes clear that we need to maximize the efficiency of our energy and resource use. We must find new sources of energy and resources (read money) than we currently have access to, and we have to ruthlessly eliminate ineffective energy and resource use. But most importantly, the model shows that we have no time to spare. The physics model is thus the blueprint for the ten planks for re-solidifying American Jewry. But before we can proceed with our platform for community-wide change, we need to take a good look at the current state of Jewish demographics in America.

Notes

1. As cited in Gary Rosenblatt, "'Eminem' Jews Rap Establishment," *The Jewish Week*, May 2, 2003, Frank Lunz argues in a report on the Jewish identity of those born between 1981 and 2000 that "most traditional communications and marketing strategies are not reaching the vast majority of young Jews." Frank Lunz, *Israel in the Age of 'Eminem* (New York: The Andrea and Charles Bronfman Philanthropies, The Alan B. Slifka Foundation and The Michael and Judy Steinhart Foundation, 2004), http:// www.shalomdc.org/getfile.asp?id=11162, accessed June 2006.

2. The use of marketing models to describe and change social behavior is called social marketing. For an introduction to this field see Philip Kotler and Eduardo L. Roberto, *Social Marketing: Strategies for Changing Public Behavior* (New York: Free Press, 1989).

3. Philip Ball, *Critical Mass: How One Thing Leads to Another* (London: Arrow, 2005).

4. The data for the graph on the percentage of children who consider themselves Jewish is from a private communication with Bruce Phillips, May 2006.

5. *NJPS* 2000–2001, p. 18.

6. *JPPPI Annual Assessment* 2005, p. 51.

7. The amount of energy needed to change one kilogram of water to ice (at a pressure of one atmosphere) is 335 kilojoules. The heat needed to return water vapor to liquid water is 2260 kilojoules.

8. Personal communication with Judith Veinstein, June 2006.

9. In her memoirs, the renowned Holocaust Scholar Lucy Dawidowicz writes: "My parents nag me to go to *shul* on holidays. They make sacrifices to keep their traditions, but they don't mean anything much in my life.... That's why I don't like to stay home. I don't want to hurt my parents [but] I can't take their advice." Lucy S. Dawidowicz, *From That Place and Time: a Memoir, 1938–1947* (New York: W.W. Norton, 1989), p. 115, quoted in Berel Wein, *Faith & Fate: the Story of the Jewish People in the Twentieth Century* (Brooklyn: Shaar Press, 2001), p. 12.

10. Wein, *Faith and Fate*, p. 229. Wein argues that mass assimilation in America began in the 1950s.

11. Wein, *Faith and Fate*, p. 16.

12. Jonathan D. Sarna, *A Great Awakening: The Transformation that Shaped Twentieth century American Judasim And Its Implications For Today* (New York: Council for Initiatives in Jewish Education, April 1995), p.31–33.

13. Chareidi means "one who trembles," in this case before God.

14. Marvin Schick, *A Census of Jewish Day Schools in the United States 2003–2004* (New York: The AVI CHAI Foundation, 2004), p. 17. http://www.avi-chai.org/Static/Binaries/Publications/Second%20Census%202003–04_0.pdf, accessed June 2006.

15. Ibid, p.17.

16. Marshall Sklare, Marc Bosk and Mark Zborowski, "Forms and Expressions of Jewish Identification," *Jewish Social Studies* 27 (1955): 20, cited in Nathan Glazer, *American Judaism* (Chicago: University of Chicago Press, 1989), p. 111.

17. United Jewish Communities, *National Jewish Population Survey 2000–01 Orthodox Jews: A United Jewish Communities Presentation of Findings*

(New York: United Jewish Communities, February 2004), p. 10, http://www. ujc.org/getfile.asp?id=4983, accessed June 2006.

18. Sharon Strassfield and Kathy Green, "In Praise of Jewish Day Schools," in *The Jewish Family Book: A Creative Approach to Raising Kids*, eds. Sharon Strassfield and Kathy Green (New York: Bantam Books, 1981) and Jonathan D. Sarna, *American Judaism: a History* (New Haven: Yale University Press, 2004), p. 279.

19. Schick, *A Census of Jewish Day Schools*, p. 17.

20. There is no example since the arrival of Jews in America of a flourishing Chareidi community that did not have some measure of support from the non-Orthodox Jewish community. See Howard Sachar, *A History of the Jews in America* (New York: Alfred A. Knopf Inc., 1992).

21. "Liberal government welfare programs, put in place by Lyndon Johnson's 'Great Society' 1960s anti-poverty programs, and retained and expanded by succeeding administrations, indirectly helped finance the emerging kollel system." Berel Wein, *Faith & Fate*, p. 320.

22. M. Avrum Ehrlich, *The Messiah of Brooklyn: Understanding Lubavitch Hasidism Past and Present* (Jersey City: KTAV Publishing House, 2004), p. 132.

23. This citation is taken from Jonathan Sacks, "The Practical Implications of Infinity," http://www.chabad.org/library/article.asp?AID=2096, accessed June 2006.

24. Nathan Katz and Ellen S. Goldberg, "The Last Jews of India and Burma," *Jerusalem Letter* 101 (April 1988), http://www.jcpa.org, accessed June 2006. See also Nathan Katz, *Who are the Jews of India?* (Berkeley: University of California Press, 2000).

25. Nathan Katz, "The Judaisms of Kaifeng and Cochin" in *Jews in China from Kaifeng to Shanghai*, ed. Roman Malek (Sankt Augustin: Steyler, 2000).

Chapter II

The Demographic Decline of American Jewry Today

"Be fruitful and multiply, and replenish the earth."
Bereishit 1:28

The following chapter will make the extent of demographic decline in American Jewry clear. Since numerous readers will be distressed by this trend, it is important to keep in mind that demographic data is like a scorecard. Population figures are not causes of anything; rather, they are the result of policies, personal decisions and the broader physical environment. The current demographic trend has disturbing implications, but these implications will only become a reality if the causes for demographic decline remain unchecked. Therefore, as we examine the population figures for American Jews in this chapter, we must think very carefully about the root causes of current trends.

The Number of Jews in America Today

The 2000–2001 National Jewish Population Survey (NJPS) population estimate that 5.2 million Jews live in America today is incorrect; the real number is closer to 4.3 million at best. The NJPS survey defines a Jew as follows

A Person:

- Whose religion is Jewish, OR
- Whose religion is Jewish and something else; OR
- Who has no religion and has at least one Jewish parent or a Jewish upbringing; OR
- Who has a non-monotheistic religion and has at least one Jewish parent or a Jewish upbringing.[1]

According to the NJPS definition of a Jew, there are 5.2 million Jews in the U.S. today and an estimated additional 100,000 who live in some sort of institutional setting, although no sample was taken of them. The problem with this figure is that it included many people as Jews who do not consider themselves to be Jewish, regardless of halachic or technical considerations. Indeed, of the 5.2 million Jews counted in the survey only 4.3 million people claimed they had a meaningful connection to the Jewish people.[2] Thus, 4.3 million is a more accurate figure for the number of Jews in the U.S. today. This figure is also consistent with David Ben Gurion's claim that a Jew is someone who considers him/herself Jewish and nothing else.[3] The 5.2 million figure is a gross distortion of the actual number of people who consider themselves to be Jewish in America today.

After the 2000 NJPS, most institutional voices breathed a sigh of relief due to the supposed stability of the Jewish population. Yet, as the above-mentioned figures demonstrate, this response is nothing short of denial: in reality American Jewry has been in steady decline since 1980. Between 1970 and 1980 the American Jewish population was broadly stable at 5.9 million Jews.[4] In 1990, the NJPS estimate was 5.5 million Jews. The official NJPS estimate in 2000 was 5.2 million. The number of Jews in America is clearly not stable. Some observers have read the data more plainly: from 1980–2000 we have lost 700,000 Jews. Yet, as bad as these estimates are, the brutal truth is far worse.

Not only has the number of Jews in America declined steadily since the 1980s, but there has also been a decline in the number of Jews who strongly identify as Jewish. Although identity is difficult to quantify precisely, there is evidence that a larger percentage of the 5.9 million Jews living in the U.S. in 1980 were Jewishly affiliated than of the 5.2 million broadly-defined Jews living in the U.S. today. There are several reasons for this assumption. First, over 90% of Jews in 1980 were the product of two Jewish parents and had some Jewish education. This is not so for Jews today. A recent Hillel survey indicated that 47% of Jewish students who claim to have "no religion" had one Jewish parent.[5] NJPS also documented that 74% of children with only one Jewish parent intermarry,[6] and that a grandchild of an intermarried couple who himself has only one Jewish parent is highly unlikely to identify him/herself as Jewish, though the NJPS might classify that person as Jewish if both his/her parents were products of intermarriage. If you intermarry, the current chances that your grandchildren will consider themselves Jewish is less than 10%. Thus, a better comparison to the 5.9 million Jews of 1980 would be the 4.3 million self-declaring Jews of today. This somewhat depressing comparison would depict a 27% drop in the Jewish population of American Jewry, or a loss of 1.6 million Jews. But that is not the entire story: if we dig deeper, the reality is worse.

In order to determine American Jewry's ability to sustain itself, we must subtract Jews who arrived in the U.S. in the last part of the twentieth century, primarily from the Former Soviet Union (FSU) from the current population estimate. Between 1980 and 2000, NJPS estimates that 335,000 of today's Jewish adults are immigrants to the U.S.[7] These immigrants had approximately 100,000 children.[8] Thus, in order to compare the 1980 population estimate to the 2000 estimate on the basis of "domestic Jews," the recent immigrant population from the FSU and their children must be subtracted from the 2000 data. The number of "domestic" Jews and their children in 1980 is thus 3.9 million, or 4.3 million minus 335,000 immigrants and 100,000 children of these immigrants. An internally consistent measurement of American Jewry's ability to sustain itself requires us to compare the 5.9 million Jews of 1980 to the 3.9 million Jews of today who were either adults in 1980 or children of those adults. The most accurate assessment of the decrease in the "domestic" Jewish population from 1980 to 2000 is thus 34%, or a loss of 2 million Jews.[9]

The derivation from the NJPS of a decline of 34% in American Jewry's numbers is corroborated by an in-depth look at New York Jewish population figures. The comparison between American population figures and New York population figures is helpful in a number of ways. First, the number of Jews questioned in both the New York and national surveys are almost the same, though the population surveyed in New York is only 24% of the national population.[10] Second, the New York survey only counts individuals who self-identify as Jews. And third, we can safely assume that there has been no disproportional migration to or from the New York area to the rest of the country. Based on these three factors, we expect the decline to be somewhat smaller than the country as a whole. The results are not as favorable as might be expected. A comparison between Jewish population figures of the Jewish Population of Greater New York Population Survey of 1984[11] and The Jewish Community Study of New York 2002[12] reveals a decline in the Jewish population since 1980 similar to the decline in America as a whole. In 1981, 1,670,700 Jews lived in the eight county New York city area of the UJA-Federation of New York[13] and in 2002, 1,412,000 Jews lived in New York, amounting to a gross drop of 15% over the two decades.[14] The survey also reports that approximately 191,000 Jews in the 2002 survey are recent immigrants from the FSU and Eastern Europe.[15] Based on the 2002 data we may also conservatively assume that these New York Jewish immigrants brought at least 50,000 children into the world. Making the same adjustments to the New York population for the immigration from the FSU and Eastern Europe as for the overall American Jewish population and ignoring any immigration from elsewhere, the domestic New York Jewish population fell by 499,700, an astonishing 29%. Given the density of the New York Jewish population, the New York numbers provide strong confirmation of an overall national domestic Jewish population decline of 34%.

The current population drop in American Jewry is truly shocking. We are accustomed to thinking of demographic change as something that only happens over the long run. We tend to think of demographic concerns as issues that might impact our grandchildren a little, and we never imagine they will impact us and our children. As John Maynard Keynes famously remarked in minimizing the need to worry about long-term consequences, "In the long run we are all dead."[16] Such flippant self-reassurance is not only wrong; it is profoundly misguided. Our domestic Jewish population dropped by over one-third in the lifetime of most people reading this book. We are witnessing demographic devastation in real time.

If the current demographic trend continues, American Jewry will have reversed over fifty years of demographic growth within thirty years. The U.S. Census Bureau projects that the U.S. population will grow from 294 in 2004 to 364 million in 2030.[17] My projection for the Jewish community is that by 2030 it will dwindle to as low as 2.5 million, which would represent less than 0.7% of the overall population and mean a loss of up to 3.4 million Jews in fifty years. If current demographic trends continue, the percentage of Jews in the American population as a whole will drop to the level it was at in 1890.[18] However, unlike in 1890, American Jewry can no longer expect a massive new influx of foreign Jews to the U.S. If American Jewry wants to stay strong, it must renew itself from within.

The drastic population decline we are witnessing in the American Jewish community today has precedents from other American groups. The French Huguenots and Dutch Reformed groups immigrated to the U.S. in even larger numbers than the Jews, yet today they are barely visible.[19] Though these groups faced different challenges than American Jewry, the main reason for their disappearance, like our decline, was intermarriage.

Intermarriage and the Decline of American Jewry

There is no doubt that the primary cause for the decline in American Jewry is intermarriage. Intermarriage is a sensitive subject from a number of perspectives. In America today we cannot bar people from marrying whom they want. We are privileged to live in a country where we have individual freedom and where anti-Semitism is so low that most non-Jews would accept a Jewish mate for their children or themselves. We must also recognize that the non-Jewish spouse of an intermarriage experiences his or her own difficulties. Intermarriage is a complicated affair but thankfully does not have to be the end of Jewish continuity, depending on how we approach it. That being said, we must face the brutal truth that, currently, intermarriage is devastating the American Jewish community. Although intermarriage is initially a symptom and not the root cause of Jewish disaffiliation, once it takes place, it leads to a physical state change. Within two generations of an intermarriage, the progeny of this union will likely have forever broken the 3,500 year chain of the Jewish people. It is that fast.

Current statistics demonstrate clearly that in America today, intermarriage is more often than not the end of Jewish continuity. Only one-third of the children raised in intermarried households are being raised as Jewish. However, even those children who are being raised as Jewish are exposed to far fewer Jewish experiences than inmarried couples provide.[20] Moreover, if a Jew intermarries, there is less than a 10% chance that his or her grandchildren will consider themselves Jewish. Also, as intermarriage rates continue to rise, future increases in this rate are already embedded, since the children of currently intermarried couples intermarry at a rate of 74%.[21]

National Jewish Population Survey 2000–01	
Intermarriage by Year Marriage Began	
YEAR MARRIAGE BEGAN	PERCENT INTERMARRIED
Before 1970	13%
1970–1979	28%
1980–1984	38%
1985–1990	43%
1991–1995	43%
1996–2001	47%

For the New York area, the numbers are somewhat lower, but are also rising.

The Jewish Community Study of New York: 2002	
Intermarriage by Year Marriage Began	
YEAR MARRIAGE BEGAN	PERCENT INTERMARRIED
Before 1970	8%
1970–1979	17%
1980–1989	29%
1990–1997	26%
1998–2002	36%

Although intermarriage statistics are relatively low due to the large local Orthodox community and the greater density of Jews within New York than the country as a whole, the intermarriage figures for New York still corroborate the national statistics. Despite the density of the Jewish population and the vibrancy of Jewish life, just 30% of the children of intermarried couples in New York are being raised as Jewish. These children also receive much less exposure to Judaism than their cousins from inmarried couples. 56% of these children being raised as "Jewish" are receiving no Jewish education, versus a solid majority of children of inmarried couples. Less than 1% of the New York children of intermarriages have traveled to Israel in comparison to the 29% of children of inmarried couples.[22] The statistics are consistent across the U.S.: every indication of Jewish affiliation is dramatically lower from inter-married couples than for inmarried couples.

Jewish Connections of Inmarried and Intermarried Jews		
	INMARRIED	INTERMARRIED
Hold/Attend Passover Seder	85%	41%
Light Shabbat candles	39%	5%
Keep kosher at home	27%	5%
Attend religious services monthly or more	37%	8%
Belong to a synagogue	59%	15%
Belong to JCC	29%	6%
Volunteer under Jewish auspices	33%	8%
Participate in adult Jewish education	31%	7%
Emotionally connected to Israel	76%	45%

Jewish Connections of Inmarried and Intermarried Jews		
	INMARRIED	INTERMARRIED
Contribute to federation campaign	41%	9%
Contribute to Jewish cause (not federation)	60%	19%

Source NJPS, p. 19.

The clear conclusion once again is that if you intermarry, you are unlikely to have Jewish grandchildren.

Another cause for the decline in American Jewry is that American Jews tend to delay marriage and therefore have fewer children than other Americans.

Percent ever married by age and sex, for Jewish and U.S. populations				
	MEN		WOMEN	
Age	*Jewish*	*U.S.*	*Jewish*	*U.S.*
18–24	10%	12%	18%	21%
25–34	48	59	64	70
35–44	74	82	85	87
45–64	90	92	90	93
65 and over	96	96	98	96
Total	72	73	79	79

Source NJPS, p. 3.

Current statistics on the average age of marriage among Jews are more worrisome if one considers that they include

Ultra-Orthodox Jews, who tend to marry between the ages of 18 and 24.

The primary impact of later marriage is a decline in the fertility rate among Jewish women. In contrast to the majority of American women, who already have children between the ages of 25 and 29, the majority of Jewish women do not have children until between the ages of 35 and 39.

Percent childless and average number of children born, by age, for Jewish and U.S. women				
	PERCENT CHILDLESS		AVERAGE NUMBER OF CHILDREN BORN	
Age	*Jewish*	*U.S.*	*Jewish*	*U.S.*
18–24	90%	70%	.13	.46
25–29	70	44	.59	1.06
30–34	54	28	1.04	1.56
35–39	36	20	1.38	1.85
40–44	26	19	1.86	1.93

Source: NJPS, p. 4.

Again this disparity is all the more striking given that the Jewish average includes the Ultra-Orthodox, who tend to have children at a young age and who tend to have six or more children.

The average Jewish fertility rate is far below the level of 2.1 needed for zero population growth. The current Jewish fertility rate of 1.86 is insufficient to sustain the current Jewish population; however, the current rate is optimistic. The current Jewish fertility rate does not distinguish between inmarried and intermarried couples, who are much less likely than inmarried couples to raise Jewish identifying children, and therefore the current Jewish fertility rate does not accurately measure Jewish continuity. A more accurate measure of the Jewish fertility rate than the current fertility rate of 1.86 is approximately 1.2, adjusted to exclude the number of children who are not likely be raised Jewish. (A rough estimate is 1.86 × (1-(.47)(.7) = 1.25.) This adjustment is also optimistic, however, since it includes intermarried couples who declare that they are raising their children as Jewish despite the evidence that these children will likely have limited exposure to Judaism. Finally, if we also exclude two parent Jewish families in which the children are being raised as other than Jewish, this rough calculation falls to 1.20.[23] The fertility rate among American Jews today is extremely low.

Another cause of the decline in American Jewry is the crisis of the Conservative Movement of Judaism in America. Although the Conservative Movement was for decades the largest of the three main Jewish movements in the U.S.[24] – in the 1960's, the Conservative Movement was poised to become not only the largest movement, but the dominant spiritual home for American Jewry – it is currently losing adherents at an alarming rate. Only 54% of Jews raised Conservative remained Conservative into adulthood.[25] 27% of the Jews raised Conservative have become members of the Reform Movement, 11% have become "just" Jewish, 3% have become Orthodox, and the remaining 5% have moved away from the Jewish community entirely.[26] The results of this exodus are already apparent. According to the 2000–01 NJPS, 34% of the respondents considered themselves Reform, 26% identified as Conservative, and 13% considered themselves Orthodox.[27] The composition of the American Jewish community has therefore changed drastically since the 1950s, when the Conservative Movement dominated American Jewry and many were convinced that Orthodoxy would disappear. The future generation of the Conservative Movement is also in jeopardy, as the Solomon Schechter Day School network – the crown jewel of the Conservative movement – has had a flat enrollment for the last five years, in contrast to the double-digit gains in overall day school enrollments, principally due to the gowth of Orthodox day schools.[28] Indeed, only just over a quarter of children currently being raised as Conservative are in a Solomon Schechter Day School.[29] The Conservative Movement is unfortunately in such a depressed and conflicted state that it seems unable to rouse itself. As it is currently constituted, the Conservative Movement is an impediment to the reinvigoration of American Jewry. I will get back to this question in Chapter x.

Addressing the Needs of Jewish Immigrants from the Former Soviet Union (FSU)

Jews from the FSU face very specific challenges that must be addressed over the next decade in order to establish Jewish continuity in this community. In New York City, one in five Jews lives in a Russian-speaking household.[30] Approximately 59% of all FSU and Eastern European immigrants settled in New York.[31] Yet, despite living in one of the most vibrant Jewish communities in America, an astounding 79% of members of Russian-speaking households have not received any Jewish education,[32] 69% do not belong to a synagogue[33] and 52% do not belong to *any* Jewish organization.[34] Russian Jews also have a heritage of lower birthrates: in Russia the fertility rate among Jews is 0.8, and in Israel it is 1.8, which is below the fertility rate for native Israeli Jews.[35] The low rate of Jewish education, the low fertility rate, and the legacy of Communism all contribute to making this a fragile Jewish community. Christian missionaries have also sensed this fragility and are targeting Russian Jews in particular. Furthermore, Jewish immigrants from the FSU carry the same attributes of upward mobility as previous Jewish immigrants, such as moving to the suburbs, yet in contrast to past waves of Jewish immigration, their Jewish background is very weak and they face far less anti-Semitic pressure, making the barriers to assimilation for this community extremely low. All of these factors make the Jewish identity of Russian-speaking Jews an urgent concern.

Thankfully, there are hints that Russian Jews desire to reconnect to their Jewish heritage. Despite the fact that 79% of people in Russian-speaking households do not have any Jewish education,

Jews from the FSU score higher than American Jews with similar levels of Jewish education on the indicators of Jewish identity. Studies show that 39% of Russian-Jewish households light Shabbat candles compared to only 30% of all Jewish households in New York.[36] Analysts have also noted that Russian Jews have a strong attachment to Israel. An impressive 97% of Russian Jews say that the State of Israel is very important to them.[37] Thus, Russian Jews show signs that they are open to developing stronger ties to Judaism. However, these links must be strengthened quickly, as the current Russian-speaking community are more susceptible to assimilation than pre-1980 domestic American Jews and their progeny. The broader American Jewish community has about ten years to address the Jewish identity of the Russian Jewish community, or the earlier projection that the American Jewish population will fall to 2.5 million in 2030 will not be a worst case scenario.

Some Positive Features of Current Demographic Trends in American Jewry.

There are small traces of good news in the demographic data. Truly, the data masks increasing commitment and observance on the part of inmarried Jews, because the less observant intermarried families are included in most measures. Day school attendance among the non-Orthodox is increasing. There is greater demand for Jewish Studies at universities. Hillel participation on campus seems to be improving. New non-traditional connections to Judaism and the Jewish people are emerging from the arts, music and literature. A core of Jews seems to be more serious about their Judaism.

Yet, even with these glimpses of light, we must confront the reality that the predictions for the Jewish population in America are bleak. Currently, hundreds of thousands of American Jews can be compared to a liquid when the environmental temperature rises above the boiling point or a solid when the temperature rises above the melting point. Those who dismiss the signs pointing to demographic devastation by claiming that we have overcome every other crisis that has affected American Judaism must face the fact that *it is different this time.* The rate of intermarriage is high and still rising, birth rates are far too low to maintain even zero population growth, the Conservative Movement has lost its way, the Reform Movement's patrilineal descent decision has has had the effect of decreasing the number of self-identifying Jews, our recent immigrants have far less Jewish identity than those of past immigration waves and there is no prospective source of new Jewish immigrants to augment our numbers once again. We must face each of these challenges if we are to remain a vibrant community.

We Must Address Jewish Population Decline Holistically

In the Passover Seder, we sing a well known song of praise, "Dayenu" – "It would be enough for us," which consists of 14 verses in which we reflect on the manifold nature of the gifts that God gave to the Israelites to instill a lasting Jewish identity in the course of the Exodus and the settlement in the land of Israel. Although we exclaim in this song that each miracle God performed would have been enough for us, all were necessary for the redemption of the Jewish people. A partial excerpt will illustrate the idea:

> *"If He had brought us out of Egypt but had not executed judgment on our enemies*
> > *It would be enough for us!*
> *If He had divided the sea for us but without leading us across to dry land*
> > *It would be enough for us!*
> *If He had granted us the Shabbat but without bringing us to Mount Sinai*
> > *It would have been enough for us!*
> *If He had brought us up to Mount Sinai but not given us the Torah*
> > *It would have been enough for us!"*

For fourteen verses we protest the need for each of the gifts that

44

were part of a multi-plank platform that was implicit in the embryonic formation of Jewish identity. Yet each and every gift was crucial and each and every one was a necessary contribution to redemption. If a single one were missing, we would not have been fully redeemed. Similarly, each challenge facing American Jewry today must be addressed if we are to revitalize our community. Our modern day "Dayenu" might read as follows:

> *The Intermarriage Rate*
> > *We need to change this!*
> *Jews are marrying too late in life*
> > *We need to change this!*
> *The low Jewish fertility rate*
> > *We need to change this!*
> *Our Hebrew schools need fixing*
> > *We need to change this!*
> *Our new Russian Jewish brethren need our attention*
> > *We need to change this!*
> *Not enough Jews are visiting Israel*
> > *We need to change this!*
> *Not enough Jewish children are in day school*
> > *We need to change this!*
> *The Conservative Movement is falling apart*
> > *We need to change this!*

As in Dayenu, we need to do it all. We cannot pluck out parts of the platform and hope that "it will be enough."

*   *   *

I have not over-stated the problem. We are clearly in a crisis. Several key factors are causing the steady decline in our population. These factors include late marriage, low fertility rates, high levels of intermarriage due to low levels of Jewish identification among a large number of American Jews, the disintegration of the Conservative Movement, the unintended effects of the Reform

Movement's patrilineal descent policy, and the unstable identity of recent immigrants from the FSU. All of these factors must be addressed together if we are to renew America Jewry, for they all impact one another. In the following chapters, I will describe a ten-plank platform that offers a systemic and comprehensive program to solidify and reinvigorate American Jewry.

Notes

1. *NJPS* 2000–01, p. 182.
2. Ibid, p.182.
3. Sachar, Howard, *A History of Israel From the Rise of Zionism to Our Time* (New York: Alfred A Knopf Inc. 1976), p. 383.
4. Jack J. Diamond, "A Reader in Demography," in *American Jewish Year Book* 1977 Volume 77, ed. Morris Fine and Milton Himmelfarb (New York: The American Jewish Committee; Philadelphia: The Jewish Publication Society of America, 1976), http://www.ajcarchives.org/AJC_DATA/Files/Vol_77_1977.pdf, accessed June 2006.
5. Linda J. Sax, *America's Jewish Freshman, Current Characteristics and Recent Trends Among Students Entering College* (New York: Hillel, 2002), p. 52.
6. *NJPS* 2000–2001, p. 17.
7. *NJPS* 2000–01, p. 21.
8. Ibid, p. 21.
9. This type of analysis is a rough version of what statisticians would call a "static pool analysis."
10. Ira M. Sheskin, "Geographic Differences among American Jews," *United Jewish Communities Report Series on the National Jewish Population Survey* 8 (October, 2004), p. 5.
11. Federation of Jewish Philanthropies of New York, *The Jewish Population of Greater New York: A Profile* (New York: Federation of Jewish Philanthropies of New York, 1984).
12. Pearl Beck, Jacob B. Ukeles and Ron Miller, *The Jewish Community Study of New York: 2002 Geographic Profile* (New York: UJA June 2004).
13. *The Jewish Population of Greater New York: A Profile*, p. 4.
14. *The Jewish Community Study of New York: 2002 Geographic Profile*, p. 21.
15. NYCS, p. 62.
16. John Maynard Keynes, *A Tract on Monetary Reform* (London: Macmillan and Co., 1923).
17. See the U.S. census website, http://www.census.gov/population/projections/PressTab1.xls, accessed June 2006.

18. Jacob R. Marcus, *To Count a People: American Jewish Population Data 1585–1984* (Lanham: University Press of American 1990).
19. Desmond Kind, *The Liberty of Strangers: Making the American Nation* (New York: Oxford University Press, 2005).
20. *NJPS 2000–01*, pp. 18–19.
21. Ibid., p. 17.
22. *The Jewish Community Study of New York: 2002*, p. 173–174.
23. The calculation is (1.86) (.96) + (1 – .47) (.7) = 1.20.
24. Marc Lee Raphael, *Judaism In America* (New York: Columbia University Press, 2003).
25. Ibid., p. 11.
26. United Jewish Communities, *National Jewish Population Survey 2000–01 Conservative Jews: A United Jewish Communities Presentation of Findings* (New York: United Jewish Communities, February 2004), http://www.ujc.org/content_display.html?ArticleID=155417, accessed June 2006.
27. Jonathon Ament, "American Jewish Religious Denominations," *United Jewish Communities Report Series on the National Jewish Population Survey* 10 (February, 2005), p. 9.
28. Marvin Schick, *A Census of Jewish Day Schools in the United States 2003–2004*, p. 2.
29. Steven M. Cohen, *A Tale of Two Jewries: The "Inconvenient Truth" for American Jews* (New York: HUC-JIR, June 2006), p. 6.
30. *NYCS 2004*, p. 66.
31. Due to the high concentration of Jews in New York, the higher relative sample size of the New York study and the assumption that new immigrants who moved to New York are representative of the 41% who moved elsewhere, most of the measures used throughout this book will rely on the New York study, *JPPPI Annual Assessment 2005*, p. 9.
32. *NYCS 2004*, p. 137.
33. Ibid, p. 117.
34. Ibid, p. 123.
35. *JPPPI Annual Assessment 2005*, pp. 374–375
36. *NYCS 2002*, p. 133.
37. Ibid, p. 109.

Chapter III

Hebrew School and More

"The very world rests on the breath of children in
the school-house." *Talmud: Shabbat 119b*

*Plank #1: It is imperative that we fix our supplementary Hebrew
schools so that they convey both knowledge and the love of Judaism and the Jewish people effectively. Still, a perfect Hebrew school
experience is not sufficient to instill an adequate understanding of
Judaism. Parents must encourage involvement not only in Jewish
education but in youth groups and camping as well.*

The Hebrew School Experience

As I sat in Hebrew school as an eight year old (many years ago),
bored silly, I would sometimes stare out of the window and have
a recurring fantasy. I imagined that all of us neighborhood Jewish
kids would be called into a big auditorium. There, an impressive
looking gentleman would approach the microphone. He would
tell us how important it was to be Jewish and how proud we should
be to be continuing our heritage. Then, he would tell us on behalf
of the Chicago Jewish community that during the time set aside
for Hebrew school, we could now have free ice time, just for us,

49

at the nearest ice skating rink, with all the hockey equipment supplies we wanted. The only catch was that we had to memorize our Haftorahs for B'nai Mitzvah when we were thirteen. He would then congratulate us for being Jewish. When the snow had melted, I would have the same basic fantasy except with baseball fields in mind.

My dream was never fulfilled. Instead, I spent five years and over 1,000 hours in a Hebrew school at which I learned very little. The Hebrew classes of my childhood were not only poorly taught and boring, but also had no discernable curriculum. Every year we seemed to start from scratch with a new set of boring books. Everything about the school just seemed tired. By the time I reached my Bar Mitzvah, years of Hebrew school had succeeded in little more than making me ambivalent about being Jewish. In the movie *My Big Fat Greek Wedding*, Nia Vardalos, the main character, had a similar distaste for Greek school. But at least she learned Greek.

The Problem with Today's Hebrew Schools

The model of the Hebrew school of today – like in my childhood – is tired. The reason for this is simple: the "modern" concept of Hebrew school (interchangeably "congregational school" or "supplemental school") still follows the 1920 design by Dr. Samson Benderly of the New York Bureau of Jewish Education. Until recently, few schools had even tinkered with this original model. As a result, parents and children have been voting with their feet. In the late 1960s, when I went to Hebrew school, 44% of Jewish school-age children attended Hebrew school.[1] In 2001, only 30% to 35% of school age children attended Hebrew school.[2] There has also been a strong push by parents to cut the number of weekly hours of Hebrew school.[3] Rather than changing the model, many young Jews are simply giving up on Hebrew school.

Even more distressing is the negative impact that poor Hebrew schools can have on young Jews. Indeed, despite the positive correlation between attending supplemental school and later identifying as a Jew, a significant minority of attendees also end up deeply disenchanted with Judaism.[4] In a well-crafted study of New York Jews, half of respondents who said that they had a significant negative experience in a Jewish institution that was a "turnoff" to Judaism named Hebrew school as that institution. Of those respondents with the lowest level of Jewish involvement, twice as many report a significant negative experience in relation to the rest of the sample.[5]

People inside and outside the Jewish community are increasingly aware of the negative impact of poor Hebrew schools on many young Jews. Outside the Jewish community, the head of a Jews for Jesus group reported that he preferred to missionize Jews who attended Hebrew school versus those who did not. He believed that existing Hebrew schools sometimes alienated Jews but left them wondering why there was not more to the spiritual side of life. In his view, the little knowledge an adult Jew remembers from congregational school could be used to make the case for Christianity. In contrast, he felt that Jews who had not attended Hebrew school were more likely just to remain secular. Within the Jewish community, people are also coming to the conclusion that some Hebrew schools are counter-productive to the Jewish people. In 1992, the Council for Initiatives in Jewish Education commissioned "The Best Practices Project: Supplementary School Education."[6] The result ironically confirmed the subjective experience of former Hebrew school attendees by highlighting how few models of excellence existed and how truly extraordinary those schools were at the time. Most Hebrew schools are not the positive force in Jewish life that they ought to be.

Why Hebrew Schools Matter

Hebrew schools matter because they are and have been the principal and often sole source of Jewish education for millions of American Jewish children over the past eighty years. If American Jewry were to fail, future historians would place substantial blame on the idea of Hebrew school. It is not just that congregational

schools have been ineffectual, it is that parents somehow came
to believe that Hebrew school alone could build Jewish identity
without parental involvement and other positive Jewish activities.
The evidence is clear that Hebrew school combined with informal
Jewish experiences is far more effective than Hebrew school alone.[7]
The potential is there. If we can harness their potential, Hebrew
schools can be a major force in the revitalization of American
Jewry.

Improving Hebrew Schools

Hebrew schools can and must be improved; we can no longer
ignore the problem. Jewish leaders resist making an investment
in Hebrew schools. The accepted wisdom is that Hebrew schools
simply cannot be fixed. For many, day schools, where students
learn both secular and religious studies under one roof, are the
only answer to the problem of poor Hebrew schools. The reality
is that many American Jews would not choose day schools, even
if they were affordable. Many Jewish parents want their children
fully integrated in public and non-sectarian private schools. For
these families Hebrew school is the only answer. We cannot abandon these families. We must build a viable Hebrew school system.
Just as Willie Sutton explained that he robbed banks because
"that's where the money is," we too must focus on congregational
schools because that's where the Jewish kids are. To ignore children who do not attend day school is unacceptable.

A Move Towards a Hebrew School Renewal

Finally, we have taken some steps towards addressing the failure
of Hebrew schools. In late 1999, after several years of inertia, the
newly created Commission on Jewish Identity and Renewal (CO-
JIR) of the UJA-Federation was persuaded that the time had come
to tackle the problem head on.[8] Having spoken so long about
the need, I was elected Chair of the newly formed Task Force on
Congregational Education. With great excitement we sent out
a very broad Request for Proposals seeking bold, adventurous,

exciting new ideas for transforming Hebrew schools. I was thrilled when 23 proposals were received. Unfortunately, as I read them, I felt like I was back in Hebrew school. The visions were too small and the plans were mostly ho-hum. Not one committee member could find one proposal that had any hope of effecting systemic change. Thus, in the in fall of 2000, the committee rejected all of the proposals and began to plot how to bring positive, transformative change to the Hebrew school. We listened to every expert we could persuade to speak to us. We spoke to Hebrew schools and we spoke among ourselves as Hebrew school graduates and parents. In the end, we focused on four drivers for positive change, all of which we deemed critical:

1. Almost every Hebrew school needs to be reinvented;
2. We need to invest in Hebrew school principals. No school can flourish without effective leadership;
3. Hebrew school teachers require and deserve top quality training. Too many Hebrew school teachers have no formal training beyond their own Hebrew school experience;
4. We need measurement tools to objectively identify the strengths and weaknesses of individual Hebrew schools. Failing Hebrew schools need to be flagged.

Two of the major findings of the Task Force on Congregational Education were that there are few Hebrew schools that could not be significantly improved and that most demonstrate the same types of problems. Indeed, it was surprising to discover how little variation there was in how Jewish supplemental education is taught. Yet, with no state or federal laws with which to comply and no organized teachers' unions with which to bargain about change, there is no need to stick to the same tired curriculum and methods.

Congregational schools are free to experiment with both curriculum and pedagogy. Whereas some might teach a lot of

Hebrew, others could teach just enough to read the prayer book. Some could focus on ritual while others might focus on text learning. Teaching methods are also open: some schools could have fewer teachers but more computer assisted learning while others could be built on a tutoring orientation (a program whereby college students teach Hebrew or explain Jewish concepts to younger children). Schools might also experiment with regional cooperation: nearby Hebrew schools might cooperate on field courses or to create regional Hebrew high schools (of which there are far too few). Well-versed members of the congregation might volunteer to teach certain classes. Schools could meet concomitantly with Shabbat services. The list of possibilities is endless and changes would not cost all that much more than the status quo.

With no external constraints, the challenge to renewing Hebrew schools is to gather a critical mass of congregants, teachers, parents, clergy and even students to redesign each Hebrew school as appropriate for each congregation. We have to transform people's dissatisfaction with Hebrew schools and take immediate action. Thankfully, it seems that a lot of constituencies are ready to do just that. For those who wish to make immediate changes, the central movements and local boards of Jewish education have under-used templates for a variety of curriculums and programs. But longer-term change should not return to a cookie-cutter approach. Every congregation must design a school that works for its members without compromising content or quality. Luckily, a few new Hebrew schools across America serve as excellent examples of community-tailored Jewish learning that works.

Some Successful Hebrew Schools

During Rosh Hashanah a decade ago, Rabbi Rick Jacobs of Westchester Reform Temple, a suburban New York congregation, gave a sermon that started dramatic change at his temple. His sermon was titled "The End of Religious School as We Know It." From this dramatic beginning, Westchester Reform Temple reinvented its Hebrew school to include weekly Shabbat morning family programs, enriched Hebrew language learning, parallel parent learning, and a tremendous focus on teens. Westchester Reform Temple has become very successful at keeping teens involved in congregational school well into high school.[9]

Congregation Beth Am of Los Altos Hills, California has also pioneered a new congregational school model. There they mix Shabbat study, Sunday classes and weekday classes, each with their own themes. They also involve families at all levels of the Shabbat experience through a program called Toldot Generational Learning Opportunities. During the rest of the week students are involved in art, dance, social events and weekend retreats. Staffing includes paid professionals, members and for some events, 11th and 12th graders. These initiatives at Westchester Reform Temple and Congregation Beth Am have enlivened not only the congregational schools, but the synagogues as well.[10]

Other new Hebrew schools have been created *de novo* by community members. The Tribeca Hebrew School, in trendy Lower Manhattan, was started by parents who wanted to start a school from scratch that could be attractive to all types of families without regard to affiliation. In a similar vein, my wife Susan and I started a new non-denominational Hebrew school on the Upper East Side of Manhattan. It is called The Jewish Youth Connection (JYC). Every class has fewer than twelve children and we take the drudgery out of learning Hebrew by having college student big brothers/big sisters work one-on-one in Hebrew language learning. These big brother/big sister sessions frequently blossom into junior mentor-type relationships. Because of the small class size and tutoring, there is no need for tests. We know how the children are progressing from close interaction. At JYC, family learning and Shabbat experiences are central. We transformed Hebrew school into a joy. Parents report to us that their children remind *them* that it is time to go to JYC.

There are other exciting Hebrew school programs such as the Jewish Youth Encounter Program in Riverdale, New York and in Bergen County, New Jersey.[11] These programs pioneered the big brother/big sister framework. To our north in Toronto, the Holy Blossom Congregational School has set a standard for imbuing children with a love of Jewish learning and commitment to the Jewish people. Significantly, the recent director of Holy Blossom's Congregational School attributes the excellence of the school to the honor and respect that are accorded to the teachers. Jewish educators are considered the highest echelon of the community. When teachers are honored the results show.[12]

These new Hebrew schools testify to the positive force that congregational schools can and should play in the lives of young Jews. Unfortunately, they are still few and far between. Continued inertia is due in part to the lack of community members pushing their congregations to reinvent their incumbent, tired models. Another issue is that most synagogues do not have the internal skills to transform themselves. There are, however, processes to follow through and promote change at the local level.

Effecting Change in Your Local Hebrew School Today: Five Key Drivers

The first driver to renew local Hebrew schools is to use an outside facilitator with Hebrew school expertise and organizational finesse to help the congregation work out its own best model for change. In our search at UJA-Federation of New York we found the best facilitating group to be the Experiment for Congregational Education (ECE), which operates under the auspices of Hebrew Union College-Jewish Institute of Religion (HUC). They have worked with Traditional, Conservative and Reform synagogues in a non-judgmental way. In New York we selected them to work with twenty synagogues. A second phase of the program is adding an additional twenty schools. While it is too early to provide a final evaluation, the first fruits of the Hebrew school renewal have been refreshingly positive.[13]

The second driver is to invest in our Hebrew school leadership. Without a strong leader, well supported by the clergy and the board, it is futile to attempt to improve a congregational school. The Task Force approached HUC (Reform) and the Jewish Theological Seminary (JTS) (Conservative) with the proposition of building a first ever Principals' Institute. The catch was that the two seminaries had to do it together. In an act that surprised everyone involved, including HUC and JTS themselves, all agreed to the condition. In July 2005, the Leadership Institute for Congregational School Principals opened in New York with 52 participants and tremendous energy. The Institute is a two year part-time program, with a full-time component during the two summers. Such a program can be run for one or two cycles each decade by the larger Jewish communities, which should be sufficient to cover all of the local principals. Smaller communities can also join with the closest large communities to create regional Principals' Institutes as needed.

The third and most expensive driver in the plan to reinvent Hebrew schools is improving the quality of Hebrew school teaching. A study found that 80% of Hebrew school teachers had no professional training in either Jewish studies or education. This would never be permitted in any other teaching environment. We need high quality continuing adult Jewish education for our teachers. The continuing education must include both Judaic studies as well as teaching skills. The cost for this component is high because unlike rewriting the blueprint for Hebrew school or a Principals' Institute, training needs to be continuous.

A necessary condition for improving the quality of Hebrew school teaching is elevating the status of Hebrew school teachers. Because teaching our children is a great responsibility, we must honor teachers by recognizing them in the community, and compensating them appropriately. As a general rule, Jewish educators do not get enough respect and appreciation in the community. Supplemental school teachers get even less. Some are are driven from the field by the lack of respect given to them by parents, the low pay and the absence of basic benefits. Rewarding Hebrew school teachers means higher costs, but we cannot educate our children on the cheap. Central Synagogue in New York has taken the radical step of employing its Hebrew school teachers on a full time basis. Holy Blossom Hebrew School children benefited from the synagogues greatly by virtue of its treatment of teachers as professionals, and by its interest in developing their professional capabilities. Other synagogues that can afford to do so should emulate this course of action.

The fourth driver, measuring the quality of Hebrew school programs, is in some ways the most sensitive. Incredibly, up until now there has been little or no objective measurement of how well any Hebrew school is doing. This is a shocking reality, especially given the fact that there are approximately 250,000 students in an estimated 1,400 congregational schools in the U.S.[14] Measuring the success of a Hebrew school is perfectly compatible with promoting community-based curricula. The measure should determine how well the school is accomplishing its own stated goals, irrespective of whether they are teaching enough Hebrew to navigate the prayer book, emphasizing spoken Hebrew and connection to Israel, or exploring only the cultural aspects of Judaism. Even if a school decides that its approach to Shabbat is just to bake *challah* on Fridays, we at least need some measurement of whether the *challah* smells and tastes good and whether the process of baking is a positive Jewish experience for the students. The results of these measurements need to be reported to the board of the Hebrew school and to the congregation. We cannot continue to avert our eyes from poorly performing schools. The consequences are too great. Focusing on mandates and standards, as movements have done up until now, is a mistake; we need to look at results.

An additional driver is to encourage more choice of supplemental schools. Day schools, Jewish Community Centers and other communal organizations should be urged and funded to start new schools. These schools may take very different forms from congregationally sponsored Hebrew schools. Tribeca Hebrew School is a very different model precisely because it is not congregationally sponsored. These schools too should not escape serious evaluation. Historically, Jewish groups outside of congregations have been reluctant to set up Hebrew schools due to a fear of seeming to compete with synagogues. The reality is that when it comes to Jewishly educating our children, the more choices the better.

The first-time reinvention of Hebrew schools may take the better part of a decade, but it must be made the highest communal priority. Furthermore, we cannot fall into the Benderly trap of creating a new structure and thereafter ignoring whether it succeeds or fails. Each decade American Jewry should declare one year "The Year of the Hebrew School." During that year, every congregation or Hebrew school sponsor should take an in-depth look at its school. For a deeper description of this reinvention process, visit *www.eceonline.org*.

Beyond Hebrew School

Reinventing Hebrew schools is the first part of building a solid American Jewry. But it is nowhere near enough. Energetic and revitalized Hebrew schools must be coupled with deep parental involvement and informal Jewish education via youth groups and camping. Ari Goldman has argued that we use the Suzuki violin teaching format for Jewish education. The key to the Suzuki method is that parents are totally involved in their children's musical education. Parents attend the lessons, stay with children while they practice and take their children to classical music concerts. Music becomes a mutually enjoyable experience and a shared family value.[15] Million of young people have learned to play and enjoy music through the Suzuki method. It can work for Judaism as well. Parental involvement is the key. If children think that Hebrew school is just about punching a ticket so that they can have a Bar/Bat Mitzvah, they will treat their Jewish education accordingly. Parents must take Hebrew school seriously. They cannot simply drop their child off at synagogue on their way to the golf course. They have to go inside and learn with the child. Without the parents' involvement Hebrew school is bound to fail.

Youth Groups

Parents should also be vigorously encouraged to expose their children to informal Jewish education through youth groups and camps. The research is clear: Hebrew school by itself is not enough. Supplemental schools must consider themselves as sources for youth groups and be open to different types of Judaism. These youth groups can be movement based, such as United Synagogue Youth (USY), National Federation of Temple Youth (NFTY), National Conference of Synagogue Youth (NCSY), Israel oriented Bnei Akiva and Young Judea, or the secular B'nai Brith Youth Organization (BBYO). Youth groups can be very effective in making Judaism or Jewish peoplehood relevant to the broader world by taking Judaism out of the synagogue and putting it into real life. Youth groups seem to be more influential than Hebrew school on a statistical basis. But as we will see in camping as well, it is probably because the more motivated Hebrew school students choose to participate in youth groups.

	Married a Jew	*Being Jewish very important*	*Very attached to Israel*
Participated in a Jewish Youth Group	75%	57%	37%
No Participation in a Jewish Youth Group	49%	27%	17%

Source: Cohen and Kotler-Berkowitz, p. 10.

Sadly, youth groups are sorely under-funded. Each movement needs to re-prioritize to provide youth groups with plentiful resources. Without USY, my Hebrew school experience alone would have left me alienated from Judaism. USY made being Jewish fun and engaging.

Camping

Camps must also be part of the equation. Currently, fewer than 10% of Jewish children attend Jewishly oriented summer camps.[16] Even among the Jewish camps, the level of Jewish content is uneven. Residential camps, for example, have the greatest potential for transmitting Jewish education informally. By living in a fully Jewish environment, children experience the rhythm of the day and the week in a positive Jewish context. Everything from ethics in sports to Shabbat meals can be imbued with Jewish meaning. Residential camp is the ultimate "bubble experience."

	Married a Jew	Being Jewish very important	Very attached to Israel
Attended a Jewish Camp	77%	56%	41%
Did Not Attend a Jewish Camp	46%	25%	14%

Source: Cohen and Kotler–Berkowitz, "The Impact of Childhood Jewish," p. 10.

The major hurdles for making overnight camp a normative experience for Jewish children are the high cost (often in excess of $7,000 for eight weeks) and the allure of non-Jewish camps. In terms of cost, we need to come up with a way to subsidize the first time a child attends a Jewish camp. Many Jewish camps already provide scholarships for about 20% of their campers.[17] We also have to help enrich camp programs so they can be fully competitive with general camps. Jewish camps will also need to further specialize in sports and other activities in order to compete with general camps. This trend is emerging, with Jewish camps being established to specialize in the arts, music, drama, basketball, baseball, soccer and wilderness experiences.[18]

The Conservative movement's Camp Ramah Network, which has provided children with a high quality experience for decades, is an example of the critical importance of camps. Indeed, the last three generations of ordained clergy of the Conservative movement are mostly past campers. Camp Ramah, one of the crown jewels of the movement, can even be said to be the real initiator of the Solomon Schechter Day School network, as campers left the summers with an appetite for more Jewish learning.

Day camps can also offer Jewish content. While they may not offer the intensity of residential camps, they can infuse a Jewish sensibility into sports, meals, and games. Many day camps already have one or more overnights during the week. A Shabbat weekend extension program in conjunction with a youth group could be a wonderful experience for the campers. The Foundation for Jewish Camping is pioneering new ideas for both day camps and residential camps (see www.jewishcamping.org).

Some camps had great success in tapping into the pool of traveling Israeli teenagers, pre- and post-army, and employing them as counselors. These young Israelis are usually charismatic role models that inspire campers to be more mindful of their connection to Israel. These encounters can be transformative for young American Jews. More camps should reach out to this Israeli resource. For many campers, hearing about Israel from an Israeli might whet their desire to visit Israel.

Shabbat Dinner in Your Home
One of the simplest and most effective ways of promoting a secure Jewish identity is making Shabbat dinner every Friday night a sit-down, at-home meal, shared by the entire family. There is a

substantial body of research that indicates that families that eat together are happier and that their children are happier, stronger and smarter as well.[19] The more meals a week a family eats together the better. Yet in today's over-programmed world it is hard for everyone to be on the same dinner schedule every day. Shabbat dinner on Friday night can be the exception, an occasion for everyone to sit and enjoy the sacred time by talking and eating together. The expression "more than Jews having kept Shabbat, Shabbat has kept the Jews" (Achad Ha'Am) has a great deal of truth in it. If I may be allowed some license with the expression, I would suggest the following: "The more that the family preserves the Shabbat dinner, the more the Shabbat dinner preserves the family."

*   *   *

In this platform we have defined a holistic approach to raising a Jewish child solid in his or her Jewishness. We need to care enough about our children's Jewish education not to rest until we have fixed our Hebrew schools. We need to care enough as parents to be deeply involved in shaping our children's Jewish experiences and making sure that children enjoy "doing Jewish."[20] This means youth groups and camps. It also means "doing Jewish" as a family. Enjoying Friday night dinner together, every Friday night, is a first step. Further steps can be participating together in synagogue or being involved with Jewishly oriented volunteer projects together. If we do not show our children we care about being Jewish, how can we ask our children to care?

Returning to our physical metaphor for building a Jewish identity, the environment must be consistent to maintain a Jewish identity. Expecting Hebrew school alone to create a Jewish identity is like expecting water in a 70° Fahrenheit environment to freeze because a 31° Fahrenheit breeze passes through every so often. The water will not freeze, but if it could think, it would be very confused. The key is in making the child's environment consistently Jewish and consistently positive. It is right to conclude that a child that has attended seven years at a quality Hebrew school and has participated in a youth group and in a Jewish camp, also while enjoying Friday night dinner every Friday with her/her family, is highly likely to be a solid Jew as an adult.

Notes

1. Nathan Glazer, *American Judaism*, p. 158.
2. Robert Louis Goodman and Eli Schapp, *What are the Numbers of Jewish Educators and Students in Formal Jewish Educational Settings?* (New York: Council for the Advancement of Jewish Education, 2002), http://www.caje-cbank.org/research-njps2.pdf, accessed June 2006.
3. For the pre-Bar Mitzvah aged students, time spent in Hebrew school has decreased from 10+ hours per week to 4–6 hours per week. See JESNA, *A Vision for Excellence Report of the Task Force on Congregational and Communal Jewish Education* (New York: JESNA, 2000), p. 10, http://archive.jesna.org/pdfs/cc_visexc.pdf, accessed June 2006.
4. For the positive correlation, see Steven M. Cohen & Laurence Kotler-Berkowitz "The Impact of Childhood Jewish Education on Adults' Jewish Identity: Schooling, Israel Travel, Camping and Youth Groups," *United Jewish Communities Report Series on the National Jewish Population Survey* 3 (July, 2004), pp. 10–11, http://www.ujc.org/content_display.html?ArticleID=155417, accessed June 2006.
5. Bethamie Horowitz, *Connections and Journeys: Assessing Critical Opportunities for Enhancing Jewish Identity* (New York: Commission of Jewish Identity and Renewal – UJA-Federation, June 2000), pp. 100 and 176, http://www.jewishdatabank.org/CJ2003.pdf, accessed June 2006.
6. Barry W. Hertz directed the project.
7. Horowitz, *Connections and Journeys*, p. 173.
8. My personal thanks to Marion Blumenthal, Alisa Rubin Kurshan and Deborah Joselow for supporting the task force on congregational education. I would like to thank Marion Blumenthal in particular, who, as the then Chair of CoJIR, embraced the idea and worked hard to find the monetary resources. Sara Nathan, my successor as Task Force Chair, has advanced the effort much further.
9. Rob Weinberg, "Creating and Enacting Shared Visions for Congregational Education" *Jewish Education News* (Winter, 2006).
10. Rob Weinberg "Programmatic Innovation in Religious Schools of ECE Congregations – Two Examples," (Unpublished article, 2005).
11. The Jewish community owes Sylvia and Carl Fryer and Rabbi Avi Weiss, the originators of the JYEP concept, a debt of great gratitude.
12. Michele Lynn (former director of Holy Blossom Congregational School), personal discussion with the author, January 9, 2006.

13. UJA-Federation of New York sponsored a preliminary evaluation of the program and so far the results have been positive, however, we must wait a few more years before can properly measure the full impact of the program.

14. Robert Louis Goodman and Eli Schaap, *What are the Numbers of Jewish Educators and Students in Formal Jewish Educational settings?* (New York: The Coalition for the Advancement of Jewish Education, 2002), p. 1, http://www.caje-cbank.org/research-njps2.pdf, accessed June 2006.

15. Ari Goldman,"Suzuki Judaism," *The Jewish Week*, September 16, 2005.

16. For a full discussion of Jewish camping, see Amy L. Sales and Leonard Saxe. *"How Goodly Are Thy Tents": Summer Camps as Jewish Socializing Experiences* (Lebanon: Brandeis University Press, 2004).

17. [6] According to Sales and Saxe, 19% is the precise percentage. Sales and Saxe, *"How Goodly Are Thy Tents,"* p. 36.

18. Jerry Silverman, "Where Jewish Leaders are Bread," *Jerusalem Post*, December 9, 2004.

19. Miriam Weinstein, *The Surprising Power of Family Meals* (Hanover: Steerforth Press, 2005).

20. Richard Joel coined this phrase during his tenure as Executive Director of Hillel.

Chapter IV

Day Schools for More Jews

"A village without a school should be abolished."
Talmud: Shabbat, 119b

Plank #2: The Jewish day school system must be exponentially expanded. 29% of American Jewish children are currently attending day school, of which 70% – 80% are being raised Orthodox. We need to adopt the explicit target of educating at least 50% of American Jewish children in day schools by 2030, of which at least 50% should be from non-Orthodox homes. To enable this growth, the entire structure of day school funding must be altered.[1]

Why Day Schools Matter

The number of years a child attends day school has a greater impact on adult Jewish involvement and inmarriage than any other variable, including being raised in an Orthodox home.[2] The day school movement is perhaps the most successful initiative in the 350 year history of American Jewry. The Orthodox, especially the fervently Orthodox, pioneered the day school movement. Whereas in the early 1940s, there were under 19,000

Jewish students in day school, by 1958, day school attendance had increased to approximately 43,000 students.[3] This number more than quadrupled by 1998 when there were 185,000 students in day schools. And there was another spurt at the turn of the century. By September 2003, there were some 205,000 children enrolled.[4] It is marvelous to see that the growth in day school students in that five year period exceeded the entire enrollment of day schools in the early 1940s. This is more exciting given that the overall American Jewish population, as we observed in Chapter 11, has shrunk since the 1940s.

Because almost all Orthodox children attend day schools, there is no doubt that the growth of Orthodoxy correlates positively with the growth of day school enrollment, however, there has also been a significant growth in non-Orthodox – primarily community – day schools. These community day schools could not have been established without parents and other community members foregoing the path of least resistance to devote a massive amount of time and money for the good of their children and the Jewish people. As a result of their efforts, eighty new day schools have been opened in the five year period ending in 2003.[5] This is a tremendous accomplishment.

The unexpected success of day schools is an example of what a community can do when it recognizes that day schools are a wonderfully bright ray of sunshine in an otherwise cloudy demographic horizon. To reach our target of 325,000 students attending day schools (about 50% of total Jewish school-aged children), we need an increase of 120,000 non-Orthodox students, which would bring the Orthodox/non-Orthodox ratio to nearly 50:50. The following chart underscores the success of day schools and the challenge that we must overcome in order to radically improve our Hebrew schools, keeping in mind that few Hebrew school students continue past the sixth year.

There is no better assurance for the future of American Jewry than a first through twelfth grade day school education.

Years of Jewish Education Received	Married a Jew	Being Jewish Very Important	Very Attached to Israel
Day school: 7–12	96%	86%	67%
Day school: 1–6	82%	59%	38%
Hebrew school: 7–12	76%	51%	36%
Hebrew school: 1–6	63%	36%	21%
Sunday school: 7–12	60%	35%	12%
Sunday school: 1–6	42%	28%	13%
No Jewish education	33%	16%	12%

Source: Cohen & Kotler-Berkowitz, pp. 10–11.

Day Schools: An American-Jewish Synthesis

Day schools are, of course, far from perfect but at their best, they are happy places that seamlessly combine Jewish education, secular studies, and extra-curricular studies. Aside from the continuity benefits, day schools, with their demanding dual curriculum, sharpen the mind. Delving into the subtleties of biblical studies prepares the children to better comprehend literature as they mature. Talmud studies engender a discipline and logic in reasoning that can be applied to all areas of study. Conversely, excellence in secular studies sheds new insights into traditional texts. The early immersion learning of Hebrew as a second language is not only a major gift; it also prepares students to approach additional languages without apprehension. There is also evidence that early immersion enhances other cognitive skills and makes learning subsequent languages easier.[6] Ideally, all day school students graduate with excellent skills in both Jewish and secular studies. Unfortunately, there are still too many sub-par day schools. As a community we must work to ensure that all schools are excellent in all areas.

Day schools also strengthen children's Jewish identity within an American context. In day schools, Judaism becomes a part of each student's daily life; it is not compartmentalized to an after-school – and therefore less important – activity. Judaism becomes second nature, not secondary. There is no conflict between Hebrew school and extracurricular activities, nor any complex shuttling of children from general school to Hebrew school to extracurricular activities to home. Day schools leave time for both Jewish and American activities. Day schools also harmonize the school, national and Jewish calendars: children learn about and experience the Jewish holiday cycle, Jewish year and American civic holidays. Day schools teach children to be proud of being Jewish and proud of being American, with a solid grounding in both aspects of themselves.

Day schools create an environment grounded in the moral and ethical values that will prepare our children to be righteous as well as successful in the Jewish community and America at large. Day schools provide everyday opportunities to do *tzedakah* and *gmilut chasadim* (acts of loving kindness). Parents and students frequently come together to work on projects to help the poor or the elderly. These projects and the day-to-day activities of the day school foster a sense of community and caring that is extraordinarily nourishing.[7] The results of the positive environment in day schools show. Day school graduates have proven to be very successful in life. Day school graduates are accepted into the top universities and become doctors, lawyers, entrepreneurs, CEO's, teachers, military officers and government officials. Day school education is an incredible gift to our children, the Jewish people, and American society at large.

Objections to Jewish Day Schools

Four major objections to day school education are usually raised. The first objection is the assumption that they will preclude the Americanization of Jews. By attending day schools, Jews will come to be viewed as separate from the general population; in other words, day schools will ghettoize Jews. In my view, this argument is simply not valid. The concept of an American "melting pot" has been replaced by the metaphors of an American "mosaic," "orchestra" or "chorus of multiple voices." Today, ethnic groups and religious communities seek to preserve and promote their heritages while celebrating the unity and diversity of America. Attending Jewish day schools fulfills this goal. What is more, a growing number of American families are also sending their children to private schools that reflect the values and culture of their local community.[8] In this respect, Jewish day schools are no different than Catholic schools or Greek Orthodox schools in America. But most importantly, there is little evidence that day school attendance hinders Jews from participating in American society after graduating. Day school graduates are proud Americans, serving in the U.S. Armed Forces, running for local, state and national offices, and joining in patriotic activities.

The second objection is that day school education is not adequate to prepare Jews for the modern world. Jewish parents are concerned that the day school curriculum, which includes half a day of Jewish studies and the other half of secular studies, is an inadequate preparation for higher secular education. This assumption is simply not true. Day school graduates perform consistently well on all major standard tests throughout the U.S., and successfully pursue higher education. And, as already noted, not only do many day schools have an outstanding secular curriculum, the Jewish curriculum also enhances those skills children need for secular learning. From a purely academic perspective day schools are an excellent choice for bright and motivated children. From the perspective of Jewish continuity, they are the best choice.

The third objection – raised frequently by parents – is that their children will become rabbis or simply "too religious." In practice, however, the subject of religiosity has only rarely been divisive among non-observant families with day school children. Acceptance of families at their own point of religiosity is a fundamental principle of community day schools and is accepted at most other non-Chareidi schools. At many co-educational Orthodox day schools, a substantial proportion of the students do not come from observant family backgrounds and are fully embraced as part of the community. Nevertheless, as a natural outgrowth of a family's commitment to Jewish education, day schools do promote increased family-oriented Jewish experiences, such as having a traditional Friday night dinner together.

The fourth objection is cost. Affordability is a primary restraint to day school enrollment growth among the non-Orthodox. It is also a source of hardship among the more fervently Orthodox. An old joke among Orthodox Jews is that the form of birth control most couples use is yeshiva/day school tuition. Unfortunately it is no joke. I know a number of couples from both the Orthodox and Conservative Movements who decided to forgo having a third or fourth child due to worries over the cost of day school. In the relatively affluent town of Lawrence, New York, Modern Orthodox parents have implored the local public school district to take over the general studies portion of their day school's program because of the rising cost of day school tuition.[9] The Lawrence request is unlikely to be adopted, as the courts have turned down every attempt to get government funding of religious schools, but the cry for help to pay day school tuition is audible. Among the non-Orthodox, who tend to have fewer children, the decision to forgo the much cheaper alternative of public school is also a very real impediment to achieving Plank #2's goal of 50% of day school children being non-Orthodox.

The Cost of Day Schools Today

Day schools are plagued by the problems of affordability. Typical day school tuition exceeds $12,000. And though most day schools offer substantial scholarship programs, typically amounting to 15–20% of day school income,[10] these programs still exclude a large number of potential day school children for several reasons. Some parents fall between the cracks, theoretically ineligible for financial aid, but practically unable to pay full tuition. Others who consider applying for financial aid are so put off by the process that they do not apply, or withdraw their children when the burden becomes too great. Even middle and upper-middle income families, especially those with more than two children, struggle to pay the tuition bill or choose not to send their children to day school so as to be able to afford other needs.

Unfortunately, with the way day schools are currently financed, most are structurally unable to lower tuition or provide aid levels that are appropriate. This is due to the higher cost of covering the curriculum of general and Judaic studies as well as the cost of the longer school day. Day schools that try to cut costs in either area undercut the critical reason for sending children there by offering a sub-par education in both general and Jewish studies. With higher costs than other schools – which continue to rise – quality day schools are likely to become less, not more, affordable. At some point, rising tuition will lead to slower day school enrollment growth or worse, slippage. We need to act now to totally reorient the day school operating finance system.

Making Day Schools Affordable

I propose that we overhaul day school financing completely. Instead of the current system I would introduce what I call the

"egalitarian tuition plan" (ETP), a system based on community responsibility. We should aspire for everyone in the community to be a partner in the cost of educating the next generation of American Jews, even if we cannot currently actualize the principle. The concept of the ETP includes some aspects of a tuition payment structure that was developed by the Manhattan Country School in 1970 and is still employed currently at the Manhattan Country School.[11] However, the ETP is more radical and comprehensive than the Manhattan Country School plan, as is appropriate given the importance of day schools for the future of the Jewish people.

Current Day School Funding

In order to demonstrate how the ETP would work, let us consider the way that most day schools are funded today. Let's take Aleph Bet Day School, a typical school with 300 students, an $11,000 average annual tuition, a $12,000 average cost per student, with 120 children on some level of scholarship which varies greatly but averages $5,000. Obviously, these numbers are estimates for purposes of this example and will vary widely from school to school.

Aleph Bet Day School Typical Tuition Plan / Operating Plan Summary	
Gross Expected Tuition Revenue (300 x $11,000)	$3,300,000.00
Scholarship Allocation (120 x $5,000)	(600,000.00)
Net Tuition Revenue	2,700,000.00
Cash Costs of School Operations	(3,600,000.00)
Annual Fundraising (of which $300,000 from non parents)	900,000.00
Surplus / Deficit	0.00

The operating statement highlights the unfairness of the system. The school starts every year at a deficit, which means that the board and principal must spend significant time on fundraising in order to cover the $900,000 deficit via special appeals and an annual dinner. Due to financial constraints, financial aid is probably less than it should be (after what can be an embarrassing process) and not everyone who should be contributing to the school is doing so at an appropriate level. Further, others remain outside the day school because they earn too much to get aid but cannot find $11,000 after-tax dollars (probably $17,000 pre-tax dollars) each year to pay for each child's education.

So let's discard the current financial system and start from scratch. Historically, Jews have recognized Jewish education as the responsibility of the entire community. In the United States, the same view is taken for public education, which Americans pay for primarily through property taxes with some state aid, unconnected to the number of children in the families of property owners or state tax payers. While some voters complain about having to support public education and communities reject school bond issues and tax proposals from time to time, by and large the overwhelming majority of U.S. citizens recognizes the communal responsibility of education. The equally American and Jewish value of communal responsibility for education should be the basis of the ETP system. Ideally, this would mean that every American Jew should contribute an appropriate amount of their income to local Jewish educational institutions, independent of the number of children in their family. While this would dramatically decrease or eliminate tuition costs, there is no binding way to compel all Jews to contribute anything at all. However, a suitable and voluntary alternative for day schools and parents would be to set up a model equitable system that retains the current basis for tuition funding, but also has an open structure, which over time will attract outside sources of funding.

The Egalitarian Tuition Plan (ETP)

The structure for a practicable alternative to current day school funding is as follows. Aleph Bet Day School would set tuition at $3,000 per student. This is an amount that almost all families would be expected to pay except those with the most extenuating circumstances. Day school education should have a basic cost to be valued by the family. All families would be required to send a financial statement to a third party independent accounting firm or other financial consulting firm (in order to maintain the confidentiality of the information). The accounting firm would then use a formula provided by the school to allocate the total net tuition budget to each family, according to its income level. The formula would likely include a baseline below which parents would pay no more than tuition and an adjustment so that families with more children paid a lesser share for each additional child in the school over two children. No one would be forced to pay more than 50% above the full cost of their children's day school education. Other parties interested in the success of the day school could ideally join in as full participants without the tuition factor or (as is more likely, at least at first) make a fixed contribution to the pool.

If there were no other additions to the revenue pool, the summary operating statement would look like the table on the following page.

So far we have assumed that no new money has entered Aleph Bet: no contributor has been motivated to add a penny or become a full partner and accept an allocation. Is Aleph Bet better off? The answer is clearly yes. No one is embarrassed about asking for financial aid as everyone files the first two pages of their tax return with an independent accountant and everyone pays an appropriate proportional share of the budget cost. Everyone now has a right to be heard on budgetary issues; there are no second-class citizens. There are also no longer very high-income parents who are paying tuition but shirking responsibility to contribute to the school. The parents are modeling collective responsibility

Aleph Bet Day School Egalitarian Tuition Plan / Operating Statement Summary	
Gross Expected Tuition Revenue (300 × $3,000)	$900,000.00
Scholarship Allocation (20 × $1,500)	(30,000.00)
Net Tuition Revenue	870,000.00
Cash Costs of School Operations	(3,600,000.00)
School Operations Cost to be Allocated	(2,730,000.00)
Contributions from Non-Parents	300,000.00
Egalitarian Allocation of Remaining Cost of Education to Parents	2,430,000.00
Surplus / Deficit	0.00

for education and creating an inviting environment for outsiders to feel as though they can equitably join in the enterprise. The annual dinner becomes much less about "*machers*," although we will always need them, and more a celebration of each family's embrace of the collective financial responsibility to educate our children according to our means to do so. Every family can come to the dinner, because every family has made an appropriate contribution.

A few schools across the U.S. have recently adopted measures that have some resemblance to ETP, with great success. In 2005–2006, the Gross Schechter Day School in Cleveland implemented a major tuition reduction by cutting tuition in half to $5,500.[12] As a result, it was short $630,000 from its annual budget. In order to make up for the difference, the school raised money from two major donors to cover a third of the outstanding balance, money from its local Federation and local endowments to cover another third, and a major fundraising campaign for which the school collected tax-deductible donations from parents and friends to cover the final third. Through these alternative sources of funding, the Gross Schechter Day School funding plan has successfully covered its costs. The Gross Schechter School's financial plan is not only fiscally viable; it has been a major impetus for the growth of the school. During its first year, the school's preschool was completely full and only one child left the school. In contrast, prior to the implementation of the tuition reduction, schoolchildren were leaving the school due to the high cost of tuition. In 2003–2004, the school lost 23 children whose parents paid full tuition; 22 of the 23 went to public school. The implementation of a system on the path towards the ETP is working very well at the Gross Schechter Day School in Cleveland.

A major part of the Gross Schechter Day School's success is that it has implemented a long-term program of tuition reduction. Although a few schools and communities have lowered tuition, most have done so only on a short-term basis and therefore have not reaped the benefits of this initiative. According to my interpretation of a UJC study on day school funding, short-term tuition reduction is not financially effective, nor does it improve day school enrollment in the long or intermediate term, since parents know that they will soon have to pay just as much as they were paying before.[13] In order for tuition reduction to have an impact, it must be implemented over the long-term in conjunction with a detailed program of alternative funding. When this is the case, as the experience of the Gross Schechter Day School demonstrates, the results are excellent. ETP takes this success to another and broader level.

The Fiscal Advantages of ETP

The annual ETP contributions may lead to substantial tax benefits. It may be possible to structure the collective responsibility

allocation in excess of tuition as a tax-deductible charitable contribution. However, it is likely that if the collective responsibility allocation is absolutely mandatory it will not be deductible.
Schools might therefore experiment with making the contribution
voluntary, but heavily encouraged. It is also possible to create a
supporting membership association that would be open to all
members of the community but would be mandatory for parents.
This supporting tax-exempt entity would pledge to equitably allocate the excess of costs over tuition revenues at one or more
local schools. Such a framework would be workable but would
certainly require an Internal Revenue Service ruling to ensure that
membership contributions to the association were tax deductible
for those taxpayers whose children attended the school. If the
supporting membership association concept were to not receive
a favorable IRS ruling, a back-up tax solution would be to enlist
our Jewish communal lobbying organizations to unite behind the
ETP. This would move the Jewish community beyond the endless
debate over school vouchers. In this scenario, our Jewish lobbying
groups should put all their resources behind convincing Congress
to authorize the tax deductibility of egalitarian tuition plans for
all religious schools. There is no reason for the Jewish community
not to be united on this issue, as this is not about vouchers. There
have been many proposals to make college tuition partially tax
deductible, with the core debate being over costs, not theology. A
college tax deduction was included in a tax bill passed by Congress
in 1992 but vetoed by then President Bush. It is likely that supporters of Catholic schools would also be strong supporters.

Beyond the potential for tax deductibility, the ETP would
facilitate new sources of money for day schools. Given that every
day school parent will be making an appropriate allocation of their
resources to day schools, each day school parent should become a
loud supporter of George Hanus' "Five Percent Answer," in which
every American Jew is asked to allot 5% of his/her estate to an
endowment fund for an established day school in their community.[14] This initiative will not have a meaningful effect for twenty

to forty years, until donors pass away and their wills are executed. There is a tremendous wealth transfer slated for this time frame in the United States. It is not unrealistic to expect several billion dollars of principal coming from this initiative if it were widely adopted. Of course, we all wish each person who makes such an election in his/her will a long life. While it is highly unlikely that this initiative will make a difference until after 2030, it can make a very significant difference past that time. As the story goes, Honi HaMa'agel once saw an old man planting a carob tree. Honi asked the old man when he thought the tree would bear fruit. "After seventy years," the old man replied. "Do you expect to live seventy years and eat the fruit of your labor?" asked Honi. "I did not find the world a desolate place when I entered it," said the old man, "and as my father planted for me before I was born so did I plant for those who come after me."[15] If people do not put this type of election in their wills now, this funding source will not be there for the next generation.

Impediments to the "Five Percent Answer," such as the risk that designating a percentage of one's estate to charity will cause the valuation of the estate to be examined by the Attorney General in certain states, can be circumvented with appropriate planning. If there is such a concern that one's estate will be open to delay and litigation, potential contributors should make an estimate of their estate and set a specific dollar amount for the day school scholarship allocation in their will. Just as we should want to give our children the gift of Jewish day schools, we should also work to spare them some of the future costs of educating their children. The "Five Percent Answer" presents a communal response that is relatively painless.

The 5% solution could make day schools affordable to more Jewish families. However, the sums that are likely to be aggregated will only be part of the answer. Let us optimistically assume that $10 billion is raised by 2040 and that 5% per year can be spent from the return on investment of the funds. This would leave $500 million to be divided among the 50% of Jewish children who we hope will be in day school. Based on an assumption of 650,000 school-aged Jewish children, 50% being 325,000, the subsidy would be $1,540 per student in 2040 dollars.

Finding New Sources of Funding for the ETP

Another possible stream of funding for the collective responsibility allocation is the Jewish Federations. Some day school advocates have heavily criticized Federations for not being larger supporters of day schools. Other contributors to Jewish Federations argue that the whole system was set up to fund the human needs of Jews in their local communities, overseas and particularly in Israel. Generally about 40%-50% of the net money from Federation campaigns is expanded to meet overseas needs through the Joint Distribution Committee and the Jewish Agency. The remainder of the money has traditionally gone to local Hebrew Homes for the Aged, local Jewish poverty councils, local agencies providing services to families in distress, food delivery to the poor and elderly and other pressing human needs. Federations usually support local JCCs, cultural organizations and burial societies as well. Over the last fifteen years, Federations have moved toward allocating increasing amounts to formal and informal Jewish education. In some communities where there are few day school students, such as Cleveland, the Federation allocation can be meaningful. Cleveland's Federation provided an allocation of over $1,300 per student in a recent year.[16] Communities with larger numbers of students in day school, such as Baltimore and New York, provide relatively low allocations per student. In Baltimore, less then $300 is allocated per day school student and in New York, the allocation is less than $150 per student.[17]

The unfortunate reality is that even if all of the Jewish Federations in the U.S. were to allocate *all* of the funds they spend in the U.S. just to day schools, the subsidy per student based on the current 205,000 students would be approximately $1,950, and based on Plank #2's goal of 325,000 students, the subsidy would come out to a bit more than $1,200 per student. So this massive reallocation of the Federation's monies is not a solution. Of course, hypothetically, if Jewish Federations were to actually adopt such a policy many critical social service agencies would shut down, an eventuality which no day school proponent could support. The reality is that every local Federation campaign is built by the broadest possible coalition of contributors who are moved by the Federation's support of human needs. Most Federation contributors believe that it is the responsibility of the affluent American Jewish community to provide significant support to needy communities abroad. To shift the campaign mostly to day schools would cause the collapse of these financial campaigns. It is inconceivable that such a significant shift would ever actually happen.

All of this is not to say that Jewish Federations should be excused from dramatically increasing support for day schools. The goal must simply be balanced with recognition of the needs of other *tzedakot* and the nature of the donor base of Federations. Beginning in 2007, and continuing for 7 years, each Federation should increase its allocation to day school education by 1.5% of its total campaign. By 2014, this would result in Federations allocating an additional 10.5% of their total campaign to day schools. Assuming that the campaigns of Federations can grow by 1.5% per year, this would mean freezing most allocations to other needs for the period. This is a very hard thing to do and will have a very real effect on meeting pressing human needs. Federations are working very hard to see any campaign growth at all. However, this undertaking will energize some segments of the Jewish community to join in the Federation campaigns or to increase their funding of Federations. Assuming that the combined Federation campaigns can grow from the current $800 million range at the same 1.5%, the overall campaign would be $888 million. This growth in income is probably the most that can be realistically expected from Federations. The additional $88 million should be allocated only to those schools adopting the ETP, to insure that the Federation funds are allocated in an equitable manner. This stream of funding would provide almost $480 per student nationally based on current enrollment in 2014, but only $270 per student if we reach the enrollment goal of this plank. In the final analysis, Jewish Federation funding would contribute more to publicly recognizing day school as a Jewish communal priority and encouraging the ETP rather than drastically reducing current tuitions.

The other major source of funding and student growth for our day schools is the 30,000 to 50,000 American Jewish students in private schools. These numbers have been estimated by a variety of observers but there is no hard data. For example, in some independent private schools in the New York City area, 30% to 60% of the student population is Jewish. In many cases, the Jewish parents of these students are very affluent but are not attracted to Jewish schools. For these parents, tuition is not an issue because they are already paying private school tuition as well as frequently making contributions to their schools. Our day schools need to achieve a level of excellence that will attract a large share of these students. The way to reach 325,000 students and a 50% share of non-Orthodox students is not by slashing education budgets but by achieving and maintaining a level of excellence in education and equitably sharing the costs through the ETP.

The one major risk of ETP is that richer day school parents will create day schools with wealthier families and thereby circumvent the ETP concept of sharing the burden. Thus, I am proposing to place a cap on the tuition gradient that any family can be involuntarily allocated in order to reduce this risk. Of course, those families should be told their full contribution amount and be encouraged to donate the difference. Integral to modeling joint Jewish communal responsibility and to receiving communal support, day schools must in turn accept upon themselves broader obligations to the Jewish community. Day schools must become resources for local Hebrew schools, including teacher training and curriculum development. Day schools could host synagogue consortium supplemental Jewish high schools and perhaps formally facilitate the opportunity for some of their teachers to teach in these schools.

Day schools must also provide additional entry points for children. Currently, it is very difficult to enter Jewish day school from a public or non-Jewish private school after first grade. Day school students advance very quickly in their Hebrew skills, which is the key to Judaic studies. However, if we are successful in enlivening Hebrew schools and coupling them with youth groups and camping experiences, we should be pleasantly surprised to find that a significant number of children will want a more comprehensive Jewish formal study program. Day schools must say yes to these children. A small minority of Jewish Elementary day schools and high schools have intensive *mechinah* (preparatory) programs for such students. All day schools need to adopt *mechinah* programs and actively recruit for them. The schools that have such programs functioning have found that after one or two years of intensive work, these new entrants can be fully brought into the mainstream of day school students. Happily, by graduation most of these students have fully caught up with a lot of work. These *mechinah* students often become Jewish leaders later in life.

*   *   *

Quantum growth in Jewish day school enrollment is critical to the future of American Jewry. The easy part is that day schools are much of the time joyful and successful places. More than any other vehicle, day schools harmonize the competing interests of being a proud Jew, proud American and active participant in extra-curricular activities. The hard part is funding day schools. We have seen that there is no one magic solution, but that several approaches combined would make the funding issue more manageable. We must make the "Five Percent Answer" broadly accepted by day schools. The ETP should be structured in a way to maximize the likelihood that the IRS will determine that the allocated costs over the stated tuition is tax deductible under current law. If not, we need to unite and focus on changing the law for the benefit of all religious schools. Achieving the goal of

325,000 students in day schools at a 50:50 ratio of Orthodox to non-Orthodox would transform American Jewry.

Notes

1. My experience as a member of the board of directors of The Partnership for Excellence in Jewish Education and as a member of the Fund for Jewish Education (a joint venture of UJA-Federation of New York and the Gruss Life Monument Fund) informs this platform. However, the views expressed in this chapter are entirely my own and do not necessarily reflect the views of the organizations I have been involved with. My opinions have also been heavily shaped by my experience as the parent of four day school children.

2. Eliyahu Katz and Mordichai Rimor, *Jewish Involvement of The Baby Boom Generation: Interrogating the 1990 National Jewish Population Survey* (Jerusalem; New York: Louis Guttman Israel Institute of Applied Social Research, 1993). Sarna, *American Judaism*, p. 279.

3. Strassfield and Green, "In Praise of Jewish Day Schools," and Sarna, *American Judaism*, p. 279.

4. Marvin Schick, *A Census of Jewish Day Schools*, p. 1.

5. Ibid., p. 1.

6. Recent studies demonstrate that bilingualism enhances academic achievement and overall language proficiency, and positively correlates with the ability to formulate scientific hypotheses, cognitive flexibility, deductive reasoning skills in math, meta-linguistic abilities, and better scores on reading tests. Maria Estela Brisk, *Bilingual Education: From Compensatory to Quality Schooling* (Mahwah: Lawrence Erlbaum Associates, 2006), p. 82.

7. Speech by Joshua Elkin to a Day School donor gathering in Pikesville, MD on February 5, 2001.

8. Protestant Christians, Catholics, Russian and Greek Orthodox Christians and Muslims all also have their own private schools that foster both religious and cultural identity and learning. Wikipedia, "Private Schools,"http://en.wikipedia.org/wiki/Private_school#Types_of_private_school_in_North_America, accessed May 2006.

9. Marvin Schick, "The Message from Lawrence," *The Jewish Week*, September 16, 2005.

10. According to the Peer Yardstick™ developed by the Partnership for Excellence in Jewish Education (PEJE), the typical day school allocates 15–20% of its tuition income to scholarship aid.

11. The Ford Foundation published a description of this plan in 1980. The

Getting Our Groove Back – How to Energize American Jewry

Manhattan Country School web site describes the current plan and some history. See: www.manhattancountryschool.org.

12. I would like to thank Kimball Rubin, the president of Gross Schechter Day School, for sharing his school's creative initiative with me.

13. JESNA/UJC, *Day School Tuition Subvention, Reduction and Scholarship Programs Affordability Working Group Project* (New York: JESNA/UJC, June 2003), http://archive.jesna.org/pdfs/affordabilityreport.pdf, accessed June 2006.

14. "Free Jewish Day Schools," ACF *Newssource*, September 26, 2002, http://www.acfnewsource.org/religion/free_jewish_schools.html, accessed August 27, 2006.

15. Babylonian Talmud, Ta'anit 23a.

16. Jack Wertheimer, *Talking Dollars and Sense about Jewish Education* (New York; Jerusalem: The AVI CHAI Foundation, 2001), http://www.avi-chai.org/Static/Binaries/Publications/AC050.dollars&sense.print_0.pdf, accessed May 2006.

17. Wertheimer, *Talking Dollars and Sense*. See also the budget of UJA-Federation of New York, www.ujaedny.org.

86

Chapter v

Israel Trips for all American Jews

"From each Jewish heart an invisible path leads to the Land of Israel." *Baderk Shiminovitz, 1923.*

Plank #3: Israel trips for young Jews need to become a cultural norm. All American Jews aged 25 should have visited Israel on an organized, high-quality trip by 2030. Summer teen and college trips, birthright israel, gap year and semester/junior year abroad trips all need to be combined into a seamless offering for young Jews.

Israel: A Land and A People

It is no surprise that Israel must be a key component of reinvigorating American Jewry. The Land of Israel is integral to the Jewish national mission and the soul of every Jew. When Abraham our Patriarch received the call to start the Jewish religion, his first mission was to travel to Israel, the land God promised to him and his descendants. After four hundred years of slavery, God fulfilled his promise, and took the Jews out of Egypt so that they might establish themselves in the Land of Israel. Once the Jews had established a kingdom in Israel, the prophets were compelled to admonish them constantly that only if the people were virtuous would the land bring forth plenty; if the people engaged in idol worship, a famine would ensue. To this day we recite the Shema, which reminds us in essence to be good, and the land will reward you, be bad and the land will punish you. The spiritual and physical identity and wellbeing of all Jews is tied to the Land of Israel.

Jewish history is the story of exile and return to the land. Seven hundred years after entering into the land, in the sixth century B.C.E., the Babylonians destroyed the first temple and exiled the Jews. Seventy years later, under the leadership of Haggai, Zechariah, Ezra and Nechemia, Jews reestablished themselves in the land of Israel and built the Second Temple with the financial support of Jews who remained in Babylonia. Six hundred years later, the Romans crushingly defeated Israel, exiled the people, destroyed the Temple and Jerusalem and scattered the Jewish people, but they did not destroy the Jews or their love for Israel.

Since the destruction of the Second Temple and the subsequent exile, Jews across the world in every generation have longed for Israel. Medieval Jewish commentators spoke lovingly and in great detail of the Land of Israel they had never seen. During the Early Modern period we have accounts of Jews traveling across the known world to get to the Land of Israel.[1] In the eighteenth century C.E., the greatest rabbi of the Mitnagdim, the Vilna Gaon, and the founder of Hassidism, the Bal Shem Tov, wished to die in Israel. Neither succeeded, but both sent students to settle there in the early part of the 19th century C.E. Later that century, Jews from Yemen crossed the desert on camel and on foot to reach Israel. During the last two thousand years of exile, Jews from across the world have longed and departed for Israel.

Love for the Land of Israel enabled the inception and survival of the modern Jewish state. The early Zionists, a great deal of whom declared that they did not believe in God, could not escape their love of Israel. Despite ever more violent pogroms and an increasingly desperate economic situation, they rejected a plan to settle Jews in Uganda, as only the land of Israel would do. Twenty years later, the British Foreign Secretary Lord Balfour, a non-Jew, recognized the bond that ties Jews to the Land of Israel. One of the reasons he gave for making his declaration in support of the establishment of a Jewish state was that Jews worldwide were still praying daily for rain in its season in the Land of Israel. Since 1917, the love of Israel has given Jews the strength to fight for an independent state against overwhelming odds. After the devastation of the Holocaust, Jewish survivors struggled to settle in Israel. In 1948, the 600,000 Jews living in Israel stood their ground on their land despite the invasion of six Arab armies determined to drive the Jews "into the sea." Over 1% of the Jewish population at that time was killed in Israel's War of Independence, but we won. The modern state of Israel exists as a haven for Jews around the world. For most of us it is now only a plane ride away.

This is not to suggest that there has always been Jewish unanimity when it comes to the policies of particular governments of Israel. Over the years some American Jews have disagreed with the policies of various governments to expand settlement activities in the occupied territories. But in the summer of 2006, when Hezbollah attacks came from Lebanon and the very existence of the state was in question, there was overwhelming American Jewish support for Israel's right and responsibility to defend itself.

Visiting Israel Today: Building Connections

A trip to Israel is a unique way of awakening the Jewish connection in visitors. While there is no "magic bullet" to instill immediate and ever-lasting Jewish identity, trips to Israel are tremendously galvanizing and often lead to other Jewish experiences. The following chart indicates the importance of Israel to American Jewry.

	Married a Jew	Being Jewish very important	Very attached to Israel
Traveled to Israel as a teen or young adult	80%	67%	53%
Did not travel to Israel as a teen or young adult	51%	29%	17%

Source: Cohen and Kotler-Berkowitz, "The Impact of Childhood Jewish Education," p. 11.

Even if one takes into account statistically that most Jews who go to Israel have had some Jewish education, and had camping and youth group experiences, the impact of an organized Israel trip on fostering Jewish identity is spectacular. The reason for this is simple: trips to Israel bring Jewish history and the land to life.

Trips to Israel impress upon young visitors the miracle of the modern state despite, or perhaps even because of, its present challenges. It is clear that the modern state of Israel will not appear as a utopia to any visitor. There are wide swaths of poverty apparent to a casual observer. Israelis can be quite brusque in dealing with Americans. Politics in Israel is hardball without helmets. The educational system is constantly on the verge of collapse. The economy is grossly over-regulated and over-taxed, and it seems as though Israelis are making ends meet only through escalating overdrafts of their checking accounts. Relations between Arab Israelis and Jewish Israelis, as well as among the factions of Israeli Jews, seem to grow tenser by the hour. There are regular threats from the Gaza border to the south and the Lebanese border to the north. And, of course, there is the constant fear of terrorism. Yet it is precisely the flourishing of Jewish life in the midst of all this difficulty that makes Israel so special. Furthermore, the ability to see these issues first-hand allows young American Jews to engage with and connect to the real Israel and not the version portrayed on CNN. Trips to Israel challenge young American Jews to grapple with their identity and the experience of other Jews.

Trips to Israel also bring home the beauty of the Land, the continuity of Jewish history and the diversity of Jewish life today. It is possible to miss these things if, for example, one were to take a direct flight to Eilat and spend a week on the beach, snorkeling and swimming with the dolphins. Yet such itineraries are rare. Most trips expose visitors to the Israel of the Bible, the Israel of the Second Temple and Talmudic periods, the context and complexities of the formation of the current state, the diversity of Jewish customs and the development of Israeli culture. An Israel trip also provides an excellent opportunity to experience the study of Jewish texts and to savor the sacred time of Shabbat. Almost all Jewish visitors leave Israel with a heightened sense of Jewish peoplehood. For young American Jews, one trip to Israel sheds a new light on the risk and cost of breaking the 3,500 year chain that is the Jewish people.

Trips to Israel: Good for American Jews; Good for Israel

Trips to Israel are not only an excellent way of fostering Jewish identity among American Jews, they also benefit Israel by building strong support for the state in the Diaspora. Israel remains America's No 1 foreign aid recipient and both countries' common strategic interest in fighting terror has become stronger since the attacks on America on September 11, 2001. There is nothing like a visit to Israel to reinforce that connection in the American mind. Clearly, trips to Israel are part of Israel's vital national security interests. Furthermore, the evidence from other Jewish communities in the Diaspora demonstrates that Israel would greatly benefit from receiving more American Jews as visitors. Among Australian Jews, a community which has a far smaller Jewish population than the U.S., more than 70% have gone on a trip to

Israel. The results are impressive: Australia is second only to the U.S. in gross contributions to Israel and far exceeds American Jewry in per capita giving.[2]

birthright israel

Since 1999, birthright israel has popularized the importance of a trip to Israel as a cultural milestone for young Jewish adults. Created and organized by Michael Steinhardt and Charles Bronfman, birthright israel enables young Jews to take a high quality trip to Israel. The trip is free to any young Jewish adult 18–26 years old who has not previously been on an organized, peer trip to Israel, which means that young Jews who have gone to Israel with their families or friends are still eligible for birthright. By the summer of 2006, over 100,000 Jewish young adults from the Diaspora had gone on a birthright israel trip.

Unfortunately, the impressive numbers of Jews who go on birthright represent only a fraction of those who are eligible. Over 200,000, or double the number of participants, have not been able to go on a trip because registration was cut off early when the available spots were filled. And though 65,000 American Jews have gone on birthright israel trips, at least the same number have not been able to go due to funding limitations. Too many young Jews have yet to go on birthright. In the relevant age range, from 18 to 26, demographers estimate that there are currently 900,000 Jews in the Diaspora and 630,000 Jews in the U.S. who are eligible for birthright israel. This mean, that there are approximately 100,000 18 years olds, and the same number of 19, 20, 21, 22, 23, 24, 25, and 26 years olds in the Diaspora, about 70% of whom live in the U.S., who should go on birthright israel.

The Impact of birthright israel

The research on the impact of birthright israel has demonstrated that the effect of the trip is as positive as the founders could have hoped for.[3] Perhaps the single most important impact the organizers wished to have, reversing the growing trend toward intermarriage, has been achieved. The results are clear: birthright israel trips significantly increase participants' desire to inmarry and have Jewish children. Moreover, the propensity towards inmarriage grows rather than fades over time. The reason for this growing impact, which is counter-intuitive, is that participants leave Israel with the desire to "do Jewish" more often. In short, trips to Israel draw young Jews into Jewish life and result in more Jews marrying Jews.

The success of birthright stems predominantly from the enthusiasm, passion and energy it generates. I have been privileged to attend four "Mega Events" that are part of birthright israel trips.[4] During these events, I have also spoken with tour guides, young Israelis in the army who joined the tour, and at least 50 Americans, and hardly heard a negative word about the birthright israel experience from anyone involved. The notion that the trip is a gift from the Jewish people adds a sense of gratitude that begets a spirit of camaraderie, openness and good will. Moreover, the tight programming and intensity of the trip compounds the initial excitement of the birthright concept. As one young woman remarked as she was boarding a return flight to the States, on birthright she had made three new close friends from her school whose names she barely knew before the trip. She was sure that they would do Jewish things together when they returned.

The positive feeling generated by birthright has a lasting impact on the lives of young Jews upon their return to America. My nephew, David, came back from a freshman year birthright trip totally energized and re-focused on his Jewish life. The following year, he decided to attend a summer session at Tel Aviv University and to become active in Hillel. When I saw him in Israel before his return to the U.S. from Tel Aviv University he was preparing for his trip to Atlanta for a Schusterman Hillel conference and for his new responsibilities as a Grinspoon-Hillel Student Fellow for Israel Advocacy on campus. He recently arranged to do his junior year in an Israeli institution. Though his growing commitment to the Jewish people did not develop solely as a result of his birthright israel trip, birthright brought him to a whole new level of engagement and commitment.

Another young man, by the name of Ezra, whom I met through business, surprised me one January by telling me that instead of skiing, he had decided to spend his vacation time on a birthright israel trip. I was intrigued by his vacation choice. Ezra was on a rising career path and had the funds to take any vacation he desired. He had a satisfying social life and enjoyed the New York singles scene. The opportunity to go to Israel and the fact that it was free attracted him so, on an impulse, he signed up. The next part surprised me further. Not only did the trip foster his love of the Jewish people, but it opened his eyes to the wide variety of Jewish backgrounds among Jews in both America and Israel. Ezra told me that the trip changed his whole perspective about being Jewish, about other Jews and about his life in a positive way. He rattled off several new Jewish activities that he was getting involved with following his return. Ezra's story is by no means unique: it is one that I have heard anecdotally from many birthright israel alumni, and it is perfectly consistent with the research. From Ezra and David's stories and countless others, I am convinced that we must continue to promote birthright israel as a central way of fostering connections to Israel.

Yet, despite the overwhelmingly positive impact that birthright israel's 10-day trips have on participants, longer trips have more profound and lasting effect. According to a study by demographers at Brandeis University, short trips like birthright have "little effect on ethical behavior, religious behavior, or participation in organized Jewish life."[5] In contrast, longer trips though groups such as NFTY, USY, NCSY, Bnei Akiva, Young Judea, Nesiya and Livnot U'Lehibanot have a durable, clear and strong positive impact on these aspects of Jewish identity. I am by no means suggesting that birthright israel be scrapped for these other programs, which last from four to eight weeks and for which participants pay considerable fees. The nature of the free birthright israel trips creates its own kinetic dynamic which has captured the imagination of young Jews who never thought about going to Israel before. We cannot stifle this energy, nor is it realistic to expect most prospective birthright israel participants to take a longer trip even if that were better for American Jewry. What I am proposing is that the birthright program become integrated into a wider spectrum of programs for the Diaspora so that young Jews receive the maximum exposure to Israel they are willing to accept.

Integrating birthright and Longer Summer Programs: The Israel Travel Voucher

I would like us to look at birthright israel as a baseline on which we can build. Here is how we can go about expanding the success of birthright: at age 16, each American Jewish teenager would be issued a non-transferable voucher for either $2,000 of credit for an approved trip to Israel or a free birthright israel trip. This can be the new Jewish "Sweet Sixteen" for both sexes. The birthright israel trip could only be taken after the recipient turned 18. The $2,000 credit voucher, which is somewhat below the cost of a free birthright israel trip, could be used during high school or college to defer the cost for an approved 4–8 week summer trip or applied toward a semester/junior year abroad in Israel. The voucher would expire upon the recipients' 25th birthday.

The design of the voucher is important. It maintains an advantaged incentive for birthright israel trips as these trips remain free, but it eliminates birthright israel eligibility concerns as attendance in longer, more comprehensive programs which should have better outcomes is fully encouraged. Given the lower cost of schooling at Israeli universities, the voucher may make semester/junior year abroad study feasible for many students and would also help to re-invigorate junior year abroad programs. In 1998–1999, the academic year prior to the start of the second Intifada, there were 1,800 Americans matriculating in Israeli universities contrasted with about 18,000 American Jewish students studying abroad. [6] The voucher could have a significant impact on this ratio. Finally, the fact that something of value will expire by a specific date certainly should encourage its use.

There is reason to believe that the benefits of the Israel Voucher, if split among American Jews and Israel, would far outweigh its costs, particularly for Israel. If one assumes that all of one year's age group travels annually and that half travel via birthright israel at an assumed cost of \$2,500, whereas the other half use the \$2,000 voucher (70,000 people × (.5) (2,500) + 70,000 people × (.5) (2,000) = \$157.5 million), the total cost of the Israel voucher would be around \$157 million annually. If one were to split the cost evenly between the Israeli government and American Jewry, Israel's share would be \$78.75 million, an unbeatable price given the rate of return on the investment. Indeed, \$78.75 million is less than two tenths of one percent of Israel's annual government budget, a sum of \$40.5 billion based on the current shekel/dollar exchange rate.[7] Yet other than the cost of the plane fare, the rest of the \$157 million expenditure will be in Israel, boosting the economy. It can be safely assumed that the 35,000 birthright israel attendees on a ten-day trip will spend at least \$150 per person, or \$5.2 million, and that the attendees on longer trips will infuse an average of at least an additional \$1,000 per person into the economy, or \$35 million. This \$1,000 is a conservative estimate as it would include not only out-of-pocket expenditures, but also program costs in excess of \$2,000. Finally, it is safe to assume that an American Jewish community in which everyone had been to Israel would contribute at least \$150 more per household to Israel. This alone would result in \$290 million flowing into Israel and boosting its economy. In summary, for an investment of \$78.75 million, Israel has the following return:

Voucher and birthright israel expenditures other than expenses of $24.5 million assumed outside of Israel	$133 million
$150 spent per birthright israel traveler	$5 million
Assumption of $1,000 spent over voucher amount on longer term programs	$35 million
Increased American contributions based on $150 per household	$290 million
Cementing the strategic relationship with American Jewry	Beyond quantification

Setting aside the non-quantifiable benefits to Israel of playing its role in preserving American Jewry, the annual return to Israel's economy is over seven times the budgeting cost. The remaining $78.75 million is up to American Jewry to fund. The U.S. Jewish Federation system via United Jewish Communities (UJC) is already funding $10 million. Five million dollars is in direct funding and an additional $5 million is funded indirectly via the Jewish Agency. It is fair to assume that UJC could increase its $5 million direct contribution to $10 million, half via its own belt tightening and half via allocations from local Federations. American Jewish philanthropists are currently contributing approximately $15 million. This would mean raising $48.75 in additional annual money. While this sum represents a lot of money, it is not an insurmountable amount to raise. We will, however, defer the particulars of how to do this until we reach Plank #5 which deals with the broad fundraising challenge for American Jewry.

Impact of the Israel Voucher

While the cost of the Israel Voucher is affordable the effect would be electrifying; it would likely increase trips to Israel exponentially.

In fact, there is reason to think that contrary to some of the other planks, this one has the potential to be fully implemented within five years. My reason for being so optimistic is as follows. In *The Tipping Point*,[8] Malcolm Gladwell notes a number of phenomena in which small numbers of participants engage in an activity and then suddenly, the number of participants increases at an amazing pace.

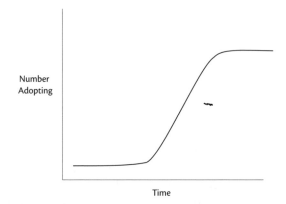

The item adopted could be watching a certain television show, using a cell-phone, using an iPod, wearing a certain fashion or any other cultural norm. We have spoken of these sudden changes in phenomena as phase transitions or the movement of matter from one state to another. Gladwell points out another ingredient to rapid social change that is relevant to Israel trips. It is very helpful if there are people who are "connectors" who can rapidly disseminate an idea and make it seem cool at the same time. Connectors are not just trendsetters, they are also acquainted with a lot of people, either directly or indirectly.

There is no better group of connectors than teenagers and young adults. The number of birthright israel attendees is approaching critical mass. Past participants are almost unanimous in believing it is a wonderful experience. Australian Jews have proved that Israel trips can become a cultural norm. An Australian who has not gone feels the need to explain why that is the case. The American and Israeli Jewish community should declare, "There is no limitation; we want everyone to visit Israel. It is your birthright. If you want to go to Israel, you can: here is your voucher. Ten days with birthright israel is wonderful. A longer trip is even more wonderful. It is up to you. Just get yourself to Israel and have a great time."

* * *

Israel trips are an essential part of the platform to re-vitalize American Jewry. The whole vision of Israel trips needs to be enlarged and allowed to encompass birthright israel as well as longer programs. Vouchers for all acceptable Israel experiences are the key. The success of this plank can be quick and the effect could embolden American Jewry to fully implement the rest of the platform for renewal.

Notes

1. Elkan Nathan Adler, *Jewish Travelers; a Treasury of Travelogues from 9 Centuries* (New York: Hermon Press, 1966).
2. *JPPPI Anuual Assessment 2004–2005*, p. 411.
3. Leonard Saxe, Charles Kedushin, Shahar Hecht, Mark I. Rosen, Benjamin Phillips, Shaul Kelner, *Evaluating birthright israel: Long Term Impact and Recent Findings* (Waltham: The Cohen Center for Modern Jewish Studies, 2004), http://www.cmjs.org/files/evaluatingbri.04.pdf, accessed June 2006.
4. The Mega Event is the one evening (or in some cases the trip is so large that the Mega Event is split over two evenings) when birthright groups are brought together for an evening of song and celebration.
5. Saxe, Kedushin et al., *Evaluating birthright israel*, p. 5.
6. *JPPPI Annual Assessment 2004–2005*, p. 222.
7. *Encyclopedia Britannica Almanac 2004* (Chicago: Encyclopedia Britannica Corporation, October 2003). Also note that the government of Israel is already contributing approximately $14 million toward birthright trips for North American Jews.
8. Malcolm Gladwell, *The Tipping Point: How Little Things Can Make a Big Difference* (Boston: Little, Brown, 2000).

Chapter VI

Three Needs to be the New Two

"To refrain from begetting is to impair the divine image."
Midrash: *Genesis Rabbah,* 34:14

Plank #4: American Jews need to have more children. Net Jewish fertility rates for American Jewish women must exceed 3.0 for American Jewry to thrive. The new cultural norm for American Jewry should be at least three children per family. To achieve this change, the Jewish community and, most importantly, parents of young adult children must encourage young people to get married sooner and have more children. Preparing children for successful marriages is therefore a necessary precondition for larger families.

Marriage age and family size are the subjects American Jews avoid most. American Jews feel free to argue about almost anything but these personal decisions. Yet without putting marriage and family size on the kitchen table for open discussion, we can not reverse the demographic crisis we are currently facing. As we derived in Chapter 11, the net Jewish fertility rate after adjusting for children of intermarriages who are not being raised Jewish is 1.25. But as low as the current rate is, this computation is actually optimistic since too few children of intermarriages are in fact begetting a third generation of children who consider themselves Jewish. Thus, even this optimistic take on our fertility rate will inevitably lead to a devastating decline in the number of American Jews, since in order to maintain a stable population over time without net immigration, any group needs a fertility ratio of 2.1[1] Further-more, a 2.1 fertility rate would not suffice to preserve American Jewry given any level of intermarriage. If we do not put intermar-riage rates (see Plank #6) and higher fertility rates front and center on all our agendas, our population will decline drastically over the next generation.

Given the current decline in fertility and the rise in the rate of intermarriage, some observers have resigned themselves to a profound population decline in American Jewry. These observ-ers advise us to adjust our mindsets and institutions to a much smaller active Jewish population in the future. In my view, this kind of anesthetic management-for-failure is bunk. It is a return to the philosophy of the ten cowardly leaders we discussed in the introduction. This is the kind of leadership that seeks to lower expectations and make us content with the notion that there is no alternative but to die out in the wilderness or go back to Egypt. Instead, we should aim for success. Fertility rates can change. In 1936, during the Great Depression, American fertility rates were slightly lower than the current level, at 2.0. Just 21 years later, in 1957, the fertility rate reached 3.6. With the second lowest fertility rate of all American religious and ethnic groups, we American Jews are in a demographic Great Depression.[2] So let's put higher fertility rates front and center on all our agendas. Let's start a Jewish baby boom.

A baby boom for Jews is not a fantasy. Birth rates among all streams of Orthodox Jewry have skyrocketed over the last decades. In the 1960s and 1970s, a typical modern Orthodox family had two or three children. Presently, a similarly situated modern Orthodox family would be more likely to have three, commonly four or more, children. The typical family size among the Chareidim exceeds six. Orthodox Jews across the spectrum have thus internalized the cultural norm that larger families are important to the future of Jewry. In Israel, the fertility rate among immigrants from the former Soviet Union has more than doubled.[3] We too can follow this lead.

A Baby Boom for American Jews

I propose extending the baby boom to all of American Jewry. But before proceeding, we should deal with the two broad philosophical objections commonly levied against raising the birthrate: the current crisis in world overpopulation, and the idea that no community should infringe on a woman's choice to have or not to have a child.

Some would argue that in an era in which natural resource depletion is a pressing issue, zero population growth (zpg) should be the standard. In my view, if we accept zero population growth as desirable – which not all people do – Jews should be exempt from this concern. Contrary to other populations across the world that have grown exponentially, the Jewish population has declined in the past fifty years. Jews still have a great deal of catching up to do, whether it be to restore the population lost during the Holocaust or simply to reach numbers proportionate to the level of population growth internationally and in America.

Globally, Jews have yet to regain the proportional numerical strength they had before the Holocaust. In 1940 the world Jewish population was approximately 17 million.[4] The world population stood at 2.3 billion in 1940, is presently 6.5 billion and is expected to be approximately 8.1 billion in 2030.[5] If Jews had maintained their share of the world population in 2005 as in 1940, the current Jewish world population would be 54 million instead of the current figure of 13 million.[6] For our relevant planning horizon of 25 years hence, the world Jewish population would need to be 67 million in 2030 to maintain Jewry's share of the total world population. Even at 67 million, the Jewish population would be a mere rounding error on the world population estimate. In stark terms, we Jews have done more than our bit for ZPG. It is time to recoup some of our lost numbers. I have purposely computed these numbers based on the number of Jewish souls prior to the Holocaust. However, even numerically adjusting for the murdered souls of our brethren and their progeny, the gap is still in excess of 33 million Jews.

In America, there is also reason to exempt Jews from the objective of ZPG. In 1940 the overall U.S. population and the U.S. Jewish population were 132 million[7] and 4.8 million, respectively.[8] In 2004, the U.S. population was 294 million and is anticipated to grow to 364 million by 2030.[9] In contrast, as earlier derived, the real U.S. Jewish population is presently 4.3 million.[10] If American Jewry were merely to have grown at the same rate the rest of Americans, our numbers would be 10.7 million in 2004 and 13.2 million in 2030. So even in the United States the lost Jewish population is quite large. Indeed, the lost Jewish population is probably larger, since American Jewry has benefited more than proportionally from net immigration in the last half of the 20th century. In the unlikely scenario that the world Jewish population were to exceed 67 million in 2030, then we could discuss slowing Jewish population growth. In the meantime, the reality is that we are witnessing demographic devastation in real time for the Jewish people.

A second objection to the call for larger families is the argument that the entire discussion is out of order. This stance is most clearly articulated by Anne Roiphe, the noted novelist, who derides family size discussions as some sort of "communal claim on the womb." In her view, women and couples should be totally free to choose to have the number of children they see fit to have. What is more, she argues that the notion of having six or seven children, as an abundant number of the Chareidim do, "would eat many women alive." Modern men and women need time to "listen to music, to take a class in pottery, dance or learn Yiddish."

Roiphe does not believe "that God wants us to reproduce at the expense of harmony of our souls." That being said, Roiphe does concede that such a stance "leaves the problem of Jewish survival unanswered."[11] In short, Jewish women should be free to have as many children as they want – though less is more.

In my view, Roiphe's argument is misguided in two ways. First, people, including myself, who wish to see higher fertility levels among Jews are not suggesting that every couple have six or seven children; rather, we are suggesting that most couples think in terms of a range of children they would like to raise. For example, if the range is two to three, I would most strongly encourage three children. If the range is three to four, than I would strongly encourage four children. In no way would I suggest that parents who are thinking of two to three children should leapfrog to bearing six or seven children. Second, the view that parents have to choose between children and pottery class is false. Yes parenting is tiring, and yes parents also need to have a life, but Roiphe fails to mention that children are not simply a burden – they can actually add their own harmony to our souls. Having more children is good for individuals and good for the Jewish people.

Nevertheless, I recognize that some readers will still consider the idea of promoting outside comment on their family size unwelcome. For such readers, please be assured that I mean no offense, and please skip to the next chapter. I hope, however, that most readers will continue to follow the arguments of this chapter, because ignoring the question of family size "leaves the problem of Jewish survival unanswered" and because Jewish survival is so important for the world.

Creating an American Jewish Baby Boom

We cannot snap our fingers and conjure up a Jewish baby boom; we must first examine the root causes of low fertility in our community. Marriage and family size are driven by a myriad of very personal decisions by young adults, yet these decisions are informed by the values young adults learn in the community.

Therefore, we must look into the root causes for our low fertility rates and put them on top of the communal agenda.

The first root cause of non-Orthodox Jews' low fertility rate is that they wait too long before marrying. Few non-Orthodox young Jews marry before turning twenty-five.[12] Even worse, by the age of thirty-five fewer than half of all Jewish men have ever been married.[13] In the case of women, the contrast is just as stark. Whereas almost two-thirds of young Orthodox women marry by the age of twenty-five, fewer than 10% of women who identify as Reform or Conservative are married at that age. And in the thirty to thirty-five cohort, 54% of Jewish women have yet to give birth to their first child, compared to only 28% of American women as a whole.[14] Considering that the average marriage age of all Jewish women put together includes the Orthodox, the contrast is more glaring. Young American Jewish men and women hear a loud and clear message from their parents that the "twenties are all about starting a career and enjoying life." "Settling down" can wait until the children are on a firmer financial footing.[15] The expectation that marriage is not an issue until after age thirty, is most profound among young Jewish men. Women face a more complex mix of internal and external pressures to postpone marriage and child-bearing. So let's look at the reasons for late marriage and low fertility for Jewish men and women in turn.

Why Jewish Men Marry Late and Why This Must Change

Young Jewish men do not end up "commitment-phobic" by accident. Years of parental and societal pressures to keep a clear head while finishing graduate school or achieving early career success have so influenced young Jewish men that too many are unwilling to marry before thirty. In fact, Jewish men have been affected by these pressures more than American men as a whole. Overall, the median age at which men have married for the first time has edged up from an average of 24 in the last century to 26.8 currently.[16] For non-Orthodox Jewish men, the median age at first marriage well exceeds thirty-five. Jewish men have been convinced that marrying late is desirable. This communal value must change.

Postponing marriage does not just lower Jewish birth rates; it also brings its own emotional complications for Jewish men. By the time a young Jewish man turns thirty, he has dated or had friendly relationships with so many women that it becomes harder and harder for these men to decide that any woman is "right." In some cases, these men fall into the impossible mental trap of comparing each new date with a composite of their best past relationships, seeking the best of all possible characteristics. As such, each new date is measured against a higher mental standard by the man. I have heard from more than a few men who fall into a sort of regret trap. As these Jewish men pass thirty they start to regret more and more that they left (or were dumped from) earlier relationships that now seem to be so much better than their current dates. As time passes, these men become ever more confused and it becomes more and more difficult for them to decide on what they really want in a life partner. By age forty-four, more than one out of four Jewish men has never been married.[17] This is not healthy for Jewish men, or for the Jewish people.

In order to change the current marriage pattern of Jewish men, parents need to get involved in their son's attitudes toward marriage and dating in their teen years. By the time parents are nagging their thirty-five-year-old son about when he is going to marry, it is far too late. Instead, parents should start talking to their teenage boys, in particular, about the single most important decision their children will make: finding a soul mate. We are all concerned with the happiness of our children and we know that choosing the right spouse will influence their long term level of happiness far more than which college they choose or what career they pursue. We must, therefore, prepare our children, but especially our young men, to seek soul mates and not simply enter the dating-go-round. Our children should be ready to decide on a spouse any time after college if they find the right person. All of the needless waiting for the right time should be dispensed to the graveyard of bad ideas.

As a community we should encourage young Jewish adults – and again, especially Jewish men – to marry in their early twenties – not earlier, and not much later. Marrying too early is as problematic as marrying too late. Teen marriages are to be avoided predominantly because they have high divorce rates. In contrast, marriages past twenty are far more lasting. And if marriages of individuals between twenty to twenty-four years of age have slightly higher divorce rates than marriages between people twenty-five and up, particularly in the eighth through fourteenth years of the marriage, the likelihood of very long marriages of seventeen years or more is actually better for individuals marrying between twenty to twenty-four years of age.[18] Furthermore, because these figures relate to the women's age at marriage, I believe that a sustained communal commitment of pre-marital preparation as discussed earlier would eliminate the slight medium-term advantage of marriage after twenty-five. There is simply no acceptable justification for the fact that 54% of Jewish men have not married by age thirty-five and 26% have not married by forty-four. There is no evidence that all of this waiting helps a young (or middle-aged, as the case may be) man's career. There is no evidence that it is easier to decide on a mate as one gets older. There is no evidence that men are happier with all of this waiting. And there is certainly no evidence that Jewish women are happier dating men who have no intention of marrying simply because the time is not right. We as a community need to buck the American trend of male adolescence extending until age thirty.

Why Jewish Women Marry Late and Have Children Late

Young Jewish women also face cross-currents of different pressures and accepted practices in their twenties that compound to delay their marriage. American women now have access to any career they desire and substantially outnumber men in college. As a result, the change in the predisposition to marry has been greater for women than men in America. In the 1970s, American women married at a median age of around 21. By the start of this century, the median marriage age had advanced to 25.1. While some women choose to stay single to finish their professional training, as least that number of women get involved in long-term relationships that do not end in marriage. Other women have difficulty finding a Jewish mate, because more Jewish men are willing to intermarry than Jewish women, leaving more eligible Jewish women than men. As a community, we should address all of these issues, and in particular, we should discourage both young women and young men from entering into long-term relationships that do not end in marriage, for the good of the American Jewish future, not to mention the emotional wellbeing of young American Jews.

If it is true that all American women are delaying marriage, once they are married, American women overall are quicker to start having children than Jewish women. By twenty-nine, only 44% of American women are childless, while at the same age, 70% of Jewish American women don't have children. It is not until the thirty-five to thirty-nine age range that the majority of Jewish women have had their first baby. Jewish women are not simply delaying marriage, but childbirth after marriage as well.

The post-marriage decision of when to start a family is, of course, one in which the husband and wife are both involved. However, women are particularly reluctant to have children immediately.[19] Young married women delay having children because they want to continue getting traction in their careers before taking maternity leave; others are seeking more financial security. Whatever the reason, all of this waiting also takes a heavy toll on fertility, particularly as women pass thirty-five.

Infertility Increases With Age Percentage of married women who are infertile by age group		
AGE GROUP (YEARS)	PERCENTAGE INFERTILE	PERCENT CHANCE OF REMAINING CHILDLESS*
20–24	7	6
25–29	9	9
30–34	15	15
35–39	22	30
40–44	29	64

Adapted from Menken J, Trussel J, Larsen U. "Age and Infertility," Science 23 (1986) :1389

*Historical data based upon the age at which a woman marries.

Some of the delay also stems simply from the fact that a significant proportion of these women need medical assistance to achieve fertility by the time they start trying to have children. Also, as women age, the risk of miscarriage rises dramatically.

Risk of Miscarriage (Spontaneous Abortion) with Increased Age	
MATERNAL AGE (YEARS)	SPONTANEOUS ABORTION (%)
15–19	10
20–24	10
25–29	10
30–34	12
35–39	18

Risk of Miscarriage (Spontaneous Abortion) with Increased Age	
MATERNAL AGE (YEARS)	SPONTANEOUS ABORTION (%)
40–44	34
≥45	53

*Adapted from P.R. Gindoff and R. Jewelewicz, "Reproductive Potential in the Older Woman," Fertility and Sterility 46 (1986): 1986

The older a woman is when she has her first child, the less likely she will have more than one or two children, mostly because the risk of birth defects rises at an increasing pace as women age. I have heard many women past forty sigh that they would like to have more children but that they are very relieved that the children they do have are healthy, and are reluctant to take the chance on any more. Unfortunately, the statistics bear out this attitude.

MOTHER'S AGE	RISK FOR DOWN SYNDROME	CHROMOSOMAL ABNORMALITIES
20	1/1667	1/526
21	1/1667	1/526
22	1/1429	1/500
23	1/1429	1/500
24	1/1250	1/476
25	1/1250	1/476
26	1/1176	1/476
27	1/1111	1/455
28	1/1053	1/435
29	1/1000	1/417

MOTHER'S AGE	RISK FOR DOWN SYNDROME	CHROMOSOMAL ABNORMALITIES
30	1/952	1/385
31	1/909	1/385
32	1/769	1/322
33	1/602	1/286
34	1/485	1/238
35	1/378	1/192
36	1/289	1/156
37	1/224	1/127
38	1/173	1/102
39	1/136	1/83
40	1/106	1/66
41	1/82	1/53
42	1/63	1/42
43	1/49	1/33
44	1/38	1/26
45	1/30	1/21
46	1/23	1/16
47	1/18	1/13
48	1/14	1/10
49	1/11	1/8

American College of Obstetricians and Gynecologist Technical Bulletin #108, September 1987

Since 26% of Jewish women are still childless at forty, it is unlikely that most of these women will ever have more than one child.[20] As a result of their age, Jewish women end up having fewer children than they would like.

Parents must warn their daughters of the risks of delaying having children and inform them of the ways and benefits of balancing a career and family. One of the best ways women can combine a career and a family is to have children *before* starting their careers in earnest. This approach has several advantages. It enables women to embark on their careers without having to interrupt them for maternity leaves, and it also allows mothers to spend quality time with their infants. Where having children before beginning a career is not an option, parents should encourage their daughters to choose to have children and work, as it can be done. And if they are able, grandparents should lend their daughters a helping hand. If young women were to have more support, they might be more willing to have children right away.

As a community, we should also underscore the importance of motherhood by acknowledging all the ways in which women are trying to be good mothers, whether by staying at home or by combining career and family. We need to let women and their spouses make the best decision for their families.

We should acknowledge, appreciate, and support the decision that women make to forgo a career and devote their primary attention to their families and communities. Being a full-time mother can be a wonderful and irreplaceable role that some women can and want to fulfill. Those women in our community who desire to be full-time mothers should be fully encouraged to do so. The Jewish community should catch up to the rest of the world in validating this choice, as there is evidence that many women would like to stay at home. A recent survey of female students at Yale found that approximately 60% of them expected to either cut back on work or stop working completely when they had children. A survey of women Harvard Business School graduates from the classes of 1981, 1985 and 1991 found that 31% of the women worked either part time or on contract, while another 31% did not work at all.[21] Jewish women who wish to stay at home should be encouraged to do so.

We should also validate and encourage women who are working and raising children at the same time. In a study of fifty highly successful women CEOs, senior executives and senior partners of professional firms, Moe Grzelakowski discovered that "mothers lead best." Among these high-level business women, Grzelakowski found that 70% had borne their first child by age thirty-three and all but 6% had done so by thirty-seven. Interestingly, all of those who had children past the age of thirty-seven either needed extra-ordinary medical assistance or adopted a child. Additionally, the timing of the childbearing did not seem to have an adverse effect on marriages, as more than 90% of the women surveyed were still married to their first and only husband.[22] Moreover, Grzelakowski's study also revealed how positive these executives felt about their own roles as mothers and business women. One of the women in Grzelakowski's study claimed that "the wonderful thing about today is that each woman can make her choice. You can fit as many things as you love into your life."[23] Another echoed this view: "I would hope that younger women do not get overwhelmed by the thought of having a career and being a mother. They can do both. The world is a lot more open, and there are more enabling support systems, so they can be successful."[24] According to these business women, being both a mom and having a career is not only possible; these two activities are complementary. We need to pass this message on to our daughters.

Perhaps more controversial, but no less important, the community can also become more friendly towards women who have not found spouses. 15% of Jewish women in the thirty-five to forty-four age range, which is considered the last meaningful childbearing age range, are unmarried.[25] Our rabbis need to make it clear to these women that it is not only okay for them to have children, but that the Jewish community encourages and supports their efforts. These women should feel encouraged to consider options from adoption to artificial insemination. Again, the Jewish community can look to the wider American community in this area. The trend of women who have not found suitable mates becoming single mothers is accelerating. The 2004 census data indicates that 150,000 women with college degrees fall into this category. Interestingly, those "mothers who choose solo status say that the problems that have traditionally burdened families headed by a single mother – poverty, abandonment by fathers, teenage motherhood, and parental conflict" – do not apply to them.[26] Single motherhood should obviously not be a first resort, but it should not be an ostracized practice either. We should no longer pressure women who cannot find a soul mate to remain childless, as is implicitly the case currently. We need a vocabulary for addressing these courageous women. We also need to ensure that our institutions are welcoming to women with the valor to raise children by themselves. Though we should not err on the side of unintentionally pressuring women who have not found marriage partners to become single mothers, we must not discourage them either. We will keep the right balance if we focus on being open to options that further the Jewish people, and enhance the lives of its individual members.

Parents should take an active role in talking to their daughters about the challenges and the joys of having children. Whether or not young women wish to start families prior to focusing on their careers, to use maternity leaves or take a mid term break from the job market, or choose to forgo a career to focus on their family, the emphasis should be on earlier childbirth. We owe it to our daughters to encourage them to have babies when it is safer for them and their babies. We owe it to our daughters to make sure that they understand the costs of waiting as well as the supposed benefits. And we owe it to our daughters to help their dreams of motherhood come true, no matter what. We owe it to the future of the Jewish people to make larger family size our priority.

Encouraging Marriage and Childbirth in the Community

The Jewish community as a whole can also send the message of "the more children, the better." Day schools, Hebrew schools and camps should offer multiple children discounts. JCCs, synagogues, Federations and other Jewish cultural groups should all build in a child care option at the same time as adult programming and meetings are conducted. Rabbis, teachers, lay leaders, parents and grandparents must all work to make Jewish life much more family friendly. Rabbis can also take an active lead in promoting the importance of family size and a healthy family life. They could dispense with politically oriented sermons, for say, the next ten years or so, and instead speak to their congregants about how we are to encourage earlier marriage and families with more children. These kinds of blunt discussions should also be part of every rabbi's pre-marital counseling sessions with couples. We must constantly send the message that family is important and that we need larger families. We must combine multiple initiatives to change our current cultural norm.

As a community we can also re-orient wedding planning and ceremonies towards preparing young couples for starting a family. Such a move is not only much needed but is entirely consistent with Jewish tradition. A key part of the Jewish marriage ceremony is *kiddushin. Kiddushin* is most often translated as "making holy," but the word also has the meaning of "dedication" or "devotion." To make holy is indeed to set aside (dedicate, devote) some time, action, or object to a sacred purpose. As a preparation for *kiddushin*, it is appropriate for the rabbis involved and the parents to speak openly with the couple about the couple's vision of their future and what part their Jewishness will play in that future. Before and during the engagement, rabbis and parents should encourage couples to devote holy time to imagining what they would like to achieve in their life together. The perspective should be the couple's future anniversary parties: 10th, 25th and 50th: At those parties, what would the couple like to gaze out at? How many children would they want to see? What kind of life would they envision for themselves and their children? Is there a connection to the Jewish people, and how is it actualized? How will they leave the world a slightly better place? It is possible that these discussions will cause some couples to separate because they cannot conceive a shared vision. Such an outcome should not be feared. For these couples, realizing their incompatibility pre-marriage is preferable for all involved. Yet, for most couples, focusing on the important, in place of the immediate, will solidify the relationship. I also believe that it will lead most couples to shorten the time of delaying their first baby. As a community we need to spend more time on helping the couple prepare for their life together than choosing a caterer.

Finally, we should encourage those couples who desperately wish to have children but cannot to adopt children. Adoption remains relatively rare in the Jewish community, and in most cases only one child is adopted. While there have been some efforts to support and guide Jewish couples entering the adoption process, too little has been done on an organized basis by the Jewish community. Adoption should also be considered a viable option for Jewish men who have passed their prime marrying years. We need to help all Jews have children, including those who wish to but cannot.

A final note for the reader who believes the suggestions in this plank are too radical. Any critique of fostering an American Jewish baby boom should be weighed against the following two points. First, over 70% of the Jewish population is not living with children and second, only 19% of today's Jewish families consist of families living with only their own children. If the solutions suggested here do not work, we must come up with others. The status quo means defeat. Therefore, the status quo has got to go.

* * *

We need a Jewish baby boom! Little has been done outside of the Orthodox community to emphasize the importance of Jewish family size to the future of the Jewish people. If we do nothing, there will be 54 million less Jews in the world and 9 million less Jews in the U.S. than had we grown at the same rate as our neighbors. We will not thrive unless we change the cultural norm for Jewish marriage and family size. By ignoring this issue we have harmed our children and the Jewish people. Every aspect of the Jewish community's approach to children must be altered. We need a Jewish baby boom. We need to get started tonight.

Notes

1. The rate of 2.1 happens to be the overall fertility rate of the U.S. population as a whole. Constance L. Shehan *Marriages and Families*, (Boston: Allyn and Bacon, 2003), p. 271.
2. The lowest fertility rate is found among whites who profess no religious affiliation. Shehan, *Marriages and Families*, p. 271.
3. Inna Shapiro, "Russian immigrant birthrate more than doubles in Israel," *Ha'Aretz* (English edition), July 27, 2005.
4. Jewish Virtual Library, "World Jewish Population (1882–2000)," http://www.jewishvirtuallibrary.org/jsource/History/worldpop.html, accessed June 2006, source Israeli Central Bureau of Statistics.
5. United Nations, http://www.un.org/esa/population/publications/WPP2004/2004Highlights_finalrevised.pdf, acessed June 2006.
6. Jewish Virtual Library, "World Jewish Population (1882–2000)," http://www.jewishvirtuallibrary.org/jsource/History/worldpop.html, accessed June 2006, source Israeli Central Bureau of Statistics.
7. U.S. Census Bureau, "Historical National Population Estimates: July 1, 1900 to July 1, 1999," http://www.census.gov/popest/archives/1990s/popclockest.txt, accessed June 2006.
8. Jewish Virtual Library, "Jewish Population of the United States (1654–2001)," http://www.jewishvirtuallibrary.org/jsource/US-Israel/usjewpop1.html, accessed April 2006 source American Jewish Historical Society.
9. U.S. Census Bureau, "Interim Projections: Ranking of Census 2000 and Projected 2030 State Population and Change: 2000 to 2030," http://www.census.gov/population/projections/PressTab1.xls, accessed June 2006.
10. See Chapter 11, p.2.
11. Ann Roiphe, "A Communal Claim on the Womb?," *Jerusalem Report*, December 26, 2005.
12. Jack Wertheimer, "Jews and the Jewish Birthrate," *Commentary*, (October 2005). http://www.simpletoremember.com/vitals/jews-and-jewish-birthrate.htm.
13. *NJPS 2000–01*, p. 3.
14. *NJPS 2000–01*, p. 4.

15. I would like to thank Zeeva Kramer, shadchanit extraordinaire, for her insight on the reasons why Jewish adults marry late.
16. Shehan, *Marriages & Families*, p. 132.
17. *NJPS 2000–01*, p. 3.
18. Shehan, *Marriages and Families*, p. 114.
19. With regard to how couples make decisions together as a general matter see: Elaine Grundin Denholtz, *Balancing Work and Love – Jewish Women Facing the Family-Career Challenge* (Waltham: Brandeis University Press, 2000).
20. *NJPS 2000–01*, p. 4.
21. Louise Story, "Many Women at Elite Colleges Set Career Path to Motherhood," *New York Times*, September 20, 2005.
22. Moe Grzelakowski, *Mother Leads Best: 50 Women who are Changing the Way Organizations Define Leadership* (Chicago: Dearborn Trade Pub., 2005), p. 217–219.
23. Ibid, p. 188.
24. Ibid, p. 189.
25. *NJPS 2000–01*, p. 3.
26. Amy Harmon, "First Comes Baby Carriage," *New York Times*, October 13, 2005.

Chapter VII

Funding the Platform

"If a person closes his eyes to avoid giving tzedakah it is as if he has committed idolatry." *Ketuboth* 68a

Plank #5 – American Jewry is wealthy enough to fully fund its own renewal, but it must alter current giving patterns in order to achieve this goal. Wealthy, affluent and moderate income Jews must be informed about how their financial contributions can advance the Jewish community. In order to do this we must present a clear vision of the value of Jewish giving to contrast with the compelling presentations made by universities, symphonies, hospitals and the wide gamut of general cultural organizations. American Jewry should publicly and officially recognize American Jews who give primarily and generously to Jewish causes.

We Are Blessed with Wealth

Among the very wealthy in America today, Jews represent a substantial proportion. A close reading of the Forbes 400 list of "The Richest People in America"[1] indicates that 20% of those registered seem to be Jewish or have a Jewish parent. According to the short Forbes biographies, these Jews take their charitable pursuits quite seriously. In a similar vein, *Lifestyles Magazine*'s "Global Philanthropy Register" counts 162 notable and wealthy Jews from around the world. The listed registrants typically have a net worth exceeding $1 billion and were very charitable.[2] Some members of the list reported making gifts of more than $100 million; the problem is that none of these $100 million gifts went to Jewish day schools, Hebrew schools, Jewish camps, Israel trips or other institutions of Jewish learning.* At the outset of this argument I want to triple underscore that American Jews who have benefited so much from the blessings of living in the United States should rightly include non-Jewish giving in their charitable pursuits. The problem I wish to address is that the current balance between Jewish charitable giving to Jewish causes and Jewish giving to non-Jewish causes is so skewed that American Jews are not currently investing enough to sustain our charitably focused Jewish community for future generations.

It is unfortunate that few very wealthy Jews direct a majority of their giving to organizations that work toward sustaining the Jewish people. More broadly, relatively few of those listed concentrated their giving in any kind of Jewish philanthropy. The overwhelming majority of large gifts went to universities, hospitals, medical research and cultural organizations such as museums and orchestras. The pattern for wealthy Jews is to give a small percentage of their total giving to Jewish causes but reserve their largest gift for general charities. A recent study of all publicly disclosed charitable gifts exceeding $10 million made between 1995 and 2000 sheds further light on the disparity between Jewish donations to Jewish and to general causes. Out of 865 gifts exceeding $10 million, which totaled $29.3 billion, 188 of these gifts were made by Jews, amounting to a sum of $5.3 billion.[3] In other words, American Jews, who comprise 2% of the U.S. population made 22% of all mega-gifts, accounting for 18% of the total amount of these gifts.[4] This is an awesome achievement. American Jewry should be very proud of this aspect of the report. However, the most stunning statistic from the study is also a cause for concern. Out of 188 gifts by Jews, just 18 went to a Jewish organization and accounted for barely 6% of the total funds distributed by Jews.[5] Jewish giving to general causes now far exceeds Jewish giving to Jewish causes. Other sources also corroborate this trend among the wealthiest Jews. *Avenue Magazine* of New York compiled a social "A List" that was approximately one third Jewish. To make it onto the list, an individual had to be both rich and involved in high profile charities, among other requirements. Again, only a tiny portion of these "A List" Jews focused their philanthropic giving on the Jewish community. The portion allotted to Jewish education was even smaller.

The giving patterns of affluent but not super-wealthy Jews follows the same trend as that among super wealthy Jews of more and more generous allocations to general charities, although affluent Jews contribute a much higher percentage of their donations to Jewish causes. Whereas relatively few mega-gifts in 2004 went to religious institutions, 35% of American contribution dollars overall went to religious groups.[6] Below is my estimate of the trend for affluent Jews and super wealthy Jews.

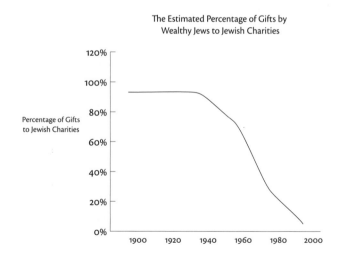

The Estimated Percentage of Gifts by
Wealthy Jews to Jewish Charities

The trend to give primarily to general causes is recent. American Jews have always – and rightly so – made contributions to broad based charities. However, in the early part of the 20ᵗʰ century, non-Jewish charities did not particularly seek out Jews (to say the least) and Jews focused inward. The current trend in Jewish giving is therefore a post-World War II phenomenon that reflects growing assimilation. As American Jews became more accepted into general American society, Jews slowly began to embrace more broad-based charities such as hospitals, galleries, museums, symphonies and universities. However, by the 1980s and 1990s, American Jews lost their initial trepidation and proceeded full throttle. According to the 2001 NJPS, 62% of American Jews gave to non-Jewish causes, and only 41% gave to Jewish causes.[7] Only 19% percent of inter-married families gave to a Jewish cause.[8] The survey did not measure the dollar amount of giving to each type of cause; however, the beneficiaries of this trend are clear. Donations to universities alone, primarily endowment gifts, comprised almost half of all Jewish mega-gift dollars.[9] Jews have become among the most generous donors of universities, and are giving less and less to Jewish causes.

By giving to high profile general charities, Jews signal their desire to be accepted into American high society. In the larger U.S. cities, it is increasingly common to see Jewish names as chairs of campaigns for symphonies, operas, museums and other cultural organizations. Whereas these charities used to seek old-line white Anglo-Saxon Protestant names to bring donations from their white Anglo-Saxon Protestant friends and associates, Jews have now become the chairs and honorees of choice. A special feature of *Architectural Record Magazine* entitled "American Museums: Reflecting the New Cultural Landscape"[10] listed the chief patrons of new museums, honoring them as the primary instigators of innovative and imaginative American Museum buildings. Of course, a disproportionate number of the highlighted patrons were Jewish. Jewish general giving is not only generous, but it has become commonplace. Institutions across America are now honoring Jews for their contributions in part out of gratitude, but also to encourage further Jewish giving.

Though I wish to emphasize again that the legitimacy of giving back to American society through charitable donations is not in question, in my view, American Jews should reconsider the balance between Jewish and general giving. Currently, the proportion of funds allocated to general giving so outweighs the proportion allocated to Jewish giving that if we continue along the current lines we are not investing enough to sustain our community and tradition of giving for future generations. Jews should also ask themselves if the general institutions to whom they are donating represent their values, and they should question the long-term impact of their donations.

Not surprisingly, however, the issue of Jews making poor allocation decisions for their generous giving is an old one. The Talmudic rabbis wrote of indiscriminate generosity during their period and pointed to even earlier incidents of this phenomenon. Rabbi Abba bar Acha said:

> It is impossible to understand the nature of this people. When they are asked to contribute to the Golden Calf, they give. And when they are asked to contribute to building the Holy Tabernacle, they give.[11]

Today more than ever American Jews face the classic question that our sage Hillel addressed when he said, "If I am not for me, who will be for me? If I am only for myself, what am I? If not now, when?"[12] The answer to Hillel's question is different for every time and place. In my view, it is imperative today that we American Jews think very carefully about how we are currently allocating our money. It is time to give more to causes that promote the future of American Judaism. We need to rethink donating to universities and other cultural institutions, we need to ensure that our Jewish giving goes to essential Jewish causes and we need to value those Jews who give generously to Jewish causes.

Donations to Universities

Jews are among the most generous donors to universities. Having recently completed a college tour with my son, I was astounded by the number of new buildings and new schools being named after Jewish donors. At the University of Chicago, Cornell and Northwestern, to name but a few, the medical schools are named after Jewish donors. At NYU and the University of Michigan the business school are named after Jewish donors. Countless Jews have endowed university chairs. At the University of Pennsylvania, Jews have created half a dozen endowed professorships in the arts and humanities alone. Jews have also endowed research institutes and departments in universities across the country. Almost all of the major Ivy League universities have received substantial donations from Jews. A review of gifts to universities by Jewish donors in 2006 alone quickly exceeds $200 million. Imagine what even a quarter of that money could do for American Jewry: it is enough to transform all of our Hebrew schools and fund all major youth groups; enough to make one year of Jewish camping affordable for all American Jews; enough to send 100,000 young Diaspora Jews to Israel on a birthright trip, enough to dramatically improve the day school movement and enable thousands of children, who otherwise could not afford to, to attend day schools. Instead, Jews are currently making breathtaking contributions to universities where their emphasis is on large and medium-sized perpetual endowments.

Though Jewish giving to universities is a testament to Jewish integration in American society, Jews should consider very carefully whether making mega-gifts to endowment funds is the best place for their contributions. In my view, those Jews who wish to donate to universities should concentrate on operating funds. The reasons are twofold. First, endowment funds are by definition perpetual assets of universities, yet universities are changing institutions. Do you want your money to continue to fund institutions when these no longer represent your values? We Jews should ask ourselves this question in light of the history of universities in America. Fifty years ago, our best universities routinely and systematically discriminated against Jews. At many schools an explicit quota of Jews was adopted and rigidly enforced. American universities also refused to hire Jewish faculty.[13] Though such practices are no longer acceptable, today some universities continue to be ambivalent towards Jews. At a few universities there is such a profoundly anti-Israel (and often anti-Semitic) environment that Jewish students once again feel unwelcome (see Plank #9). With such a history, it is impossible to know what the campus environment for Jews will be like in 50 years; Jews should therefore seriously consider whether unrestricted endowment gifts are appropriate. Second, but no less important, most universities that receive mega-donations from Jews are extremely wealthy institutions in their own right. As of 2004, the top five university endowments exceeded $70 billion.[14] These universities commanded more than 20% of higher education endowments. Thus, it is far from clear that donating to wealthy universities with an ambivalent record on Jewish issues is the most beneficial use of Jewish wealth.

One of the major attractions of university giving is that donors feel assured that their gifts will have an enduring legacy. Universities, like research hospitals, have a reputation for fiscal prudence, financial probity and long lives. Having one's name on a university building or a school of medicine is also an express entry card into higher "A List" social echelons. Jewish giving to universities should continue in a proud fashion, but at this challenging time in American Jewish history, it must be part of a measured and proportionate mix that includes Jewish charities.

Let's Stop Giving to Non-Essential Jewish Causes

Unfortunately, the dilemma of Jewish giving is not just that we give a disproportionate share to general causes; it is also that too much Jewish giving is allocated to well-meaning, but non-essential Jewish causes, that is to say, causes that do not directly help to promote the future of the Jewish people in America and the world. These are Jewish museums across the U.S. and certain Jewish secular initiatives in major Jewish centers like New York City, where these programs could be self-supported. Though all of these causes are worthy, American Jews should consider how effective they are in safeguarding the future of American Jews around the world. Some initiatives that are being funded are simply not necessary. We should not fund any more Holocaust museums, given the amount of excellent educational material currently available to educators across the country. We should also stop funding local Jewish museums that are not likely to attract visitors, and we should reconsider whether to support Jewish community centers that no longer function as Jewish institutions. Likewise, Jews and the Federations should no longer be sole funders of social service agencies that once served the Jewish community, like hospitals, senior residences, and immigrant social service centers, but now serve primarily other Americans. Instead, Jews should participate in funding these institutions alongside other communities. If a cause is not likely to have a major impact on fostering Jewish identity and community, ensuring Jewish physical survival, or improving the lot of Jews in need, it should be deemed non-essential and cancelled, postponed or partnered with other communities of donors.

A more troubling issue is that of organizations that claim to represent the Jewish people, but in practice operate as self-focused fundraising machines. A prime example of this phenomenon is the current activity of the Anti-Defamation League (ADL). Though this organization has a proud history, it is unclear that its current direction reflects the priorities of Jews in America. In 2005, the ADL adopted the fight against the "Christianization of America" and more specifically against Evangelical Christians as one of its primary initiatives. This choice is very hard to explain when the real threat to American Jewry comes from American Islamic fundamentalism and the Hard Left, but certainly not Christianity. There is thus reason to suspect that the ADL's de-

Christianization campaign serves the ADL more than American Jews. However, the ADL is not the only organization to make this mistake; other Jewish defense leagues are equally obsessed with the perceived threat of Christian evangelism. This focus is totally inappropriate for several reasons. First, the religiosity of Americans benefits rather than threatens Jews. In 1999, over 90% of Americans said they would vote for a Jew as President, but only 49% said they would vote for an atheist.[15] Second, since the United States regularly ranks as one of the most religious countries in the Western world, and as Tocqueville said, "There is no country in the world where the Christian religion retains a greater influence over the souls of men than America,"[16] the ADL's fight is likely to fail. America is 86% Christian, 8% other – including Jewish – and 6% with no religion.[17] Moreover, it is probable that the ADL's battle against the "Christianization of America" would harm the American Jewish community immeasurably, since Evangelical Christians already resent the secularization of America. Finally, despite the ADL's claim to represent the Jewish community, many if not most Jews do not view Christianization as a major issue. Simply put, de-Christianization campaigns are a waste of precious Jewish resources.

Let's Stop Supporting Overlapping and Inefficient Agencies

Another source of wasted Jewish giving is the continued support of redundant agencies. There are too many examples of local and national Jewish organizations that provide overlapping services. These organizations do not have economics of scale or are just poorly run and therefore ineffective. Were some of these organizations to merge, the resulting entities might be stronger, enjoying broader bases of support. It is imperative that we ask whether there is a need for both the American Jewish Committee and the American Jewish Congress. Would a merger in fact not only create efficiencies but also eliminate confusion when both organizations lobby the same government official with somewhat different positions? Would more than 10% of American Jewry, which both organizations purport to represent, know the difference? The overlapping Boards of Jewish Education across the United States are other clear examples of this phenomenon. Sadly, overlap is usually the result of a second agency being created because the first one was ineffective and no one was willing to reorganize it or had the courage to shut it down. Communities can no longer allow such redundancy. We must either merge overlapping agencies or break them down into their useful components and merge those. Undertaking such systematic downsizing will save our community tens of millions of dollars. These funds should be re-deployed toward programs and organizations that will improve the future of American Jews. But in order to do this, Federation leaders need to muster the will for change. We must also muster the self-discipline to avoid undertaking wasteful white elephant projects that deplete scarce communal resources. We need ever-greater courage to recognize wasteful projects that are currently under way and shut them down. In Congress, there are always fervent supporters for "bridges to nowhere," who glibly explain why a bridge from nowhere to no place is in the best interest of the country. We must fight these voices. We simply cannot afford to get caught up in false assumptions or political horse-trading.

We must also have the courage to cut ineffective programs. As it stands, the Federation supports some legacy agencies that have become ossified. The reason for this is habit and fear. Though the number of these redundant organizations is small, they still have proud pasts and strong (and affluent) supporters who threaten to cut their important Federation gifts if the Federation cuts a particular agency's allocation. Therefore, Federation board members and allocation committee members often find it less painful to just keep funding these agencies, though they are ineffective. Yet, as analysts have noted, "The tyranny of the status quo must be overcome. Past and outdated policy orthodoxies, organizational inertia and vested interests must not hinder essential policy creativity, organization renewal and leadership rotation."[18] Federation leaders have to be brave and cut tired programs. Community members and donors should be told the truth about the current functioning of their agency of choice for giving.

Unfortunately, however, the current philanthropic practice is to perpetuate the status quo. I have attended too many meetings where a majority of the meeting's participants understood that monies were not being put to highest and best use, but rather only to acceptable use. The primary reason for this policy is to avoid criticizing inefficient agencies. Most Jews involved in philanthropy steer clear of criticism as a rule for several reasons. First, the criticism frequently rebounds in a very personal way and veers away from the issues at hand. Second, lay leaders are unpaid volunteers, and therefore most would prefer to avoid the firestorms of controversy. Third, Jewish professionals, also wish to avoid controversies that are time consuming and distracting. Sadly, the path of least resistance is to just go along with stale programs because of inertia. Unfortunately, maintaining the path of least resistance leads us to managing the decline and diminishment of American Jewry.

In order to avoid the inefficient use of funds, Jewish organizations should designate one year every decade during which each organization's board conducts a serious internal evaluation of its effectiveness and asks itself whether it is advancing the Jewish people or not. If not, the honorable path to take is to cease draining monetary resources and human talent that could be redeployed elsewhere. In some cases, local Federations will also need to muster the courage to "assist" local agencies in this task. But, in order to accomplish this task on a wide scale we must also address the question of efficiency within the community as a whole. It is time for every Jewish organization and their donors to articulate their organization's mission anew with the view that every group is responsible for advancing the Jewish people. Organizations can no longer be allowed to make decisions that advance their own interests, but harm other Jews or American Jewry as a whole. If organizations are required to focus on what is good for the Jews as a whole, I am sure we will find our collective vision for the future is more unified than we suspect.

Promoting Giving to Causes that Advance the Jewish Future

One of the most important ways of increasing Jewish giving to Jewish causes is honoring donors who advance the Jewish future on a community-wide basis. We should recognize philanthropic leaders who are funding the renewal of American Jewry, since their efforts are not the normative path for the super wealthy and honoring their efforts should help to expand the base of mega-donors that is urgently needed for a Jewish renewal. This can easily be accomplished if American Jewry, by itself or in conjunction with the President of the State of Israel establishes a Society of Chaverim that honors mega-donors. The term "chaver" which translates as "friend" or "member" has been used since the Middle Ages to designate individuals who have provided extraordinary service to the entire Jewish community. In recent times, Kibutzniks referred to each other as "chaver," which they understood as the Hebrew equivalent of comrade, though the term has now fallen into disuse. I suggest that here in America we restore it to its original meaning: the best friends of the Jewish community.

The selection of Chaverim should reflect the honor of the appellation. An elite group of well-recognized senior Jewish leaders should be formed to vote on inducting a small group of mega-donors who have provided very meaningful contributions to Jewish causes into this Society of Chaverim. Each voting member would be forbidden from voting for a substantial donor to an organization with which he/she was closely involved. Members of the Society would then also vote on subsequent inductees. Members would come from every authentically Jewish group ranging from

Orthodox, Conservative, Reconstructionist, Reform, Secular and "Just Jewish." To give the Society some pomp and circumstance, it may be appropriate to have the names formally approved by the President of the State of Israel and to have him or her preside over the induction ceremony. The title Chaver should then be used on a Jewish community-wide basis to refer to that individual. This title is, of course, honorary since the U.S. Constitution prohibits either foreign governments or U.S. states from bestowing titles such as "Sir" or "Lord" on U.S. citizens.[19] Yet, there is a precedent for such an honorific title in the US; every American lawyer appends Esquire to his/her name, which originally was a title that referred only to candidates for knighthood. Salvation Army adherents also use their "military" titles as official, which take precedence over their "normal" title: e.g. "General Dr. Edward Rollins." We should be blessed with a multitude of future Chaverim.

There is no reason why we could not start the society of Chaverim today. I would suggest that the first class of candidates to the Society be a group of individuals who are widely recognized for their broad support of Jewish causes. In the inaugural year, the inductees must be as widely known and recognized in the philanthropic world as the names of Babe Ruth and Ty Cobb were in the world of baseball when the Baseball Hall of Fame was created. However, unlike the baseball hall of fame, which honored ball players after their retirement, the Society of Chaverim should be comprised of active philanthropists. We should hope that members will be spurred to new achievements in Jewish giving. Ideally, the Society of Chaverim should grow so that becoming a Chaver (or Chavera) is an honor to which every wealthy Jew will aspire.

Today Jews face the challenge of convincing wealthy Jews to shift a substantial share of their giving to Jewish causes. To this end I would like to suggest a hypothetical conversation between a potential mega-donor and a Jewish philanthropy. In it I will lay out the major arguments that Jewish charities have at their disposal to persuade mega-donors to "give Jewish."

Convincing Jews to "Give Jewish:" A Hypothetical Dialogue

Nathan Asker: Thank you for taking the time to let me talk with you about The Jewish Education Organization or as we affectionately call it "JEO." (The reader can name this type of organization from any of the planks. JEO could be a day school, Hebrew school group, youth group movement, birthright, an Israel teen trip, Jewish camping organization or any other Jewish educational organization.)

Phil Thropist: I want to stop you right there. Why should we give our money to a Jewish group? Yes, we are Jews, but we are also grateful to this wonderful country and community for creating the environment that has enabled our company to prosper. We have recently been approached by the local hospital, which wants to upgrade its emergency room, the city symphony, which has a serious deficit, and the university, which our daughters attended, which is in the midst of an endowment campaign.

Ann Thropist: I don't want you to get the wrong impression though, we are proud to be Jews. We used to belong to a synagogue, and we send in a gift to the local Jewish Federation. It's just that there seem to be a lot of wealthy Jews donating money. Why don't you ask them?

Nathan Asker: You both ask a lot of good questions and make valid points. I am not here to denigrate the other causes you have mentioned, or to argue that you should only give to Jewish educational causes. But I am going to compare the impact of your gift to JEO with the impact of your other donations and explain to you why there is an urgent need for giving to Jewish causes. Simply put, your gift to JEO has the potential to make the world a better place. It is…

Ann Thropist: Sorry to interrupt you, but I am not sure you meant what you said. Our gift to JEO can make the world a better place? I could understand it if you said JEO would benefit Jews, but if we want to change the world, shouldn't we give to the other more broad-based organizations we are considering?

Nathan Asker: No, I really meant what I said; the best, most assured way that you can improve the world in a lasting way is to give to an organization like JEO. I say this for two interrelated reasons. First, the Jews have been and continue to be a moral compass of humanity despite the fact that we are 0.2% of the world population. Therefore, simply preserving the Jewish people will make the world a better place. Second, one of the traditions that make Jews a moral compass of humanity is the special value of giving, called *tzedakah*, which must be preserved and extended. *Tzedakah* is frequently translated as "charity" but it is really much better translated as "righteousness."

Phil Thropist: I agree we Jews are egocentric but how can we claim to be a moral compass for humanity? That sounds far too grand.

Nathan Asker: Actually it is not – even if it does sound a bit ethnocentric. Let me quote from a great non-Jewish scholar who wrote a book entitled *The Gifts of the Jews – How a Tribe of Desert Nomads Changed the Way Everyone Thinks and Feels*:

> [We cannot] imagine the great liberation movements of modern history without reference to the Bible. Without the [Jewish] Bible we would never have known the abolitionist movement, the prison-reform movement, the antiwar movement, the labor movement, the civil rights movement, the movements of indigenous and dispossessed peoples for their human rights, the antiapartheid movement in South Africa, the Solidarity movement in Poland, the free-speech and pro-democracy movements in such Far Eastern countries as South Korea, the Philippines, and China. These movements

of modern times have all employed the language of the Bible; and it is impossible to understand their great heroes and heroines – people like Harriet Tubman, Sojourner Truth, Mother Jones, Mahatma Gandhi, Martin Luther King, Cesar Chavez, Helder Camara, Oscar Romero, Rigoberta Menchu, Corazon Aquino, Nelson Mandela, Desmond Tutu, Charity Kaluki Ngilu, Harry Wu – without recourse to the Bible. Democracy grows directly out of the Israelite vision of individuals, subjects of value because they are images of God, each with a unique and personal destiny. There is no way that it could ever have been "self evident that all men are created equal" without the intervention of the Jews. [20]

Or consider Mark Twain's insightful words on the Jews' impact on the world written more than 100 years ago:

If statistics are right, the Jews constitute but one percent of the human race. It suggests a nebulous dim puff of stardust lost in the blaze of the Milky Way. Properly, the Jew ought hardly to be heard of, but he is heard of, has always been heard of. He is as prominent on the planet as any other people, and his commercial importance is extravagantly out of proportion to the smallness of his bulk. His contributions to the world's list of great names in literature, science, art, music, finance, medicine, and abstruse learning are also way out of proportion to the weakness of his numbers. He has made a marvelous fight in this world, in all the ages; and has done it with his hands tied behind him. He could be vain of himself, and be excused for it. The Egyptian, the Babylonian, and the Persian rose filled the planet with sound and splendor, then faded to dream-stuff and passed away; the Greek and the Roman followed, and made a vast noise, and they are gone; other people have sprung up and held their torch high for a time, but it burned out, and they sit in twilight now, or have vanished. The Jew saw them all, beat them all, and is now what he always was, exhibiting no decadence, no infirmities of age, no weakening of his parts, no slowing of his energies, no dulling of his alert and aggressive mind. All things are mortal but the Jew; all other forces pass, but he remains. What is the secret of his immortality?[21]

We Jews have made even more contributions to humanity. The Apostle Paul, a Jewish man, and a yeshiva *bochur* no less, reformulated Judaism into Christianity, which made a universalized form of Judaism available to all peoples. Until Paul, all of the believers in Jesus were observant Jews. Islam also descends from Judaism: it incorporates both the Jewish Bible and the Christian Scriptures as holy texts. The intense friction between Islam and the Jews is also a relatively recent phenomenon.

Jewish tradition has also influenced Western law and politics. The concept of property rights, which emerged in the Middle Ages and rescued Europe from feudalism, can be directly credited to the European intellectual class's adoption of Talmudic property rights.[22] Likewise, the notion of "rule of law" which determines that actions by the state and sovereign are subservient to a higher constitutional law derives from the Jewish Bible and the Talmud. Thus, yet another Jewish precedent influenced the European intellectual class in the 15th and 16th centuries and helped them to develop constitutional monarchies across Europe.[23] As Thomas Cahill argued, secular democracy also has a Jewish signature. I could even argue…

Ann Thropist: Whoa! Have some tea before the next rhetorical flourish. I am willing to agree that the Jews historically have had a positive impact on the world. But that was then and this is now. The best of Jewish values have already been deeply inculcated into Judeo-Christian and secular American society. We American Jews are privileged to live in this time and in this country. Perhaps the time has come for us to accept that we have made our contribution and just let assimilation take its course. Perhaps we should cede what Mark Twain called our "immortality."

Phil Thropist: Ann, perhaps we should dispense with all this history, take out our checkbook and give JEO a modest donation. Nathan, you can call on us next year as well.

Nathan Asker: Look, I am here to ask for a substantial donation, not a token donation to assuage your guilt or to cut this solicitation short. The stakes are too great. Your wife's question is a good one. We Jews have done a lot. But we are not close to having accomplished our mission. Today we offer an essential quality to American society: we feel responsible for others. Perhaps it is that we have been the foil of an uncountable number of bad ideas in the course of history; perhaps it is our natural gadfly role; perhaps it is our being a 3,500-year-old society built on the basis of responsibilities (sometimes called commandments or mitzvot) and not rights. All these factors have contributed to making us worry about our neighbors, our communities, our world and even our enemies. We are not permitted to stand by idly in the face of evil. You are part of this tradition: the very reason that you are sitting with me, and will sit with so many non-Jewish organizations, is that you feel a sense of responsibility.

We Jews also still have a lot of important things to tell the world about current problems – be it the environment, globalization, economics and even marital relations. And if we Jews speak with several voices, we are still doing our duty, as plurality is also part of our tradition. The key to our contribution to the world is that all of our voices are grounded in a 3,500-year-old tradition of responsibility, righteousness, caring and concern. The prospect of our voices disappearing from American society is enough to make me cry. It is for this reason that I am not embarrassed to ask you to give a lot of money to JEO; I hope you now understand – after all, you are good business people and there is no better bargain then giving to an organization like JEO. We will teach children and young adults the importance of *tzedakah*. We will teach them to give time and money to hospitals, medical research, and groups that help humanity. If we do our job right, over time money will also flow into some of the organizations you spoke about, more than you could ever give yourselves. If we are successful in ensuring that future generations of Jews come into the world, Jews will continue to set the standard of giving. In a certain way I might say that it would be in the long-term best interests of universities, symphonies and other general cultural organizations to encourage their Jewish donors to give to Jewish causes that will result in future generations of Jewish givers. So, please don't send me away with a token gift. Please give enough to make a difference.

Ann Thropist: If we give the gift to JEO you are asking for, we will not be able to make the gift to the university endowment campaign. I have to think about that.

Nathan Asker: Most of the wealthy Jews I speak with have given to universities. One study indicated about half of all Jewish mega-giving went to universities. Universities are great places to support but you should really consider how you want to give and what you want to accomplish. People question why Harvard, which has a $26 billion endowment, is in need of more endowment funds. Princeton also has an endowment of $1.7 million per student.[24] Some schools can make the case for more endowment funds, but if you are giving to the mega-endowed schools, you need to ask yourself if you are giving to make a difference or for personal prestige. If you do choose to give, you might consider giving to operating funds that will be spent for purposes you endorse and not on endowments that generate spending of 4%–5% per year of the principal amount. By the way, I am also not a big fan of endowments even in the Jewish community, other than for scholarships. Endowments tend to lessen accountability. The more any entity can rely on its own endowment, the less it needs to make its case to the outside world. Annual campaigns require organizations to make their case every year. I emphasize again that I am not asking you to abandon your support of general charities. Support them for what they do and enjoy their perks. But you should also know that right now the Jewish people need your support in a substantial, immediate and urgent way.

Phil Thropist: Let's say for a moment that we do give a substantial amount to JEO; how do we know you will raise enough for your endeavor to succeed?

Nathan Asker: I will not kid you and say that success is assured. We have no "secret to immortality." We have a lot of work to do. At the same time, I feel that many Jews believe that we are currently at a pivotal point in our history and that this is the moment to take a stand. But in addition to your money, I am going to need to call upon you to help make the case to those other wealthy Jews who know and respect both of you.

Ann Thropist: You mean in addition to our money you want our time?

Nathan Asker: Yes. I hope that I have convinced you of the importance of our mission. Never before has there been a Jewish Diaspora community as affluent and influential as American Jewry at this time. We are on center stage. The spotlight is on us. We have flubbed our last few lines, but we will rally and perform magnificently. We have never failed before. The good news is that others are beginning to clear the trail for you. In addition to the Steinhardts, Schustermans, Bronfmans, Wexners and Grinspoons of American Jewry and others who have been pursing the renewal agenda for a while, there are fresh arrivals joining the mission. In 2004, a group of families donated $45 million to improve Jewish day schools in the Boston area. In 2006, a family in Maryland committed $15 million to an existing community day school and a foundation that will distribute approximately $25 million per year emerged from the estate of Jim Joseph. These and other gifts are part of what is hopefully a sea change in Jewish giving. We want you to be a part of this great endeavor. In the Talmud, there is a sage who noted that "Better to be the one who asks many givers than to give just yourself."[25]

Phil & Ann Thropist: We need to rethink our priorities. We will spend more time together talking about the points you made. We will be back in touch.

Nathan Asker: That is all I could ask for. Thank you for your time.

Although the conversation above was conducted with a wealthy couple, it does not matter whether the donation being discussed is $100, $1,000 or ten million; all American Jews need to prioritize their charitable giving. We must all maximize the impact of our gifts. In order to do so, treat yourself as a foundation. Decide what dollar amount or percentage of income is appropriate to donate, then allocate your charitable budget by category. This method enables all givers to think strategically about how to give and what amount to give. Some may prefer to give a little to a lot of causes. Others may prefer to concentrate their giving on just a few *tzedakot*. In any event, this process makes giving more rational and provides a framework for each family to give until it feels good. And, if an individual or couple finds that they are not spending all of their charitable budget, they should seek out worthwhile organizations or increase their giving to current recipients. Conversely, if their charitable budget is entirely spent, they can reevaluate their budget to determine if the amount is appropriate. If it is appropriate, they can feel comfortable in saying no to new solicitations. Even the Talmudic sages realized that giving too much was not a good idea.[26] Adding discipline to our charitable giving will lead us to make individual allocation decisions that will ensure the future of Jews in America. Every gift is important, but in the near term, the wealthiest American Jews need to make mega-gifts that can make a strong impact quickly and can set an example for all American Jews. We need to fund a Jewish renewal before it is too late.

*   *   *

The wealth and generosity of American Jewry is apparent. Unfortunately, too little Jewish generosity is flowing into causes that promote the future of the Jewish people. We need to create mechanisms that enhance Jewish-focused giving among Jews. We cannot afford to waste resources on inefficient or legacy Jewish agencies. We must engage in creative destruction and/or reorganization of these agencies in order to free resources for more pressing needs. Jewish organizations need to put the overall Jewish community and not their own interests first. With vision, we will have more resources to build the Jewish future. None of us is exempt from this responsibility.

Notes

1. "The Richest People in America," *Forbes Magazine*, October 10, 2005.
2. Pullout section, *Lifestyles Magazine*, Summer 2005.
3. Gary A. Tobin, Jeffrey R. Solomon, Alexandra C. Karp, *Mega-Gifts in American Philanthropy: General & Jewish Giving Patterns between 1995–2000.* (San Francisco: Institute for Jewish & Community Research, 2003), p. 1, http://www.jewishresearch.org/PDFs/MegaGift_03_web.pdf, accessed June 2006.
4. Ibid., p. 1.
5. Ibid., p. 1.
6. Beckey Bright, "In a Year of Disasters, Americans Continue to Give, Polls Find, "*The Wall Street Journal Online*", November 25, 2005. The article cites data from the Giving U.S.A. Foundation 2004 report, which defines mega-gifts as gifts over $1 million. In contrast, in their study *Mega-Gifts*, Tobin, *et al.* define a mega-gift as a donation of $10 million and over.
7. *NJPS 2000–01*, pp. 13 and 19.
8. Ibid., pp. 13 and 19.
9. Tobin *et al.*, *Mega-Gifts*, p. 19.

10. Suzeanne Stevenswith Sarah Cox,"Museum Additions American Style" Section *Architectural Record Magazine,* (November 2005).
11. Babylonian Talmud, Shekalim 2b.
12. Pirke Avot 1:14.
13. James O. Freedman, "Ghosts of the Past: Anti-Semitism at Elite Colleges," *The Chronicle Review* (December 1, 2000), http://chronicle.com/free/v47/i14/14b00701.htm, accessed June 2006.
14. John Hechinger, "When $26 Billion Isn't Enough," *The Wall Street Journal,* December 17–18, 2005.
15. Samuel P. Huntington, *Who Are We? The Challenges to America's Identity* (New York: Simon & Schuster, 2004), p. 88.
16. Alexis de Tocqueville, *Democracy in America,* trans. Henry Reeve (New York: A.A. Knopf, 1980), pp. 314–315.
17. Huntington, *Who Are We?* p. 11.
18. *JPPPI Annual Assessment 2004–2005,* p. 13.
19. See "The Constitution of the United States," Article 1, Section 9, Clause 8 and 10.
20. Cahill, *The Gifts of the Jews,* pp. 248–249.
21. Mark Twain, "Concerning The Jews," *Harper's Magazine,* March 1898.
22. Max I. Dimont, *The Indestructible Jews; Is There a Manifest Destiny in Jewish History?* (New York: Signet, 1973), p. 264.
23. Ibid., p. 265.
24. John Hechinger, "When $26 Billion Isn't Enough." *The Wall Street Journal,* August December 17, 2005.
25. Babylonian Talmud, Babba Bathra 9a.
26. Babylonian Talmud, Ketubboth 50a.

* Just prior to the printing of this book, Yeshiva University announced that it had received a $100-million gift from Ronald P. Stanton, a New York City industrialist. I hope that Stanton's example leads to many other mega-gifts within the Jewish community.

Chapter VIII

Intermarriage and Patrilineal Descent

"There is no greater sin than to cause one's nation to disappear from the world." Zerubabel Levinsohn, 1853.

Plank #6: American Jewry's response to intermarriage and to the children of intermarriage must be coherent and must include clear boundaries for belonging to the Jewish people across all movements. We must be realistic: a continued high intermarriage rate will sap the vitality of American Jewry. The Reform Movement must modify its policy of patrilineal descent with the objective of getting Jewish fathers of mixed marriages much more involved in raising practicing Jews. We need to welcome those couples that do decide to intermarry, but with an unconcealed and unabashed agenda of encouraging the non–Jewish spouse to convert to Judaism.

The Roots of Intermarriage

The intermarriage of one Jewish individual is rarely a sudden occurrence. Rather, an individual's choice to intermarry is a function of the depth of their Jewish education and experiences, the density of the Jewish population in the relevant geographic area, and commitment to "in-dating." An American Jew who chooses to intermarry typically shares many of the same goals and values as his/her non-Jewish fiancé(e) and is therefore open to building a family with him or her. Intermarriage is also a sign of the success of Jewish acculturation to the American environment and acceptance by Americans

Intermarriage in America

Intermarriage in America today is the result of the amazing social progress of American Jews. While only decades ago, most non-Jewish Americans strongly disapproved if their child wished to marry a Jew, ninety percent of Americans now say that they would welcome a Jew marrying their son or daughter.[1] Not only are Christian Americans willing to marry Jews, but Americans of all kinds of divergent heritages, whether Japanese-American, Indian-America or African-America, are marrying each other at an increasing pace. The current consensus in America is that people can fall in love across race, ethnic group, and creed and that nothing should stand in their way. As a result, Jews are justly sensitive to the charge that discouraging intermarriage is a form of bigotry, since for many non-Jews, Jewish aversion to intermarriage is problematic. How can Jews claim to be tolerant and then be unwilling to allow their child to marry a non-Jew? Jews who intermarry also have difficulty understanding their friends' and relatives' consternation at their decision, a decision which they perceive as a testament to their openness to different cultures. This view of Jewish intermarriage must change.

Jewish inmarriage is not a form of bigotry. As Melvin Konner, a distinguished anthropologist, argues, Jewish inmarriage is the only way to preserve Jewish culture. Konner describes the Jewish people's vulnerability to intermarriage through the following insightful metaphor: "Non-Jews suspect that Jewish insularity is a kind of reverse bigotry, or at least a superiority complex, and for some Jews this is true. But for most who care about Jewish religion and culture, who want to see it survive, it is simply a matter of numbers. Consider: If you let a drop of red liquid – borscht, say, or syrup-sweet Manischewitz wine – fall into a pitcher of water, you can watch it disappear, and after it is gone the water will seem unchanged. A 50 percent intermarriage rate by Jews would draw off about 1 percent of Christians; in the extremely unlikely case that all the resulting families became Jewish – fewer than half do – the effect on the Christian community would be negligible. But the loss to the Jewish community is devastating."[2] Intermarriage hurts the Jewish community in America; in contrast, it has little impact on the survival of any other non-Jewish American community.

The Impact of Intermarriage on Jewish Identity

We need to recognize the brutal truth that intermarriage is a scourge to the vitality of American Jewry. Only 30% of the children of intermarriage are raised as Jews. Most of these children receive only the most limited Jewish education, and experience few Jewish family or community traditions. Less than half of intermarried families have any kind of Passover Seder, compared to 96% of families with two Jewish parents. Just 19% of intermarried parents with young children belong to a synagogue, compared to 80% of in-married parents with young children. The list of statistics that show the contrast between the Jewish observance of in-married and that of intermarried couples is almost endless. The brutal truth is what it is.[3] We cannot put a gloss on it.

Recognizing the Impact of Intermarriage

Because intermarriage is clearly devastating the Jewish people, American Jewry cannot permit rabbis and cantors to abuse their ordination by sprinkling holy water on mixed marriages. Judaism does not sanctify mixed marriages. Sadly, a minority of Reform rabbis – particularly outside of the New York area – officiate at intermarriages despite the Reform Movement's official position on intermarriage, according to which:

> "The Central Conference of American Rabbis, recalling its
> stand adopted in 1909 that mixed marriage is contrary to the
> Jewish tradition and should be discouraged, now declares its
> opposition to participation by its members in any ceremony
> which solemnizes a mixed marriage."[4]

Even more sadly, Jewish clergy who perform such ceremonies
are sometimes motivated by financial gain. Because few rabbis
perform intermarriage, they often charge premium rates for their
services. Although several rabbis I have spoken to claim that they
officiate at mixed weddings in order to avoid alienating the non-
Jewish spouse and encourage the couple to raise their children
as Jews, most of them offer little or no pre-marital counseling on
the issues that intermarried couples will face, options for building
a Jewish home, and how the couple will raise their children.[5] I
have also yet to hear of an officiating clergy actively following up
on a mixed marriage couple to encourage them to pursue Jewish
observance. Furthermore, usually Jewish clergy are included in
intermarriages only to placate the parents on the Jewish side. The
non-Jewish fiancé(e) typically does not feel the need for Jewish
clergy but is willing to be accommodating.

Because intermarriages are a wound to the Jewish community, Rabbis who perform these ceremonies should not be
permitted to be members of any accepted rabbinical organization,
whether their ordination is from an accredited institution or the
East Himalayan Rabbinical Seminary Correspondence School.
The Reform Movement must also enforce its stated guidelines on
intermarriage by publicly barring rabbis who officiate at intermarriages from the Central Conference of American Rabbis (CCAR)
from now on. The Reform Movement can no longer sanction
the current divergence between standards it sets and practice it
condones that sets it apart from the broader American Jewish
community. As the largest movement, it has a responsibility to
all of American Jewry. Officiants who perform intermarriage

should also be barred from being called to the Torah at any temple or synagogue and receiving any other communal honor. While such a ban may not override the commercial considerations of these officiants, it demonstrates to American Jewry as a whole that these ceremonies take place without the authentic blessing of the Jewish people.

Intermarriage will never disappear, but it cannot be sanctioned by Judaism.

Reconciling Freedom of Choice and Jewish Continuity

It is each person's sovereign right to decide whom to marry; as a community we must accept that not all Jews will marry Jews. The intermarriage rate will never drop to zero. Nor would a zero intermarriage rate be a healthy development, as it would imply that the non-Jewish majority actively rejects all social contact with Jews. There will always be some intermarriage. Even in Boro Park, Brooklyn, the most densely Jewish and most Orthodox neighborhood in all of New York City, there is a 6% intermarriage rate.[6] There is no question that all Jews must continue to have the freedom to choose whom they wish to marry.

Supporting freedom of choice does not, however, mean sanctioning intermarriage. I personally have no problem attending the wedding of a Jew and non-Jew as long as it is a civil ceremony. I would privately be sad for the Jewish people but unreservedly happy for the couple. Boycotting the wedding will have no impact on whether the wedding happens, nor should it. As previously noted, the Jewish participants' willingness to consider intermarriage is usually the result of a lifetime of experiences and decisions. We cannot accept, however, the misappropriation of Jewish symbols and rites, which make a mockery of their true meaning. The fraudulent use of these symbols and rites makes it seem like intermarriage can be fit into Judaism. Let's just be happy for the couple and drop the fraudulent Jewish veneer.

After the marriage, the Jewish spouse is still Jewish; we must therefore welcome him/her with open arms and encourage his/her non-Jewish partner to convert. We Jews already seem to be doing a surprisingly good job at the first part of this response, as 90% of intermarried Jews who have some connection to a Jewish institution feel accepted by the Jewish community.[7] We should however, redouble our efforts at welcoming these families with the open agenda that we wish the non-Jewish partner to make the commitment to join his/her spouse as a member of the Jewish people, although we must also respect his or her choice to remain true to the faith of his/her birth. The common misperception that converts hurt the vitality and strength of the Jewish people is simply untrue; converts to Judaism bring enthusiasm, new perspective and intellectual curiosity to Jewish settings. In fact, it is common for a newly converted spouse to prod his or her spouse to go to the synagogue more often and to devote more attention to Jewish home rituals such as Shabbat dinner. The NJPS survey picked up a hint of this enthusiasm in its questions about adult Jewish learning. 50% of couples that included a convert said they were involved in adult Jewish learning versus just 24% of American Jews overall.[8] American Jews could use some of this enthusiasm to inspire us.

Conversion in Jewish Law and History

Converts have always been an integral part of the Jewish people. Born Jews are commanded to welcome an individual, who, by voluntarily accepting the beliefs, practices and fate of the Jewish people, becomes a full-fledged Jew. Because Judaism firmly espouses that each person is a reflection of God in some way (*B'tzelem elokim*), *anyone* may choose to convert to Judaism. The Jewish people are not parallel to a race or nation in the modern sense, rather we are akin to an egalitarian club that accepts applicants regardless of color, education, pedigree or any other personal factor. The club does, however, have some serious and meaningful rules, which apply to all members and must be accepted before joining. It also does not recognize resignations: you may think you have quit, but the club still keeps you on the membership rolls with all of its attendant rules and responsibilities. Joining the Jewish club must therefore be taken seriously: it must be the result of an informed and voluntary choice.

Traditionally, Judaism had great respect for converts. The Jewish club has no glass ceiling for new entrants. Ruth, one of the most famous converts to Judaism, has her own book in the Hebrew Scriptures and has the honor of being the great-grand-mother of King David. Converts have also been great Torah scholars: Onkelos, the son of a Roman nobleman, translated the entire Bible into Aramaic, and some of the Tosafot – scholars who wrote commentaries on the Talmud in the Middle Ages – were also converts. Converts have even made the supreme sacrifice of martyrdom. One such individual, Count Pototzki, the righteous convert of Vilna, is buried beside one the greatest Torah scholars of all time, the Vilna Gaon. These and more examples show how much converts to Judaism can contribute to the Jewish people if conversion is embraced wholeheartedly from both sides.

The current aversion to conversion should thus be revised. Our current reluctance to accept converts is the result of the Jewish experience of living in Christian and Muslim lands in which conversion to Judaism was often likely to result in the death of the converted party as well as members of the Jewish community who were connected to the conversion. This naturally put a damper on Jewish enthusiasm for conversion. Persecution during the modern period has also made Jews wary of the motives of non-Jews. Yet this experience has not always been, nor should it be, the case. Jews in ancient times assiduously welcomed converts. Yet whether encouraged or discouraged, conversion has never been an easy process, nor should it be. Throughout Jewish history conversion has required individuals to make a life-changing commitment of existential proportions; only someone who truly wishes to be part of the Jewish people should undertake this process. We should be honored to receive those willing to embark on this path.

Challenges to Defining Collective Jewish Identity in Modern Times

Accepting and welcoming converts is not the only challenge to Jewish identity in modern times. Today across the Western world ethnic identity has become confused, due to conflicting notions about national belonging in a global world as well as to generations of mixed marriages. In response to these challenges, two dominant views about ethnic identity have emerged as solutions. The first is biological: for some, one simply inherits the ethnicity of one's parents. The second is a question of individual choice: one may inherit an ethnic identity, but one can adopt another identity through citizenship. The issue is then further complicated by two factors: first, generations of mixed marriages have produced individuals who can choose to adopt one of several ethnic identities conferred on them by birth, and second, global migration enables individuals to settle in another country. This issue has not been avoided by the Jewish community.

The challenge of defining Jewish identity in Israel demonstrates that in practice an individual's identification with the Jewish people is both a matter of descent and of choice. In 1970, the Israeli government amended Israel's Law of Return to grant automatic citizenship to any grandchild of a Jew, spouse of a Jew, spouse of a child of a Jew, and the spouse of a grandchild of a Jew.[9] This law was aimed primarily at helping anyone with Jewish ancestry in the Eastern Communist bloc defect to Israel and because this was Hitler's definition of a Jew, used to decimate millions in the Holocaust. The definition of who is Jewish according to the Law of Return has not, however, meant that all immigrants with Jewish parentage have a clear Jewish identity. A not insignificant proportion of individuals admitted under the amended Law of Return not only have no functional Jewish identity, but clearly identify as Russians ethnically and as Orthodox Christians or atheists religiously, proving that one can have Jewish parentage and grand-parentage, live in Israel, and still choose not to be

Jewish. Similarly, if parentage or grandparentage alone were used to determine Jewish identity in America, there would be approximately 10 million "Jews" in the U.S.[10] Such a figure would clearly not be meaningful if many of this number might resent being told that they are Jewish. Being Jewish is not simply a matter of citizenship, ethnicity or choice.

Jews are not alone in struggling to define the question of the role of national identity in "belonging." In an era of global migration, states across the world are struggling to adopt a suitable paradigm for determining citizenship of newborns. Some countries, such as the United States, place the emphasis on birthright. If a baby is born in the U.S., he/she is generally a citizen of the U.S., although for U.S. citizens living abroad, the rules become quite complex after the first generation. In a number of other countries, parentage determines citizenship. In Germany, for example, a descendant of an eighteenth-century immigrant to Russia who is able to prove direct lineage can return to Germany as a full citizen. The downside of awarding citizenship on the basis of descent is that it is difficult for non-Germans to ever become naturalized citizens. This is the case in many other countries.[11] In the United Arab Emirates only 25% or so of the residents are citizens.[12] No country in the world has yet come up with a perfect solution to defining citizenship.

Just as no country offers citizenship unconditionally to any applicant, not everyone who is offered citizenship in an adopted country wishes to receive it. As with any club, some might simply not wish to join or become a citizen even if they are fully qualified. On the one hand, the real or perceived drawbacks of citizenship may be factors in this decision. On the other, many are reluctant to disassociate from their past identity; it is just too strong for them. In the U.S., where naturalization is an open possibility, many green card holding immigrants choose not to become naturalized, or in other words, to nationally convert. The variance among groups is surprisingly large.

Citizenship Rate for Immigrant U.S. Residents by Nationality[13]	
Filipinos	76.2%
Koreans	71.2
Chinese	68.5
Vietnamese	67.7
Poles	61.3
Indians	58.7
Italians	58.3
Jamaicans	57.5
Germans	51.8
Cubans	49.9
Britons	44.1
Dominicans	42.0
Canadians	40.0

Likewise, not everyone wishes to become Jewish. Every nation, club or culture has some rules of membership. Concomitantly, not every person who qualifies for membership wishes to enter the club.

Since the time of Ezra, that is to say for about 2,500 years, the rules for membership in the Jewish club have been clear and widely observed. A Jew is someone born of a Jewish mother or someone who has converted to Judaism. While this may seem arbitrary, it is no more so than other definitions of belonging and citizenship, and also has the virtue of being clear and fair. And, in the days before DNA testing, it had the additional advantage of being verifiable, as opposed to claimed patrilineal descent. This definition is still valid today.

Recent Jewish Challenges to Defining Jewish Identity: Patrilineal Descent

In 1983, the Reform Movement made the decision to grant any child born of a Jewish father automatic membership in the Jewish People, a policy otherwise known as patrilineal descent. Indeed, the decision of the conference of Central American Rabbis was truly radical: it "transformed the halachic formulation of 'the child of a Jewish mother' to the 'child of a Jewish parent'"[14] in delineating the transmission of Jewishness from one generation to the next; moreover, it stipulated that no child, whether born of a Jewish father or mother, was officially Jewish until he/she completed a bar/bat mitzvah or engaged in public acts or ceremonies of Jewishness.[15] The impact was immediate: conversions to Judaism dropped by 75%. Following the patrilineal descent decision, only 5% of non-Jewish fiancé(e)s in prospective intermarriages converted to Judaism.[16] The ancient Jewish club now had some members who did not recognize other club members, creating confusion. Worse still, the overwhelming majority of those granted this new club membership threw away their membership cards. As a result, membership in the Jewish club has been profoundly devalued.

Though the Reform Movement instituted patrilineal descent as a means to combat the problem of poor Jewish identity among children of intermarriage, the result has been the exact opposite. Among the 30% of children of mixed marriages who are raised as Jews, the vast majority had Jewish mothers. Even when the Jewish parent desires to raise the children as Jews, this is only likely to happen when the Jewish parent is a woman.[17] This may seem surprising since the child of a Jewish father most often carries the father's Jewish name and is frequently assumed to be Jewish by acquaintances. Nevertheless, the factual evidence is clear: whether by virtue of genes, tradition or culture, Jewish mothers are much more effective at transmitting Judaism to their children than Jewish fathers *even if* they so desire. There are nevertheless exceptions to this rule: there are men who have taken up the mantle of transmitting Judaism; they just do not seem to do so very often, for whatever reason.[18] The Jewish Outreach Institute, which focuses on bringing Judaism to interfaith couples, recognizes this phenomenon. Although the Institute has organized classes to assist non-Jewish mothers in raising their children as Jews,[19] it has not created a course for the non-Jewish husbands of Jewish women.

Children of intermarriages between a Jewish father and a non-Jewish mother are aware that their identity is problematic. In a study of young adult children of interfaith marriages, Pearl Beck found that all the children she interviewed, whether they identified themselves as Jews or not, and whether they had any knowledge of other Jewish ritual law or not, were aware that Judaism traditionally only considers the children of Jewish mothers to be Jewish. Some of those interviewed felt that they were "fraudulent" Jews because of patrilineal descent. Others resented their Jewishness being questioned.[20] No doubt there are also other children of Jewish fathers who practice other faiths and would prefer not to be considered Jewish. These bad feelings are the direct result of membership rules that have become messy and have ceased to be universally accepted by all members of the Jewish club. Furthermore, the rule of matrilineal descent is almost universally known in America. In the Broadway production of "Spamalot," the character of King Arthur asks if anyone of the characters is Jewish. His loyal servant, Patsy, responds that he is Jewish because "my mother was Jewish." The entire audience got it. Despite the Reform Movement's ruling on patrilineal descent, the majority of Reform Jews unquestioningly accept the children of Jewish mothers as Jewish, whether they have been bar/bat mitzvah or not. Thus, the Reform Movement's 1983 policy is not fully understood by many Reform Jews.

Despite the Reform movement's policy of patrilineal descent, for better or worse, the determination of matrilineal descent is ancient, broadly accepted and widely known. A simple declaration that the rule has changed on an issue as central as personal identity

does not feel authentic. A parallel to this occurred in the 19th and
early 20th century when some radical Reform rabbis and Reform
Temples decided to change Shabbat services from Saturday to
Sunday. Though Sunday observance fitted better with the six day
American workweek of the early twentieth century, the majority
of Reform Jews in America did not accept this change. Although
the Pittsburgh Platform mentions the observance of Shabbat on
Sunday, it made peace with Saturday as the Jewish day of rest.[21]
The debates over the best day to celebrate Shabbat show that one
of the strengths of American Reform Judaism is its ability to be
open to re-evaluate its experimentation and to re-embrace tradition when this seems more fitting.

Responding to Children of Intermarried Jewish Fathers

Despite the practical failure of patrilineal descent, we should
not dismiss its objective of integrating the children of intermarriages between a Jewish father and a non-Jewish mother into the
Jewish community. A few communities, most notably Baltimore,
are using their existing assets, such as high Jewish density, and
implementing policies in synagogues and day schools to embrace
intermarried families. Baltimore Jews can be proud that 62% of
the children of intermarried couples in Baltimore are raised as
Jews, a rate approximately twice that of the rest of the U.S.[22] Simply bestowing membership on these children was not part of the
Baltimore formula for success: their numbers are the result of
sustained educational and communal efforts. There is no evidence
that simply bestowing membership has been productive anywhere;
instead it has been counter-productive, as it has deterred conversion. We need an approach which encourages Jewish fathers to
get involved in raising their children as Jews. Interestingly, the
data from recent studies on intermarriage suggests an approach
based on American Jewry's single most enhanced Jewish observance – the bar/bat mitzvah.

One of the best purveyors of Jewish identity is the bar mitzvah. Among children of intermarriage interviewed, having had

a bar/bat mitzvah is highly related to positive current Jewish identity. Less than one quarter of the total respondents had a bar/bat mitzvah when growing up. However, among those who had a bar/bat mitzvah, 90% currently consider themselves exclusively "Jewish" by religion, in contrast to only 13% of those who did not have a bar/bat mitzvah who identify Jewishly. Having a bar/bat mitzvah is also related to strong positive feelings about being Jewish; 40% of those who had a bar/bat mitzvah, compared with a negligible proportion of those who did not have a bar/bat mitzvah, said that being Jewish was "very important" to them. Whether or not a child had a bar/bat mitzvah was the result of his/her parent's – and especially the mother's – level of Jewish identity. Fifty-five percent of children whose mother had a strong Jewish identity had a bar/bat mitzvah, compared with only 33% of those whose father was strongly Jewishly identified.[23] The evidence from the survey is extraordinarily clear. If you are a child of intermarriage and you had a bar/bat mitzvah, there is a 90% chance that you consider yourself Jewish, in contrast to the 13% chance that a child would identify as Jewish as an adult without a bar/bat mitzvah. The bar/bat mitzvah is such a central milestone for American Jews that it can function as a clear line between those who are in and those who are outside of the club.

Provisional Membership:
the Alternative to Patrilineal Descent

Based on the results of twenty years of patrilineal descent, it is clear that an alternative policy to patrilineal descent must be put in place in order to achieve the Reform Movement's goal of fostering a Jewish identity among children of Jewish fathers and non-Jewish mothers. A possible alternative might function as follows: anyone born of a Jewish mother would automatically be deemed Jewish; however, the child of a Jewish father and non-Jewish mother would become a provisional member of the Jewish people until the bar/bat mitzvah, with all the responsibilities, rights and privileges of any other pre-bar/bat mitzvah Jew. The child of a Jewish father would be welcomed to enroll in Hebrew school and youth groups, to become a junior member of a synagogue and so on, and even to go to day school, as long as the only religion in which the child is being raised as is Jewish. Then, at some point prior to bar/bat mitzvah age, the child would be asked to make a choice if he/she desires to study for bar/bat mitzvah and be called to the Torah as a full member of the Jewish people. We should appropriately treat this as a major decision for the child and not attempt to coerce a decision in any way. The child and family should discuss the issue at length, both in the presence of a Rabbi and by themselves.

Once the child has decided if he/she wishes to be Jewish, we must accept the child's choice. If the child's decision is not to proceed, then his/her provisional membership would cease and the Jewish community would consider the child as not Jewish. Our response to this choice must, however, be understanding and continued friendship. After all, as the Yiddish expression goes "Shveyr tzu zayn a Yid – It's not easy to be a Jew." And if the child decides to join the Jewish people later as an adult, we should welcome him/her; however, the same conversion procedure should apply to him/her as to any other convert. If, on the other hand, the child decides to affirm his/her membership in the Jewish people, then the bar/bat mitzvah should be preceded by a private conversion before a *beit din*. Adopting such a procedure should resemble the rules for converting children in traditional Judaism, which are traditionally more lenient than those for converting adults. After the conversion, the community should consider the child Jewish without an asterisk

Modifying patrilineal descent to include conversion and bar/bat mitzvah would not only benefit the child and the Jewish community as a whole, it would also benefit the Reform Movement. Presently, only the American arm of Reform Judaism recognizes partrilineal descent. The Canadian and Israeli branches have actually lobbied the Reform Rabbinical Association (the CCAR) to reconsider the ruling. Furthermore, within the U.S., standards among Reform rabbis as to who is a Reform Jew are so blurry as to be unknowable. The Reform Movement requires that children of a Jewish father engage in some form of Jewish education. In some cities, this means Hebrew school and a bar/bat mitzvah. In other cities it means much less. So it is possible, for example, to be considered a Jew by Reform standards in Nashville or Dallas but not in parts of Chicago or Detroit, and certainly not in Toronto or Tel Aviv. Thus, even within the Reform Movement, children of Jewish fathers have an uncertain identity. It is time to face the brutal truth: the 1983 patrilineal descent decision does not work.

Instituting a process of bar/bat mitzvah and conversion to integrate children of Jewish fathers into the Jewish people is not a perfect solution. Devising a conversion process that all Jews can accept is and has been a very difficult task. For seven years, from 1977 to 1983, the Reform, Conservative and Orthodox rabbis of Denver agreed to a joint conversion program. The rabbis from all the different movements made deep compromises. When the program fell apart and was "outed," all the rabbis involved were subject to harsh criticism from their rabbinical organizations. The Orthodox rabbis received the most severe criticism.[24] Therefore, we should not get too technical about defining the process of these pre-bar/bat mitzvah conversions. Each child/family can decide where it wants to situate itself within the spectrum of the movements with less rancor than if there were an attempt at a unified conversion process. Yet even if we keep the process of provisional membership/bar mitzvah/conversion flexible, for the Jewish people it is far superior to the status quo, as it resolves the status of children of Jewish fathers within a more traditional Jewish framework, and also addresses the very real issue of intermarriage. It is therefore reasonable to expect that the process of provisional membership/bar mitzvah/conversion will mend the current rifts in the American Jewish community created by patrilineal descent.

The process of provisional membership/bar mitzvah/conversion for children born of Jewish fathers will have other positive outcomes. First, it will get Jewish fathers much more involved in creating a Jewish life for their children, since automatic patrilineal descent has led even those fathers who care about Judaism to shy away from the nitty-gritty decisions and choices that create Jewish identity. In essence, the process of provisional membership/bar mitzvah/conversion will give these Jewish fathers a biological clock of their own. If by bar/bat mitzvah age his child does not want to be Jewish, the Jewish father has forfeited his birthright. "After all, interfaith marriage is not the end of Jewish continuity. Not raising Jewish children is the end of Jewish continuity."[25] The process of provisional membership/bar mitzvah/conversion will also be advantageous for those Jewish fathers who do not want to raise their children as Jews, as it will ensure that their children will not receive mixed messages. Thus, this process will also allow fathers to actively opt out, although it will force them to recognize the consequences of their decision. This same reasoning also applies to children of Jewish fathers, as this provisional process will prevent them from having a Jewish identity involuntarily forced upon them if they do not identify as Jewish. For these reasons, one might expect that the process of provisional membership/bar mitzvah/conversion would result in more patrilineal descent Jews actually becoming practicing Jews and members of the Jewish community. Many synagogues and day schools within the Conservative Movement follow this sort of procedure on an informal basis. In South America many community day schools also admit students along the same lines. The effect of this change would serve as a step in repairing a major breach within the Jewish people.

Although altering patrilineal descent is likely to create tremendous controversy in the Reform Movement, there is no reason to believe that this controversy will not be overcome. The Reform Movement has long demonstrated its vitality and maturity by embracing reforms that work and modifying or discarding those that do not. Already the Reform Movement recognizes the conundrum it has created by instituting fluid borders between Jews and non-Jews. At the Reform Movement's November 2005 biennial convention, the president of the Movement, Rabbi Eric Yoffe, said that "by making non-Jews feel comfortable and accepted in our congregations, we have sent the message that we do not care if they convert. But that is not our message." He continued by saying that "the time has come to reverse direction by returning to public conversions and doing all the other things that encourage conversion in our synagogues."[26] The same reasoning could be used with respect to patrilineal descent. By telling Jewish fathers that their children are Jewish, the Reform Movement has had the unintended effect of creating fewer future Jews. Likewise, the Reform Movement gives the impression that it sanctions intermarriage by continuing to tolerate clergy who officiate at intermarriages. By reconsidering the policy of patrilineal descent and enforcing the Reform Movement's stated opposition to intermarriage, the Reform Movement will clarify boundaries for itself and heal the rifts between itself and all of *klal yisrael*.

* * *

Intermarriage is a fateful challenge for American Jewry. There is no doubt that it seriously compromises the viability and future of Jews in America. We must discourage intermarriage through quality Jewish education and lifelong quality Jewish experiences. Last minute attempts to dissuade adults from marrying are not likely to be successful. Yet, because of their potential negative impact for the future of Judaism, Jewish clergy cannot sanctify these marriages. Rabbis and cantors who officiate at these ceremonies make a mockery of Jewish rites and symbols and must be barred from any recognized rabbinical association. But, though Judaism does not sanction intermarriage, we must welcome both the Jew and non-Jewish spouse to our community after the wedding. Our open agenda should be to convert the non-Jewish spouse and encourage the whole family to become more deeply involved in the Jewish community. It is now clear that the Reform Movement's patrilineal descent initiative has had the unintended consequence of bringing fewer children to the Jewish people. There is also evidence that intermarried Jewish fathers trail far behind intermarried Jewish mothers in their efforts to raise their child as Jewish, even if they intend to do so. Finally, it has also been established that the bar/bat mitzvah is a defining event for children of intermarriages. Almost all children who have a bar/bat mitzvah identify as Jews when they become young adults; few who have not do so. Thus, it seems that the Reform Movement would bring more children of intermarried couples into the Jewish people by modifying its stance on patrilineal descent to a policy of membership/bar mitzvah/conversion. This modified policy would also encourage Jewish fathers to get more involved in their children's Jewish upbringing, and decrease confusion and resentment among Jews as well as among those who do not want a Jewish identity foisted upon them. In so doing, the Reform Movement would also be achieving a great *tikkun olam* by acting to heal this schism within Jewry.

Notes

1. Melvin Konner, *Unsettled – An Anthropology of the Jews* (New York: Peguin, 2003), p. 422.
2. Ibid.
3. Steven M. Cohen, *Engaging the Next Generation of American Jews: Distinguishing the In-Married, Inter-Married and Non-Married*, unpublished conference paper draft for the World Conference of Jewish Communal Service (2005), http://www.huc.edu/alumni/Engaging%20American%20Jews.doc, and Steven M. Cohen, *Jewish Educational Background: Trends and Variations Among Today's Jewish Adults* (New York: United Jewish Communities, 2004).
4. See Rabbi Don Rossoff, "Ask the Rabbi & FAQ / Intermarriage," CCAR website <http://urj.org/ask/intermarried/>, 2006.
5. Debra Nussbaum Cohen, "47% of Rabbis in 2 Movements Conducting Intermarriages," *The Jewish News Weekly of Northern California*, 22 March 1996. Although this article grossly exaggerates the number of Reform rabbis who perform intermarriages, the Union of Reform Judaism recognizes that a minority of Reform rabbis do perform intermarriages.
6. UJA, *Jewish Community Study of New York: Geographic Profile* (New York: UJA, 2004), p. 75.
7. Steven M. Cohen, *Engaging the Next Generation of American Jews: Distinguishing the In-Married, Inter-Married and Non-Married*, unpublished

conference paper draft for the World Conference of Jewish Communal Service (2005), <http://www.huc.edu/alumni/Engaging%20American%20Jews.doc>.

8. UJC, NJPS *2000–2001 Adult Jewish Education: Presentation of Findings*, PowerPoint presentation, http://www.ujc.org/content_display.html?ArticleID=118670#edu (cited June 2006), slide 20.

9. See Law of Return (Amendment No. 2), article 4A, 5730–1970 as found in <http://www.jewishvirtuallibrary.org/jsource/Immigration/Text_of_Law_of_Return.html>, accessed May 2006.

10. JPPPI, *Annual Assessment 2005*, p. 61.

11. Samuel P. Huntington, *Who are we?: The Challenges to America's identity* (New York: Simon & Schuster, 2004), 31–32.

12. See<http://en.wikipedia.org/wiki/Islam_in_the_United_Arab_Emirates>.

13. Huntington, *Who Are We?*, p. 239. Huntington takes his statistics which uses the standardized 1990 naturalization in order to eliminate any statistical differences due to an immigrant's year of entry in the United States, from Leon Borivier's study, Leon Bouvier, "Embracing America: A Look at Which Immigrants Become Citzens," *Center for Immigration Studies*, Paper 11, 1996, p. 14, table 4.3, http://www.cis.org/topics/assimilation.html, accessed July 2006.

14. M.H. Vogel, "The Resolution on Patrilineal Descent: A Theological Defense," *Modern Judaism* 6 (2) (May 1986), p. 129.

15. Ibid.

16. JPPPI *Annual Assessment 2005*, pp. 65–66.

17. Bruce Phillips, *Catholic (and Protestant) Israel: Non-Jews and Spouses and Children in Jewish Families*, unpublished paper, 2005.

18. Steven M. Cohen and Arnold Eisen, *The Jew Within* (Bloomington: Indiana University Press, 2000), p. 186.

19. *Rabbi Kerry Olitzky, "Unsung Heroes," The Inclusive*, Autumn 2005, p. 1.

20. Pearl Beck, *A Flame Still Burns: The Dimensions and Determinants of Jewish Identity Among Young Adult Children of the Intermarried 2005* (New York: Jewish Outreach Institute, 2005), p. 29.

21. See<http://www.jewishvirtuallibrary.org/jsource/Judaism/reform_practices.html>, accessed May 2006.

22. JPPPI, *Annual Assessment 2005*, p. 68.

23. Beck, *A Flame Still Burns*, p. 35.

24. Samuel G. Freedman, *Jew vs. Jew: the Struggle for the Soul of American Jewry* (New York: Simon & Schuster, 2000), chapter 2.

25. Rabbi Kerry M. Olitzky, "Optimism for the Jewish Future," *Contact Magazine*, Spring 2005, Steinhardt Jewish Life Foundation, p. 10.

26. James Besser, "Tradition with Twist of Diversity," *The Jewish Week*, 25 November 2005.

Chapter IX

A New American Minhag to Promote Jewish Identity and Learning

"Make your study of Torah a fixed habitual activity."
Pirke Avot 1:15

Plank #7 American Jewry should adopt the minhag (tradition/ practice) that each Jew reaffirm his/her bar/bat mitzvah every 18 years after the age of 13. These re-affirmations would thus coincide with critical points in an individual's lifecycle. Prior to each bar/ bat mitzvah reaffirmation every 18 years, each Jew should pursue some Jewish project, such as a course of study, a chesed (caring) commitment, a social action pursuit or any other Jewish endeavor. The cyclical 18-year bar/bat mitzvah renewal would culminate in a ceremony that could include being called to the Torah or participating in another communal ritual event. The 18-year bar/bat mitzvah renewal will create a new occasion for an individual Jew to celebrate his/her identity and re-establish his/her connection with the Jewish community.

Milestones in American Life

The majority Americans celebrate milestones. Almost every American regardless of their ethnic or religious origin celebrates birthdays, the most common milestone in American life. Even the most traditional Chareidim have taken up birthday celebrations. Yet birthdays are not a Jewish tradition, nor are they universally celebrated by Americans of other faiths and ethnic backgrounds, rather birthdays have only recently become widespread.[1] Most Americans also celebrate anniversaries to commemorate the number of years of a couple's marriage, or time spent working at a firm. A large number of Americans also now make extra festivities to celebrate round-figure birthdays such as 30, 40, and 50, which mark new stages in life. Similarly, the American culture has special names for key anniversaries that mark the years a couple has spent together. In this chapter, I suggest that American Jews think about infusing the American custom of celebrating lifetime milestones with Jewish learning and social action. Rather than just having a thirtieth, fortieth, or fiftieth birthday party, American Jews can think about celebrating their accomplishments by re-engaging with Judaism in what ever way they connect to most. In a celebration akin to the most popular and only Jewish milestone, the bar/bat mitzvah.

The Origins and Popularity of the Bar Mitzvah

As far as Jewish traditions go, the bar/bat mitzvah ceremony is a recent addition. Sometime in the 16th century, Jews in Poland and Germany established the practice of commemorating the ritual when a boy reaches the age of adulthood. Over time, the bar/bat mitzvah became more festive; the bar mitzvah boy wore new clothes and his family held a feast for extended family and guests to celebrate the event.

Sometime in the late nineteenth century, American Jews adopted the concept of the bar mitzvah as a celebration and further enhanced it. In 1922, Rabbi Mordechai Kaplan, the founder of the Reconstructionist Movement, originated the first bat mitzvah ceremony in honor of his daughter. While traditional Jews did not accept this innovation at first, over the decades virtually all streams of American Jewry embraced the bat mitzvah, albeit with significant ritual differences among the Orthodox.

Over the course of the 20th Century bar/bat mitzvah parties have tended to become ever grander and more focused on the parents. Though bar/bat mitzvahs in the 1970s and 1980s seemed to become more about the "bar" than the "mitzvah," since the 1990s communities have modified this trend. With some major exceptions, most bar/bat mitzvah parties are now somewhat less grandiose and much more child centered.

Yet, even though bar/bat mitzvah parties in America have been a bit too extravagant at times, they have always been about more than the party. During his or her bar/bat mitzvah, the boy or girl reads from the Torah, chants a Haftorah and delivers a d'var Torah (literally "word of Torah," a lesson on the Torah). For these rituals Jewish children usually have to learn to read Hebrew at least phonetically and to study the translation of the words they will chant as well as some interpretations of the reading. In order to acquire these skills, children must spend several years learning in a Hebrew school or day school prior to the bar/bat mitzvah. Most rabbis also spend quality time teaching and getting to know the bar/mitzvah candidates. As a result of the commitment this preparation entails, the decision to have a bar/bat mitzvah is probably the most important factor in instilling Jewish identity in children of intermarriages. Since only about a quarter of the children of intermarriage choose to have a bar/bat mitzvah, everyone seems to recognize that a bar/bat mitzvah is about a lot more than just receiving presents.

The Bar/Bat Mitzvah in American Jewish Life

The bar/bat mitzvah has become so central to American Jewish life that American folk culture has implicitly understood its importance to American Jews. The "Dick Van Dyke Show," "Frasier," "The Wonder Years" and countless other general network television programs have aired very positive episodes that incorporated a bar/bat mitzvah celebration. General American teen fiction, such as the popular series the Babysitters Club[2] and the books accompanying American Girl dolls[3] have also presented the bat mitzvah in a positive light. For Jews and non-Jews, having a bar/bat mitzvah is what every Jew must do.

Unfortunately, despite its popularity and importance, the American bar/bat mitzvah has become the natural endpoint of Jewish learning as opposed to a launching pad. This is not acceptable. Learning before the age of thirteen is not enough to inform adult choices in the modern era. The breadth, depth and texture of Jewish learning are not fully comprehensible to pre-adolescents, and will not lead them to develop greater connections to Judaism as adults. In fact, the first chart in Chapter IV indicates that children who attend day school until the age of bar/bat mitzvah had a substantial deficiency in Jewish identity indicators in comparison to children who continued in Jewish day schools throughout high school. The bar/bat mitzvah may be important to American Jews, but it is not enough to sustain American Jewish identity.

Adult Bar/Bat Mitzvah:
An Identity Event and the Culmination of Jewish Learning

The concept of a once-and-for-all bar/bat mitzvah is just not enough for American Jews today. In the era when bar/bat mitzvah ceremonies began, the average lifespan was 33 to 37 years. Past the age of thirteen, most young men needed to devote themselves to learning a trade, getting married and starting their own family. In contrast, today American Jews are (thankfully) living much longer and in a more and more complex modern world: the average American Jewish lifespan ranges from 77 to 81 years, and many people are active in the work force for most of their adult lives.[4] With such long and complicated lives, the idea that a bar/bat mitzvah would be enough to instill a strong Jewish identity in young Jews and prepare Jewish teens to be Jewish adults is no longer valid. Today, Jews need occasional boosts in both their Jewish identity and Jewish learning throughout their adult life.

Even secular Jews recognize the need to bolster Jewish identity. One of the most famous secular Jews of the last century, Sigmund Freud, rarely used the term identity in his writings. Nevertheless, he often referred to this concept indirectly, and grappled with his own Jewish identity on more than one occasion.[5] When the B'nai Brith society honored Freud for his many years of active membership, Freud responded to the honor by explaining his motives for being an affiliated Jew, though he was entirely secular in his beliefs. In his view, "other things…make the attraction of Judaism and Jews irresistible – many…emotional forces, all the more potent for being so hard to grasp in words, as well as the clear consciousness of an inner identity, the intimacy that comes from the same psychic structure."[6] But simply living in a Jewish setting was not enough for Freud to identify as an adult Jew, as he notes, "I became one of you, took part in your humanitarian and national interest, [and] made friends among you."[7] Freud's participation in the B'nai Brith society led to meaningful Jewish action and social bonds: it became his adult "bar mitzvah."

American Jews today also need to enhance their Jewish learning if they want to make sense of being Jewish in the modern world. This is especially true given that most American Jews are not formally observant. According to Isa Aron, a widely regarded academic scholar of synagogue life and Jewish education, "[…] learning is even more important for those Jews who value their autonomy, yet want to retain their connection to Jewish tradition. Jews who do not feel commanded by God, but who identify with the Jewish people and want to participate in Jewish life, need a foundation for understanding their Judaism and for enabling them to decide what traditions to follow…If one is going to be selective about one's Jewish practice, one had better be fully informed…. Today Jewish learning is more essential than ever. Americans, including Jews, have discovered that excessive autonomy results in isolation and excessive skepticism leads to anomie…All Jewish learning, whether it is devoted to a study of sacred texts, Jewish thought or Jewish history, enables learners to connect their personal struggles to larger social and ethical ideals…Learning creates a larger sense of community as well as a community that links Jews through time and space.[8] For modern and independent American Jews, Jewish learning may be the single most important way to stay connected to Judaism.

Because Jewish identity and learning is important for most Jews in America, whether secular or observant, the 18-year bar/bat mitzvah cycle would give those adult Jews who crave spiritual growth – but who may not feel justified in taking time for Judaism – the chance to reaffirm their Jewish identity and learn throughout their adult lives. Having this opportunity is all the more important since feeling part of the Jewish people, as well as a connection to Jewish history, is a lifelong journey. Recent studies have also shown that positive adult Jewish experiences have a very strong impact on Jewish identity. Thus, if a bar/bat mitzvah at age 13 provides the basis, later Jewish experiences have a renewing impact.[9] As Bethanie Horowitz, the author of the study "Connections and Journey" argues: "For Jewish institutions, it is crucial to learn that 60% of the people in the study experienced changes in their relationship to being Jewish over time, suggesting that Jewish identity is not a fixed factor in one's life but rather a matter that parallels personal growth and personal development. There are critical periods and moments in people's lives that offer potential opportunities for Jewish institutions to play a role, if only these institutions can be open and available to individuals in a way that meets their changing needs and concerns."[10] American Jews need more entry points during their adult life to embark on the life-long journey of connecting to the Jewish people and their traditions.

The 18-year bar/bat mitzvah has the potential to open entryways to Judaism for the 60% of Jews whose Jewish identity changes over time, and to provide a boost to what Freud calls our shared "psychic structure" and our shared "intimacy." The 18-year bar/bat mitzvah renewal cycle affords an opportunity to learn, and therefore to replenish and increase the intellectual reservoir that was pre-maturely cut off at age thirteen. This learning and doing can also help Jewish adults find personal meaning by "connect[ing] [our] personal struggles to larger social and ethical ideals." Just as the first bar/bat mitzvah experience is "all the more potent for being so hard to grasp in words," adult Jewish learning and community involvement can be profound and uplifting. The problem is that most American Jews always have a reason to focus on what they view as urgent instead of what they believe is important.

Current Adult Attitudes to Jewish Learning

Recent studies have uncovered several reasons why adults do not devote more time to Jewish learning. In Amy Sale's study of members who pay dues, but are not active in synagogue life, adults of different age brackets gave diverse answers for not getting more involved. The answers nonetheless followed an interesting pattern. Young married couples with children said that while they were happy to bring their children to events at the synagogue, they were too busy with their careers and young children to have enough personal time to spend on temple events. However, they said they were sure that once their children were older, they would have more time to do Jewish stuff themselves. Adults with tweens and teens said that they were still too busy with carpooling, child rearing and careers, but that they were sure when the children went off to college that they would have more time to do Jewish stuff. A somewhat older group of adults talked about visiting their children in college, helping them to start off in life and taking long-delayed vacations. They also spoke of continuing career pressures in an environment of constant corporate change. These couples also claimed that they were very much looking forward to getting more involved in their synagogue once things were just a little quieter. And when Sales questioned the oldest group of retirees and empty nesters as to why they kept paying dues to the synagogue but were not active, they replied that they were paying so that younger people could use the synagogue. "It was really for the younger folks."[11] For most people the pace of modern life leads them to take care of what they view as urgent rather than what they perceive as merely important. In my view, the 18-year bar/bat mitzvah renewal cycle would counteract this trend by providing milestones at key life stages to replenish and nourish our Jewish identities.

The 18-Year Bar/Bat Mitzvah

The 18-year bar/bat mitzvah would provide refresher points that are particularly well positioned throughout an individual's life. "Anytime" goes on a schedule. The timing would be as follows:

Age Stage

13	Bar/Bat Mitzvah
13+18=31	Young Adulthood
13+36=49	Mid-life
13+54=67	Retirement
13+72=85	Reflection, legacy

Interestingly, all of the bar mitzvah steps have a numerical relationship to 13.

31	$3 \leftrightarrow 1 = 13$
49	4+9=13
67	6+7=13
85	8+5=13

For those who would prefer to use the traditional bat mitzvah age of 12 as a starting point, the ages would be as follows:

Age Stage

12+18=30	Young adulthood
12+36=48	Mid-life
12+54=66	Retirement
12+72=84	Reflection and Legacy

With the exception of the first 18-year bat mitzvah, these numbers continue to have some relationship to 12 by adding the digits:

48	4+8=12
66	6+6=12
84	8+4=12

This discussion will refer to 13 as the bat/bar mitzvah age as this is the time used for almost all non-Orthodox bat mitzvahs and the majority of bat mitzvahs overall.

Celebrating an additional bar/bat mitzvah every 18 years is symbolically appropriate. In Hebrew, each letter has an associated numerical value. The two letters in חי (Chai) add up to 18:

ח	8
י	+10
חי	=18

The Jewish tradition of computing the numerical value of words and finding words with the same numerical value is called *gematria. Gematria* is sometimes used for homiletic purposes but has no value in Jewish law. In this case, the number 18, or "life," plus bar/bat mitzvah age symbolizes the passage from one major chapter to another in an individual's lifetime.

The 18-Year Bar/Bat Mitzvah at 31

The 18-year bar/bat mitzvah renewal at 31 is a time when most young American Jews are making decisions that will influence the rest of their lives. The 30s are an exciting time, an age of beginnings. Frequently young adults are at exciting points in their career, engaged in new relationships and full of energy. At the same time, many young American Jews enjoy an extended feeling of adolescence in their early thirties. Too many 31-year-old Jews, particularly men, are not yet married and too many 31-year-old Jewish women have not yet had their first baby. For Jews of this age who are not married, formal ties to the Jewish community are typically at a low ebb. Thus, establishing a milestone at this point to encourage reflection, study, social action and connection to the Jewish people is particularly appropriate. The 18-year bar/bat mitzvah will also provide a natural access point to synagogues, Jewish social action groups and Jewish institutions for learning. This young adult bar/bat mitzvah will also force Jewish groups to offer relevant and meaningful programs to attract young adults to their particular program.

The 18-year bar/bat mitzvah at 31 will also mark the transition to adulthood. For some Jewish men, a communal celebration of their lives to date may be just the event they need to formally end their over-extended adolescence. For Jewish men and women who are already married, this celebration can be equally important. It may give them pause to imagine their future together and their future children, and thereby prompt them to start a family. It is also the right time for young Jews to seek out Jewish synagogues and organizations that are responsive to their lives. And for young men and women who already have children, bar/bat mitzvah plus 18 is a good time to think about having even more children than they had previously planned to bring into the world and to consider the Jewish education they want for their children. Bar mitzvah plus 18 will help young Jewish adults build Jewish families.

The ceremony for celebrating bar/bat Mitzvah plus 18 need not be elaborate. It may be as simple as being called to the Torah. Alternatively, it might involve completing a Jewish environmental bike ride or volunteer project. Bar/bat mitzvah plus 18 need not be a large catered affair with live music. However, a dinner with close family and friends is certainly appropriate – people tend to celebrate round figure birthdays in this way. Bar/bat mitzvah plus 18 should be an occasion that Jews work towards and look forward to.

The 36-Year Bar/Bat Mitzvah at 49

The next milestone, 36-year bar/bat mitzvah, is often a time when adult Jews are re-evaluating their priorities. Most adults are set in a career; they have had all of the children they are likely to have naturally (especially in the case of women), and have lived in the same home for the longest period of time they will ever live in any one home. They have older children and most have set social connections, friendships and patterns of daily life. But though everything seems very settled at this age, the late forties is often an age full of ferment, seeking, and self-evaluation. It is the age when preconceived expectations in life collide with reality. Many men and women are deeply involved in careers that may seem less fulfilling than they felt years ago. Some may feel stuck. Women who left careers to focus on children and family may be trying to return to the job market. Women who have spent years focusing on others may also want to pursue their desire for personal fulfill-ment. At 49 years old, many American Jews are still thirsting for spiritual meaning and connection.

More than any other generation, the generation of Jews in their forties needs Jewish learning to provide the "intimacy" and the perspective that "links Jews through time and space." For some American Jews in their late forties, the collision between expectations, reality, responsibility and desire for personal fulfillment may explode into a mid-life crisis. The consequences can be divorce, estrangement or other radical personal changes. Thankfully, for most people of this age, the outlook is less catastrophic, but nonetheless powerful. They may simply experience the need for a spiritual boost. The Jewish community should respond to these needs by reaching out to Jews in their late forties and extending to them the opportunities to learn and get involved in the community. In turn, many Jews at this age will find that if they get involved in Jewish learning, they will connect to it more than before. Once one has led an adult life, it is easier to appreciate the struggles of our patriarchs and matriarchs, of David, of Eliyahu, of Naomi, and of a host of other biblical heroes. Jewish learning does not take all that long but it can be incredibly nourishing. I have been privileged to witness individuals engaged in Jewish learning at this age regain their intellectual and spiritual vigor. As one acquaintance said to me, "it put the wind back in my sails."

A commitment to Jewish learning in one's late forties can help adult Jews regain their sense of purpose and lead some to change their personal priorities. The good news about being 49 is that there is still time for most people to make meaningful changes in their lives for their own benefit and the benefit of the larger community. Two of *Time Magazine*'s 2005 "Persons of the Year," Bill Gates and Bono (aka Paul Hewson), reoriented their priorities in their late 40s. While Bill Gates dedicated himself completely to making Microsoft a dominant software company and Bono spent most of his life as a rock musician with all the accoutrements and distractions of that lifestyle, both adopted and subsequently championed causes that have the potential to improve the future of humanity in their late forties, the prime of their careers. Bill and Melinda Gates now spearhead major initiatives to improve human health in developing countries. Bono now advocates tirelessly for forgiving Third World debt and giving aid to African peoples. At the same time, neither Bill Gates nor Bono has abandoned his previous career. For both Bono and Bill Gates, humanitarian work seems to have energized and added vigor to their "day job" endeavors.[12] However, Bill Gates has announced that he intends to spend substantially less time at Microsoft and more time on his philanthropy after he reaches the age of 52.

Jews also have a long tradition of leaders and scholars emerging in the prime of their lives. Abraham and Moses were in mid-life when they received their calling. Rabbi Akiva, said to be the greatest scholar of Judaism, started learning Torah at forty. In our day, major Jewish philanthropists such as Leslie Wexner[13] and Zalman Bernstein z"l[14] first made their forays into major creative philanthropy in their forties. Both kept their day jobs as well. Leslie Wexner was inspired by thoughts of his own mortality while hiking in Aspen. Zalman Bernstein was inspired by adult Jewish learning. Both made enormous contributions to American Jewry.

The 54-Year Bar/Bat Mitzvah at 67

One of the blessings of living in America is that at the 54-year bar/bat mitzvah at age 67, we still have a lot of time to learn and to make the world a better place. Although 67 is usually retirement or post-retirement age, most Jews of this age are still in excellent health and have unprecedented time and energy to devote to learning and volunteer work. The 54-year bar/bat mitzvah is an excellent opportunity to motivate Jews of this age to re-think their priorities in a Jewish context and undertake new volunteer projects. It was shortly after retirement that Alfred Nobel read the erroneous publication of his obituary (in fact it was his brother who died), which sharply criticized and condemned him for his invention of dynamite. Nobel took the opportunity to rededicate himself. After a period of introspection, he decided to leave the bulk of his substantial fortune to establish the Nobel Prize. Today, his memory is considered a blessing. Thus at 67 there is still plenty of time to think about matters other than bequests. Adults of this age should also consider volunteering in Jewish organizations, day schools, Hebrew schools, synagogues or social action groups.

Although it is appropriate to think about bequests at this age, Jews will gain more pleasure from giving *tzedakah* during their lifetimes, and the 54-year bar/bat mitzvah is an excellent time to do so. As a jump start for the important rededication of the 54-year bar/bat mitzvah, a period of Jewish learning culminating in a family celebration is entirely in order. This celebration will also motivate younger members of the family to think about how they might imagine themselves at 67.

The 72-Year Bar/Bat Mitzvah at 85

At the 72-year bar/bat mitzvah, we can fully celebrate the (hopefully) accomplished lives of the most senior members of the Jewish community. This is a time for Jews to contemplate a life well-lived. There is no doubt that a party would be a joy for 72-year bar/bat mitzvah celebrants. Synagogues should bestow the highest honors upon these celebrants For almost all members of the Jewish community, bar/bat mitzvah plus 72 will be the last the bar/bat mitzvah, we can wish everyone five bar/bat mitzvah celebrations for his/her lifetime, though as lifespans rise, bar/bat mitzvah plus 90 may one day become relevant.

Adopting the Cyclical Bar/Bat-Mitzvah

Some readers might consider that bar/bat mitzvah plus concept too fanciful to be taken seriously by the Jewish community. This risk always exists with any new minhag. Yet over the course of Jewish history, Jews have adopted countless new minhagim that may have seemed silly to some at first. In America, many people ridiculed the bat mitzvah concept when it was first introduced, but 50 years later American Jews have accepted it almost universally. Moreover, adopting the cyclical bar/bat mitzvah concept over the next generation is perfectly plausible for institutional, psychological, sociological, and spiritual reasons.

It is in the strong interests of synagogues to adopt the cyclical bar/bat mitzvah as a means of enhancing congregational life. Only 27% of Jews say that they attend services once a month or more.[15]

The cyclical bar/bat mitzvah offers synagogues a way to reengage directly with adults in a Jewish context and on matters that do not pertain to their children. Rabbis, family educators and fellow synagogue members could also use this opportunity to reach out to non-active synagogue members. Some synagogues may wish to reach out to non-members. Synagogue attendance is the Jewish measure most subject to change over a lifetime.[16] Unaffiliated Jews might appreciate this opportunity to reconnect to their roots. While everyone will understand that the cyclical bar/bat mitzvah is a modern custom and not of the more venerable order to which the bar/bat mitzvah at thirteen belongs, its unique features will make it an attractive touch point for all Jews.

The ritual of the bar/bat mitzvah also meets most of the socio-psychological criteria required for American Jewry to adopt it successfully. In Marshall Sklare's classic work "Jewish Identity on the Suburban Frontier,"[17] Sklare closely examined Jewish life in a Jewish suburb, which he gave the pseudonym Lakeville, and came to strong conclusions about the rituals that Lakeville Jews would choose to practice. Although first published in 1967, Sklare's analysis remains valuable. He delineated five criteria that would lead to the wide-scale practice of a ritual:

1) "Capable of effective redefinition in modern terms."[18]

Sklare notes that Lakeville Jews observe Chanukah and Passover particularly widely because they have based their understanding of these holidays on the universal thirst for freedom and struggle to overcome slavery. Had Sklare been writing after the Six Day War in 1967, he might have also noted the modern tendency to identify with the perceived weak versus the strong side of a struggle. During the holiday of Chanukah, we celebrate the victory of the few over the many, the weak over the strong and the righteous over the wicked. The cyclical bar/bat mitzvah has the virtue of tapping into the lifelong search for spirituality and connectedness sought by modern Americans. Most Americans value periods of reappraisal and retrospection. American Jews can thus apply their respect for reappraising one's life to the ritual of the cyclical bar/bat mitzvah.

2) "Does not demand social isolation and the following of a unique lifestyle."[19]

The cyclical bar/bat mitzvah is certainly not a socially isolating event. Whether the pre-bar/bat mitzvah preparation is adult Jewish learning, social action, volunteer work or social action in a Jewish context, the cyclical bar/bat mitzvah involves social activities. The cyclical bar/bat mitzvah ceremony would also be a synagogue or communal ritual event. Additionally, any associated dinner party is, of course, a social event.

3) "Accords with the religious culture of the larger community and provides a Jewish alternative when such is felt to be needed."[20]

The vast majority of Americans are involved in a religious or spiritual quest. They are searching for opportunities to find connections that transcend the ordinary.[21] Because Jews are the most secular group within the American religious spectrum, adopting the cyclical bar/bat mitzvah would bring those Jews closer to the practices of the majority of Americans. The cyclical bar/bat mitzvah would also enable Jews, who already feel the same yearning for spirituality as other Americans but have difficulty relating it to a Jewish context because their Jewish education ended when they were thirteen, to undertake a Jewish spiritual journey. For those Jews who wish to relate to the cyclical bar/bat mitzvah in a non-religious way, opportunities for social action or service to the Jewish people are also an option.

4) "Centered on the child."

Sklare notes that rituals are not just practiced because children are eager to do them, but that certain rituals "accord with [the parent's] desire to transmit Jewish identity to offspring." The tone of such rituals is "optimism" and "fun."[22] While the cyclical bar/bat mitzvah is more about individual Jews than families, parents who celebrate the cyclical bar/bat mitzvah can be a positive example to their children. Participating in the cyclical bar/bat mitzvah can be an important way for parents, who might otherwise demonstrate little personal connection to Judaism, to show their children what being Jewish means to them in a concrete way. Since the cyclical bar/bat mitzvah is also a social event, Jews who celebrate this ritual can involve relatives across all generations to join in their fun. The celebration of the cyclical bar/bat mitzvah is also a way to reconnect to one's formative childhood experience of becoming bar/bat mitzvah.

5) "Performed annually or infrequently...the yearly ritual will persist more than the seasonal, the seasonal more than the monthly, the monthly more than the weekly, the weekly more than the daily." [23]

The most practiced rituals are those that celebrate an extraordinary occasion. Self-identifying Jews almost universally observe once in a lifetime rituals such as circumcision and bar/bat mitzvah at thirteen. The cyclical bar/bat mitzvah also has the virtue of being infrequent, and as a result is more likely to be observed.

The cyclical bar/bat mitzvah scores a strong four out of five of Sklare's criteria for a successful ritual. The weakest measure is in terms of its child centeredness, although the cyclical bar/bat mitzvah can positively impact children. Therefore, synagogues should welcome and promote this new opportunity for engagement. Adult Jewish learning organizations and Jewish social action and service organizations should also welcome and promote the cyclical bar/bat mitzvah. This new ritual could rapidly build its own momentum as quality Jewish engagement leads to more frequent and intensive connections between Jews, Judaism and the Jewish people.

Imagining the New American *Minhag*

Were American Jewry to adopt this new *minhag*, the results would be more positive than we can imagine. The number of Jews engaged in adult Jewish learning would grow exponentially. Moreover, the positive unintended consequences of an increase in adult Jewish learning could be larger than the intended consequences. For more than a decade, the Wexner Heritage Program has identified a core of Jewish lay leaders and given them a free education with some of the best teachers of Judaism. The lay leaders, all in their 30s and 40s, were drawn from across the ideological spectrum of Judaism. While the program must certainly be judged a success in fulfilling its stated goal to educate the next generation of American Jewish leadership,[24] the program's greatest legacy might be that it has led to the creation of scores of day schools across America. The participants had so much fun engaging in Jewish learning that many of the 1,400 alumni of Wexner left the program with the desire to give the gift of Jewish education to their children. These alumni went about forming new day schools that were relevant to their families. Wexner participants or alumni created or lead a substantial percentage of day schools formed in the 1990s.

Researchers confirm the far-reaching impact of adult education. Robert Peers, the distinguished British historian of adult education, found that "the most active periods in the history of adult education have always been periods of very rapid change.[25] Although he is careful about deterministic arguments, Peers credits the adult education movement as being one of the major causes of the industrial revolution, which transformed Britain into the greatest imperial power of the era and changed the economy of the world.

For Jews, education has always been inexorably linked to our advancement as a people. Throughout Jewish history, from Yavneh to the adult Jewish education movement in late nineteenth-century America, adult Jewish learning has always led to Jewish renewal. Adult Jewish learning enables Jews to develop in ways that are grounded in authentic Jewishness and add energy to Jewry. Moreover, learned adult Jews contribute new ways of learning to traditional Jewish education, which in turn often become part of Jewish tradition. It is my hope that the cyclical bar/bat mitzvah has this effect. This idea can usher in a new period of learning, engagement, redefinition, vitality, renewal and advancement for American Jewry.

* * *

One bar/bat mitzvah is no longer enough for Jews in America. The power of the bar/bat mitzvah as an event that marks Jewish identification and requires Jewish learning must be expanded to punctuate the passage of each person's lifetime. The dramatic increase in Jewish learning and action that this new American *minhag* can engender will invigorate American Jewry for future generations.

Notes

1. Wikipedia, "Birthday," http://en.wikipedia.org/wiki/Birthday, accessed June 2006.
2. Anne Martin, *The Baby Sitters Club – Abby's Lucky Thirteen* (New York: Scholastic Inc., 1996).
3. See American Girl doll Lindsey and accompanying book Lindsey, http://www.americangirl.com/, accessed June 2006.
4. Entry on Life Expectancy in Wikipedia.
5. Michael A.Meyer, *Jewish Identity in the Modern World* (Seattle: University of Washington Press, 1990) pp. 1–3.
6. Signmund Freud, "On Being of the B'nai Brith, " *Commentary* (March 1946), p. 23. The commentary article is a publication of his address on May 6, 1926 to the B'nai Brith Society of Vienna.
7. Ibid., p. 24.
8. Isa Aron, *Becoming a Congregation of Learners* (New York: Jewish Lights Publishing, 2000), pp. 23–24.
9. Horowitz, *Connections and Journeys*, p. 124.
10. Horowitz, *Connections and Journeys*, p. 180.
11. Amy Sales, unpublished paper, (New York, Synergy Conference on Synagogues, January 9, 2006) sponsored by UJA-Federation of New York's Commission on Jewish Identity and Renewal.

12. "Persons of the Year," *Time Magazine*, December 26, 2005.
13. Wikipedia, "Leslie Wexner," http://en.wikipedia.org/wiki/Leslie_Wexner, accessed June 2006.
14. Rabbi Shlomo Riskin, "Zalman Bernstein: An Unorthodox Orthodox Baal Teshuvah," *Jewish Action* (Summer 1998), http://www.ou.org/publications/ja/5759summer/bernsteinprofile.pdf, accessed June 2006.
15. *NJPS 2000–2001 Report*, 19, http://www.ujc.org/content_display.html?ArticleID=60346, accessed May 2006.
16. Horowitz, *Connections & Journeys*, p. 152.
17. Marshall Sklare and Joseph Greenblum, *Jewish Identity on the Suburban Frontier* (New York: Basic Books, 1967), pp. 57–59. Steven M. Cohen and Arnold M. Eisen's use of Sklare's analysis of American Jewry in their book, *The Jew Within: Self, Family and Community in America* (Bloomington, Indiana University Press, 2000) on pages 96–99, prompted me to make use of it in this chapter as well.
18. Ibid., p. 57.
19. Ibid., p. 58.
20. Ibid., p. 58.
21. Wade Clark Roof, Bruce Greer, Mary Johnson, Andrea Leibson, *A Generation of Seekers: The Spiritual Journeys of the Baby Boom Generation* (New York: HarperCollins, 1993) and Anna Greenberg, *OMG! How Generation Y is Redefining Faith in the iPod Era*, (Washington: Greenberg Quinlan Rosner Research, April 2005), p. 11. http://www.greenbergresearch.com/index.php?ID=1218, accessed June 2006.
22. Ibid., pp. 58–59.
23. Ibid., p. 59.
24. Fern Chertak, Leonard Saxe, Rebecca Silvera-Sasson, *Exploring the Impact of the Wexner Heritage Program on a Development of Leadership capital in the Jewish Community* (New Albany: Wexner Foundations, November 2005).
25. Robert Peers, *Adult Education* (London: Routledge & Kegan, 1958), p. 3.

Chapter x

Reimagining the Conservative Movement

"Seventy Faces of the Torah."
Midrash Rabba Bamidbar 15–13

Plank #8: The Conservative Movement as it is currently constituted has outlasted its historic role as a unifying force for American Jewry. As both its internal theological contradictions and institutional failures have become apparent, the movement has become locked in an unfortunate spiral of strife, recrimination, and institutional paralysis. The time has come for the Conservative Movement to re-invent itself as a community of mini-Movements bound by practice and closely attuned to its constituent members. As a result, some of the mini-Movements will accept the binding nature of halacha, some will not. Some streams of Conservative Judaism will accept openly gay and lesbian clergy, others will not, and so on. Creating mini-Movements within the framework of Conservative Judaism will encourage more centrist religious options for those who feel left out or uninspired by existing Jewish denominations.

The Crisis in the Conservative Movement

The Conservative Movement is in a crisis that demands radical action. As discussed in Chapter II, just over half of adult Jews raised in the Conservative Movement continue to consider themselves Conservative. Nearly half of all Conservative adults are age 55 or over, making the Conservatives the oldest Jewish Movement and far older than American society as a whole.[1] Between 1990 and 2000, 255,000 Jews departed from the Movement, leaving only 660,000 members in the Conservative Movement.[2] This is the equivalent to a drop off of 2,125 members per month, or one very large congregation leaving per month. If the decline in the Conservative Movement continues at this pace, it will fall behind Orthodoxy and become the third largest movement in American Judaism by 2010.

A Conservative Jew suddenly transported from the 1940s, 1950s or even 1960s would be astounded by the numeric decline of the Movement. Only forty years ago there were 2.5 million Conservative Jews. Conservative Judaism was *the* face of American Jewry; it shone brightly through the personas of Louis Finkelstein, and Abraham Joshua Heschel the leading figures at the movement's educational center, The Jewish Theological Seminary in New York. The largest Jewish women's organization, Hadassah, was the creation of Henrietta Szold, an early JTS graduate. The second largest Jewish women's organization was the Women's League for Conservative Judaism. JTS produced "The Eternal Light," a program broadcast on network radio and television. The U.S. Army adopted the Conservative prayer book as its standard for Jewish soldiers. Ramah camps were built and expanded and created demand for the nascent Solomon Schechter Day School system. United Synagogues Youth (USY) grew dramatically, flourished and quickly led to teen Israel trips. In both small Jewish communities and on college campuses, the only synagogue or *minyan* was invariably Conservative.[3] No one could have foreseen the Conservative Movement's rapid numeric decline.

The Conservative Movement is not, however, only losing

numbers; it is also going through an existential crisis. Conservative Jews are dispirited because even the Movement's most respected leaders fail to agree on the basic theological underpinnings of what it means to be a Conservative Jew. On the one hand, Rabbi Jerome M. Epstein, the religious leader of The United Synagogue of Conservative Judaism, the organization of Conservative synagogues, and others argue that the central idea of Conservatism is that *halacha* is binding upon Jews[4] – and call for a Conservative renewal by urging Conservative Jews to passionately re-embrace the *halacha*. On the other, Conservative thinkers, such as Rabbi Neil Gilman, a Professor of Jewish Philosophy at the Jewish Theological Seminary, do not believe that Conservative Judaism is a *halachic* movement; instead they argue that *halacha* is a voluntary system that one can participate in or not. Today there is simply no clear consensus on the theology of the movement.

The Theology of the Conservative Movement

One of the distinguishing factors of the Conservative Movement in the past has been its view towards *halacha*, which toed a middle line between the Orthodox and Reform perspectives. *Halacha* is the Jewish Oral Law, which takes commandments of the Torah and makes them practically observable by Jews, such as the *halacha* of Jewish dietary laws, which is a rich elaboration of the simple Torah description of prohibited and permitted foods and animals. All Orthodox Jews accept the Oral Law as part of the divine revelation at Mt. Sinai; however, whereas most Chareidim view the *halacha* as virtually unchanging, Modern Orthodox Jews view the Oral Law as divinely inspired, but shaped by the rabbis partially in response to historical forces. Therefore, Modern Orthodox Jews interpret *halacha* somewhat more flexibly, and are willing to revive past minority views if they seem necessary for today. Until recently, Conservative Jews agreed that the Oral Law is central to the existence and survival of the Jewish people, but largely shaped by historical forces. Conservative Judaism has argued that *halacha* should conform to the modern world and not vice versa. Conservative Jews therefore adopt a more liberal view of the *halacha* than either the Chareidim or Modern Orthodox Jews, while generally accepting the Torah as divine revelation. In contrast to both Orthodox and Conservative Judaism, while Reform Judaism views both the Torah and the *halacha* as divinely inspired gifts to the Jewish people, for Reform Judaism neither is inherently divine and neither constitutes a form of revelation: both are the outcome of the combined scholarship of generations of living Jews. For Reform Jews, *halacha* is therefore one point of reference; it is not a binding legal code.

In recent years, the consensus on the status and nature of *halacha* in Conservative Judaism has broken down. Rabbi Neil Gillman, mentioned above, argues that *halacha* is not binding on Conservative Jews. Furthermore, he argues that those who allege it is binding are not being intellectually honest. In his words, "if we are a *halachic* community, it has to be because we want to be, not because we have to be."[6] Other Conservative Jews argue that the question of the binding nature of *halacha* on Conservative Jews is no longer simply theological; the Movement must come to grips with the fact that "not only are the vast majority of its laity (and perhaps a not inconsequential number of its clergy) non-*halachic*, but an undeniable critical mass of Conservative Jews do not consider *halacha* to be their 'commanded' path to an authentic Jewish life."[7] Indeed, because the argument between "halachists" and "non-halachists" threatens the meaning of Conservative Judaism, some leading Conservative pulpit rabbis have tried to change the terms of the argument. Rabbi David Wolpe has declared that Conservative Judaism is not defined by an attitude towards *halacha*; rather, it is "Covenantal Judaism." For Wolpe, the idea of "Covenantal Judaism" takes the Jewish concept of covenant and uses it as a statement of principles that define the relationship a Jew has with God, with other Jews, with the Jewish people and with the rest of the world. Jewish law he adds, is part of the mix, but not its essence.[8] Countless other Conservative thinkers and rabbis have offered other ideas, yet none has emerged as a powerful overarching concept that bridges the spectrum of Conservative Jewry or provides a theological underpinning for Conservative Judaism that all Conservative Jews can accept. As a result, the question of the Movement's relationship to *halacha* is still unresolved, and Conservative Jews have become increasingly dissatisfied with the Movement and resentful of its leadership.

The Causes for the Conservative Movement's Decline

Conservative Jews feel that the Movement's lack of effective leadership and institutional failings have caused the Movement's decline. As Professor Susan Hodge writes, "It is a half joking, half bitter catchword among some of us that the Conservative *Movement* has contempt for Conservative *Jews*. The Movement also has self-perpetuating bureaucracies that are out of touch with us and don't respect or even welcome us, the ordinary Jews living our lives."[9] Dr. Jacob Ukeles, a consultant to The United Synagogue of Conservative Judaism, wrote after his involvement in a three-year effort to design a strategic plan to reorganize The United Synagogue's twenty-two separate departments and fifteen regional offices that progress has been "glacially slow."[10] As of 2006, five years have passed since The United Synagogue first identified the need for institutional reform, yet little has changed. The Conservative Movement bureaucracy makes the U.S. Department of Agriculture appear positively dynamic. To put it bluntly, the leadership of Conservative Judaism is floundering in a bureaucratic quagmire.

The Conservative Movement's recent failure to address the decline of Conservative Jewish education in a constructive way underscores the laity's criticism of the Movement's leadership. Because of a lack of vision and a spirit of frustration, some Conservative leaders have begun to gratuitously criticize the Movement's flagship day schools, the Solomon Schechter system. While correctly bemoaning the Conservative Movement's failure to devote anywhere near adequate attention or resources to congregational schools, some have gone a step further by calling for an end to the "overemphasis on day schools." Others have claimed it was a "massive failure to put the emphasis we do on day schools" and that "the damage done has been horrendous."[11] Rather than simultaneously accentuate the positive aspects of day schools and advocate additional focus on congregational schools, Conservative leaders are pitting one form of education against another needlessly. Tragically, this unnecessary fighting has contributed to the stagnation of Solomon Schechter Day School enrollment and has led many of the Movement's best and brightest leaders to focus solely on non-denominational community day schools. Moreover, none of this bickering has led the Conservative Movement to devote additional resources to Hebrew schools; rather, all recent additional resource allocations to Conservative Hebrew schools have come primarily from community organizations such as the UJA-Federation of New York and groups of national unaffiliated philanthropists. The Reform Movement has contributed most of the new methods for teaching and organizing Hebrew schools. For many Conservative Jews, the fight over Jewish education is only the most recent example of the Movement's lack of leadership.

There are also, to be fair, external reasons for the accelerating decline of the Conservative Movement. A fundamental reason for the Conservative Movement's success from 1945 until the 1970s was that the Movement corresponded to American society's general desire for "moderation" and "homogenization" and occurred at a time when Americans generally, and Jews specifically, moved to the suburbs. As Marshal Sklare argues, in his book *Jews on the Suburban Frontier*, the combination of these two phenomena created the perfect environment for Conservative Judaism to flourish. Sklare claims that the Conservative Movement was in a way tailor made for the "Lakeville" or suburban Jew. The 82% of Lakeville Jews who were born Orthodox but wished to flee Orthodoxy were looking for a synagogue environment that was comfortable and not so concerned with theology. These Jews were naturally drawn to Conservative synagogues, because they had a lot of Hebrew in the service, including all the traditional parts of the service (such as *Musaf*), and a Jewishly observant and devout rabbi. Conservatism's primary virtue was that it did not fall under either "extreme" of Reform or Orthodox. In recent decades, however, American society has become more comfortable with diverse and more narrowly focused groups. Few people still feel the need to moderate their views to become part of a larger group, and emerging adults no longer need a "compromise synagogue" between their practices and the practices of their parents. Instead, young Conservative Jews today want a Judaism that focuses on their own spiritual needs. The result of this social shift has been the steady decline of Conservative Judaism over the past two decades.

Unfortunately, it seems as though the Conservative Movement leadership has deliberately ignored the societal changes around them. The Conservative Movement leadership can be compared to the character "Hem" in the widely read parable of "Who Moved My Cheese."[12] In this story two "little people," Hem and Haw, discover that after many years of finding and enjoying cheese from one spot in a large maze, one day the cheese is suddenly no longer there. In fact, the cheese had been slowly diminishing over time; Hem and Haw had simply not noticed. But although Haw leaves his old spot – albeit with much tribulation and some self-doubt – and ultimately succeeds in finding a new spot with more cheese than ever, Hem refuses to leave. Instead, Hem nurtures his confusion and resentment about the possible reasons why there is no more cheese but takes no action. He just keeps blaming others for the movement of the cheese, and yet is still somehow comforted by being able to go to the same place where there used to be cheese even though it no longer offers any food. Although the parable holds out some hope, Hem presumably starves to death. Conservative Jews in the pews and working pulpit rabbis have been witnessing the slow decline in the Conservative Movement's leadership for years and are understandably more and more angry and resentful towards the Movement's central organs. Others have just voted with their feet.

Additional Controversies that threaten the Conservative Movement

The Conservative Movement is currently grappling with two issues that threaten its ability to remain unified. These issues are the ban on gays and lesbians entering rabbinical school and the coexistence of egalitarian and non-egalitarian congregations within the Conservative Movement.

Currently, the Conservative Movement is polarized between those who do and do not support the coexistence of egalitarian and non-egalitarian synagogues. In approximately 90% of North American Conservative synagogues, men and women participate equally in all aspects of prayers and Torah reading. These synagogues refer to themselves as egalitarian. In the other 10%, women's participation is limited to some degree by traditional *halachic* constraints that relate to women leading services, being counted in the *minyan* and participating in the Torah service. Men and women sit together in all Conservative congregations. At the December 2005 biennial conference of the Conservative Movement, Rabbi Menachem Creditor was both enthusiastically supported and bitterly resented for a speech that urged the Movement to expel non-egalitarian Conservative synagogues from the Movement. On the one hand, Creditor's supporters feel that it is impossible to coexist with non-egalitarian synagogues as a matter of principle; on the other hand, Creditor's critics, especially Canadian Conservative rabbis, who are the spiritual leaders of most of the non-egalitarian congregations, found it hard to comprehend that the Movement leaders were threatening their congregations with expulsion when they had been part of the Conservative Movement for decades and were practicing what was the normative Conservative Judaism of just a few decades ago.[13] This particular rift not only involves a dividing line within American Conservative Jewry, but also highlights the split of American non-Orthodox Jewry from its international brethren on key issues. For example, Canadian Reform Jews have not recognized the American Reform position on patrilineal descent. Furthermore, Canadian Reform

Jews have not been successful in getting the CCAR to reexamine the issue. In the Conservative case, some American Conservatives are lobbying to expel the Canadians if they do not comply with the American view.

The second major issue threatening to split the Conservative Movement is the question of gay and lesbian rabbis. Although it seems clear that a decisive majority of both Conservative laity and rabbis endorse the acceptance of openly gay and lesbian individuals to Conservative rabbinical and cantorial schools as well as collegial assemblies, a change of policy in favor of gays and lesbians nonetheless faces very tough hurdles from a purely *halachic* perspective. And, while some Conservatives believe that *halacha* should simply be set aside on moral grounds, others who deeply believe in Conservative *halacha* contend that there are grounds for a revision of *halacha* known as a *takana*, and that this course of action must be pursued before any official pronouncement can be made. In the meantime, the current policy is that gays and lesbians are not admitted to Conservative rabbinical school; however, if a Conservative rabbi post-ordination "comes out," he/she may continue to be a member of the Rabbinical Assembly and a practicing rabbi. Although the status quo has functioned in practice, the issue nevertheless threatens to split the current Conservative configuration, because advocates of both approaches to gay and lesbian clergy feel passionately that they will not be able to stay within the Movement if the decision goes against their view.

The narrowing of vision of the Conservative Movement has resulted in other departures from the Movement. Many of the offshoots of Conservatism were once some of the most exciting groups within the Movement. Groups such as the Union for Traditional Judaism, the *Havurah* devotees, and the Reconstructionists are offshoots of Conservative Judaism, and new or revitalized synagogues are led by ordained Conservative rabbis who have either left the Movement or founded new institutions pointedly unaffiliated with the Conservative Movement. Neither B'nai Jeshurun ("BJ") or Kehillat Hadar, both of New York, Shaar

Hashamayim of Montreal nor Ikar of Los Angeles, could find a place within the Conservative Movement for their vibrant and rapidly growing congregations.[14] These new offshoots are a boon to American Jewry, but a loss to Conservative Judaism.

Jewish Commitment among Conservative Jews

With all of the controversy and confusion about what it means to be a Conservative Jew, only half of Jews who call themselves Conservative actually belong to a Conservative Synagogue (or any synagogue for that matter).[15] It is, however, critical to note that although the number of Conservative Jews who do affiliate with a synagogues continues to decline, their Jewish commitment is high and arguably rising, if measured by their commitment to Jewish practices. The intermarriage rate among "synagogue" Conservative Jews was 17% from 1980 to 1990, and only 12% a decade later. This rate is far below the overall American Jewish average of 46% for 1991–2001. Thus, though the number of Conservative Jews is declining, their commitment to Judaism is increasing. The fundamental question for Conservative Jews should be: how can more Jews find Conservative Judaism meaningful? In my view, the Conservative Movement should review how the Reform and Orthodox Movements responded to existential challenges with radical solutions that enabled them to rebuild their bases.

Reform and Orthodox Responses to Existential Threats

Over the past century both Reform and Orthodox Jewry have responded to existential threats, resulting either from a decline in leadership or unresolved controversies, by allowing their constituents a margin of freedom. As a result, neither Orthodox nor Reform Jewry today is uniform; rather, both encompass a broad spectrum of practices within boundaries defined by the center. This response has revitalized both groups enormously.

Reform was able to avert demographic collapse by abandoning a fixed theology. During the 1930s and 1940s, the Reform Movement's membership dwindled to fewer than 10% of American

Jewry. (Reform's crisis then was worse than today's Conservative crisis.) In response to this drastic decline, the Reform Movement jettisoned its highly ideological and partisan Pittsburgh Platform of 1887 and replaced it with a framework for Reform Judaism instead of a fixed theology. This approach permitted Jews with very different theological stances to coexist within the Reform Movement and even the same synagogues. Moreover, during this period, Reform laity gathered the courage to completely change the way the Movement's institutions were led. The laity called on leaders to honor different positions within Reform Judaism rather than making religious decisions binding on all Reform Jews.[16] Thus, at the December 2005 Union of American Hebrew (Reform) Congregations convention, the prayer services ranged from yoga-oriented silent prayer groups to a *minyan* that closely resembled a left-wing Conservative service. By abandoning a fixed theology, Reform has re-made itself into a vibrant, dynamic, and wide open movement that would be unrecognizable to a Reform Jew of the 1920s.

Orthodoxy's incredible and unexpected revival in the past several decades has taken place for two principal reasons: first, its willingness to include more diversity under the umbrella of orthodoxy and second, a wider focus on day schools. Although some outside observers perceive Orthodox Jewry as monolithic, it is actually diverse and growing in its diversity. In addition to the four variations of the fervently Orthodox we discussed in Chapter I, there are at least three other groups: Centrist Orthodox, Modern Orthodox and a nascent "Egalitarian-light" Orthodox. Each of these groups feels that their members are "commanded" by *halacha* and a passion for lifelong Jewish learning. At the same time, these groups also exhibit significant variations at the level of basic practice and regarding certain ideological foundations. For example, the chasidic concept of "the Rebbe" differs greatly from the concept of "Rabbi" or "Rav" in other streams of Orthodoxy. A chasid is essentially born following a certain rebbe because a chasidic devotee follows the rebbe of his clan. In all other streams, an adult individual presumes the right to select a rabbi whose approach to Judaism is consistent with his personal beliefs. These groups also vary considerably in the role of women within the synagogue service and within the community.

Orthodoxy today incorporates different roles for women. In all streams to the left of the Chareidim, women's roles in formal prayer services and in learning have grown significantly. Women on the left wing of Orthodoxy have also been pushing for rabbis to revive formerly minority opinions that would enable Orthodox women to participate in the Torah service portion of prayers. Thirty years ago Orthodox women formed the first "women's davening groups." In these groups, women prayed separately from men and conducted the entire service, including the Torah portion, themselves. Some *halachic* adjustments were made to the standard service, but some Orthodox women felt spiritually invigorated by having "a service of their own." Recently, a few left-wing Orthodox *minyanim* have adopted the hybrid regular service/women's davening group for Shabbat morning first introduced by Congregation Yedidiyah of Jerusalem. In this service, men and women pray *shacharit* (the morning prayer) separated by a *mechitsa* and led by a male cantor. Men and women then go to separate rooms for the Torah service that enables women to participate fully in the reading. After the Torah service, both sexes come together again for *mussaf*. In the last few years, the search for *halachic* innovations to permit more women's participation has lead to the Shira Chadasha/Darchei Noam[17] style service wherein women actually lead prayers for some portion of the services (at the same time as men present on the other side of the *mechitsa*) such as Kabbalat Shabbat and Pesukei DeZimra. Women there also participate fully in the Torah service, with the men present on the other side of the *mechitsa*.[18] Women's learning has grown tremendously in all streams of Orthodoxy. In many streams, a year of post-high school Jewish learning for women has become as de rigueur as for men. Though a Chareidi man would find it anathema to pray at a Shira Chadasha style *minyan*, and a woman used to Yedidiyah might be unwilling to attend a Chareidi service because she would find it unfulfilling, both of these Jews would consider themselves Orthodox and commanded by *halacha*. This lack of uniformity is played out in other areas, from dress to educational methods: there is no one Orthodox rabbinical organization that can claim to speak for all Orthodox rabbis. There are several meaningful Orthodox rabbinical associations, in contrast to the Conservative and Reform Movements, which each have only one.

This lack of uniformity has allowed the Orthodox to broadly delineate and differentiate what might at first glance seem like a small range of the Jewish denominational spectrum. All streams of Orthodoxy have embraced day schools. If there is one reason for the reinvigoration of Orthodoxy, it is day schools, as noted in Chapter III. But more importantly, the intense drive for Jewishly educating children energized all parts of the movement. With this, Orthodoxy became by far the fastest growing movement in America over the last twenty years.

The Conservative Movement has the potential to undergo a similar radical transformation, if its members are willing to fundamentally reconceptualize their understanding of what it means to be a Conservative Jew and install an entirely new leadership. This transformation will make Conservatism the first post-denominational movement. While this may sound like a contradiction, upon closer examination it is not. Post-denominationalism is not the same as non-denominationalism. Non-denominational Jews are those who do not belong to any movement because they are simply less attached to Judaism. They may be Jews married to non-Jews, children of intermarried Jews or simply disaffected from Judaism. Most non-denominational Jews are on the exit lane from American Jewry. By contrast, post-denominational Jews may be highly interested in being Jewish but feel disaffected from the Movements as they are currently configured. Many of these Jews are lapsed Conservative Jews who have not found a new denominational home in which they are comfortable.[19] Also, unlike non-denominational Jews, post-denominational Jews have core

Jewish peoplehood values such as culture, an interest in Israel, a wish to perpetuate the Jewish people and a desire to educate their children Jewishly. At the same time, post-denominational Jews have a wide variety of narrow approaches to the religious part of being Jewish. The "Conservadox" have a somewhat expansive view of traditional *halacha*, but consider *halacha* binding. Other post-denominational Jews approach God through more purely spiritual practices. As important as Judaism is to them, these Jews do not view the strict observance of traditional *halacha* as a way to help them find meaning in their lives.

Reinventing Conservative Judaism

Because there is no way that the Conservative Movement can encompass the entire spectrum of post-denominational mini-Movements in a theologically consistent manner, it should stop trying to bind all of its members to one theology. Instead, it should create boundaries that leave room for a wide range of practices. Present Conservative leadership feels encroached on by members on the left and the right only because it wants to resolve the differences between them by drawing a straight party line somewhere down the middle. The narrowness of the middle, however, is only the result of the Conservative leadership's own lack of imagination. As the case of vast variations within the Orthodox and Reform Movements demonstrates, the middle can also be wide. Consider the following analogy from the physical world. The length of any coastline such as the Costa del Sol, or the Cliffs of Cornwall, will vary considerably depending on how it is measured. If a surveyor measures the coastline by advancing 1000 yards per measurement, he would get a much different measurement than if he advanced up the coastline 10 yards at a time. In the latter case, more nooks and crannies would each become meaningful parts of the measurement, which would be substantially larger. The measure of the coastline would be larger still if the surveyor advanced one yard at a time.[20] For American Jews there are many meaningful crevices and nooks that are defined away by the leadership of the

Conservative Movement when they try to measure their boundary as one straight line from top to bottom. Instead, the beauty of a theological landscape only becomes clear when each sub-peninsula (i.e. mini-Movement) on the coast displays its own texture and magnificence. When the Conservative Movement decides not to resolve major theological questions such as the gay/lesbian issue, the key women's participation issues, the binding nature of *halacha* and Schechter Day School versus Hebrew school controversy, the middle will become very large indeed.

In lieu of a uniform theology, the Conservative Movement must declare several boundary principles which are in the reach of practicing and non-practicing Conservative Jews as well as post-denominational Jews. I will propose a list of these principles, but such a list is obviously up to a new Conservative leadership to devise.

1. Observance of Shabbat, Jewish Holidays and kashrut in some form;
2. Weekly synagogue attendance;
3. Commitment to making Torah learning a life long endeavor;
4. Commitment to a serious Torah education for children, meaning day school or effective Hebrew school in conjunction with youth groups, camping and Israel programs;
5. *Tzedakah*, ethical behavior and social action;
6. Commitment to Israel;
7. Traditional determination of Jewish peoplehood (i.e., matrilineal descent or conversion).

This is not a large list and it is not particularly ideological. One can believe or not believe in *halacha* and embrace each principle; however, all new Conservative Jews should be able to recognize and appreciate the commonality of those who abide by these seven principles. Within the framework of these seven principles, there is a lot of room for variation. Some mini-Movements within the new Conservative umbrella will deem other additional principles to be binding. It may be that some Conservative Jews will not feel comfortable davening in another Conservative synagogue linked with a different mini-Movement; this should not be viewed as an obstacle, as it happens all the time among the Orthodox. Likewise, some Reform Jews don't understand yoga *minyanim* while others do not like mostly Hebrew services. Perhaps different mini-Movements will want to establish their own rabbinical seminaries. That too is okay. The more seminaries there are, the more avenues to approaching Jewish learning there will be. Some mini-Movements will feel comfortable with openly gay and lesbian rabbis and some will not. Some on both sides can feel loyal to the common principles of the *halacha*. We can also hope the rancor over the binding nature of *halacha*, which is now largely theoretical, will quiet down as Conservative Jews press towards a common practice of the common denominators of Judaism.

The Conservative Movement can flourish by creating a high-quality common infrastructure for a highly engaged community of Jews who have different beliefs yet also respect each other. The Conservative Movement must make its Hebrew schools engaging and effective, as described in Chapter III. Conservative synagogues must also create a seamless integration of youth groups, summer camps and Israel programs for its youth. Everyone can agree on the imperative of these steps. The Law Committee of the Conservative Rabbinical Assembly, which presently issues opinions that are either ignored by the laity or which divide the Movement, should be abolished. In its place, a Fences Committee should be established to define the boundaries of the Conservative Movement. Each mini-Movement would establish its own Law or Practice Committee. These smaller Law Committees would be more responsive to their mini-Movements, which will hopefully lead their constituent members to actually take their rulings seriously.

The Conservative Movement should shift its focus away

from theology toward creating comfortable places for Jews to express their Judaism. The overall Fences Committee should not be empowered to opine on the rightness or wrongness of the mini-Movements' legal rulings; rather, it should only determine if a constituent mini-Movement has violated one of the fundamental principles or add a principle if there is a broad and deep consensus within the overall Movement to do so. Constituted as such, the new Conservative Movement will no longer have the urge to expel groups that do not express majority opinions, as long as they express authentically Jewish ideas and abide by the seven principles. By shifting away from ideology, theology and theoretical debate, Conservative Judaism will create comfortable places for Jews to express their Judaism. In short, all the streams of the new Conservatism can commonly support these comfortable places.

Some Conservative synagogues may offer multiple comfortable places which each have their own approach. A few avant-garde Conservative synagogues such as Ansche Chesed of New York already offer several different *minyanim* on Shabbat morning and thus already function like a microcosm of what could be the new Conservatism. If different groups can and do happily coexist in the same physical space by focusing on being a community bound by practice as opposed to the purity of ideology, imagine how well they could live together within the same Movement. And, since the focus of the seven principles is to create a realistic common denominator, Conservative Jews who do not and would not want to keep all aspects of *halacha* can still find their place within the Movement. The goal of these principles is to eliminate the "contempt" that Jews in the pew currently feel from the elite intelligentsia of the Conservative Movement. A focus on practice would also end the present and embarrassingly ineffective push for "compliance," and replace it with a push for cooperation, education and growth from wherever a Conservative Jew stands. Conservatism must change its attitude from shunning Jews to inviting them into the Movement.

In April 2006, the Conservative Movement took a step towards renewal by appointing a non-rabbinic chancellor to JTS who had no previous official tie to the Conservative Movement. Professor Arnold Eisen, previously of Stanford University, will assume his new post on July 1, 2007. This appointment carries much promise and *some* risk. Professor Eisen is an outstanding scholar and passionate and engaging speaker who will bring a new spark to the Movement. However, since Professor Eisen's appointment, the Law Committee is still moving forward on a global decision on the issue of openly gay clergy, thus demonstrating that the Movement is continuing to make divisive decisions without first clarifying the core principles of Conservative Judaism. There is a great risk that leaders in the Conservative Movement might be tempted to think that they have made their bold move by appointing a non-rabbi as chancellor of JTS, and thus shy away from re-imagining the Movement, be it by synagogue members, the intermediate organization, or the rabbis. Any change in the Movement must embrace all disaffected segments of the Movement through an open architecture that is as expansive as possible.

Ideally, a new post-denominational Conservatism will link all of its tributary streams into one diverse Movement that links all Jews through "time and space."[21] This new form of Conservatism will nurture Jews spiritually through practices that create powerful emotional sources and bolster, as Freud terms it, the "shared Jewish psychic structure" that supports a strong Jewish identity. If that can be accomplished, Conservative Jews can focus on theology later. The new leadership of the revitalized Conservative Movement can demonstrate that there is not just one meaningful and acceptable ideological stance between Reform and Orthodoxy, but an abundance of comfortable places along the spectrum. The new Conservatism would not be an ideology in the sky but an achievable set of practices that will dramatically strengthen American Jewry and challenge Orthodoxy and Reform to continue to grow.

* * *

The Conservative Movement is currently locked in a self-defeating cycle of self-criticism and introspection, which is focused on reconciling irreconcilable theological positions. The Conservative tailspin is further compounded by organizational and management failures. These developments have alienated rank and file members. American Jewry needs the Conservative Movement to reinvent itself as a broad-spectrum association based on practice, not theology. The new Conservatism can be a comfortable home to a host of mini-Movements, each offering a more personal meaning to its members. The focus of the broad new Conservative Movement should be on increasing Jewish practice and involvement in a way that will challenge its members to reach achievable goals. Through these efforts, Conservative Jews will pioneer and illuminate the vastness of the terrain between Reform and Orthodoxy.

Notes

1. United Jewish Communities, *National Jewish Population Survey 2000–01 Conservative Jews: A United Jewish Communities Presentation of Findings* (New York: United Jewish Communities, February 2004), http://www.ujc.org/content_display.html?ArticleID=155417, accessed June 2006.
2. Steven M. Cohen, "Change in a Very Conservative Movement," *Sh'ma* (February 2006), p. 6.
3. Many of these points were taken from a sermon by Rabbi Samuel Fraint of Moriah Congregation of Deerfield, Illinois, given on the first Day of Rosh HaShanah 2005.
4. Rabbi Jerome Epstein, "Defining a Conservative Jew," *Sh'ma* (February 2006), p. 14.
5. Rabbi David Lerner, "Toward a Passionate Conservative Judaism," *The Jewish Week*, December 30, 2005.
6. Gabriella Birkner "Conservative Call for Openness," *The Jewish Week*, December 9, 2005.
7. Jeffrey E. Schwartz, "To the new Chancellor," *Sh'ma* (February 2006), p. 2.
8. Rabbi David Wolpe, "What is Conservative Judaism," *The Jewish Week*, December 16, 2005.
9. Susan E. Hodge, "To the new Chancellor," *Sh'ma* (February 2006), p. 1.
10. Jacob Ukeles, "Reinventing the Conservative Movement," *Sh'ma* (February 2006), p. 7.

11. Hodge "To the new Chancellor," p. 1 and Gary Rosenblatt, "All Eyes on Rabbi Tucker at Panel," *The Jewish Week*, January 20, 2006.

12. Spencer Johnson, *Who Moved My Cheese: An Amazing Way to Deal with Change in Your Work and in Your Life* (New York: G.P. Putnams Sons, 1998).

13. Gabrielle Birkauer, "Conservative Leaders Call for New Openness," *The Jewish Week*, December 9, 2005.

14. Professor Jonathan Sarna's address to the Rabbinical Assembly, March 6, 2005.

15. *NJPS Conservative Jews*, pp. 8–9.

16. Sarna, address to the Rabbinical Assembly.

17. Shira Chadasha of Jerusalem was the first to use the method, which was later adopted by Darchei Noam of New York.

18. Mendel Shapiro, "Qeri'at ha-Torah by Women, A Halakhic Analysis," *The Edah Journal* 1:2 (Spring 2001).

19. Steven M. Cohen, "Non Denominational and Post Denominational: Two Tendencies in American Jewry" *Contact Magazine* (Summer 2005).

20. James Gleick, *Chaos: Making a New Science* (New York: Viking, 1987), p. 96.

21. Arons, *Becoming a Congregation of Learners*, pp. 23–24.

Chapter XI

Combating External Threats

"The Jews are the world's canary. Canaries are taken down to
mines because they quickly die upon exposure to noxious
fumes. When the miner sees the canary dead, he knows there
are noxious fumes to be fought [or he too will die]. So it is with
the Jews. Noxious moral forces often focus on the Jews. But
their ultimate targets are the moral values that the Jews represent. Non-Jews who share Jews' values…make a fatal error
when they dismiss anti-Semites as the Jews' problem." Dennis
Prager, "What Bitburg Revealed about the Jews,"
Ultimate Issues, Summer 1985, 1.

*Plank #9: Since this book examines the current challenges facing
American Jewry as a whole, it would be incomplete without addressing the external threats we face today. Although, after World War II,
American Jewry entered a period of relatively limited domestic anti-
Semitism, unfortunately, over the past decade this trend has changed.
While traditional right-wing anti-Semitism has diminished, far left
and radical Islamic anti-Semitism have grown at a worrisome pace:
challenging Israel, Jews and American society as a whole. Jewish
organizations have not sufficiently adjusted their focus to these*

two new and often allied sources of anti-Semitism. Consequently, many Jews are not properly informed about the threat current anti-Semitism poses, or else they do not take it seriously. This must change. American Jewry must come to terms with the seriousness of current threats posed by radical Islam and the far left to Jews, to Israel and to the world, and build coalitions with other threatened groups to combat them.

The Problem We Thought We Wouldn't Have to Face Again

Of all of the chapters in this book, this is the one that most pains me to have to write. Only a decade ago, like most American Jews, I was optimistic that virulent anti-Semitism was a thing of the past. Anti-Semitic incidents were down sharply across the globe,[1] the ongoing Oslo peace process had quieted anti-Israelism, the United Nations repealed its resolution defining Zionism as racism, and Jordan signed a peace treaty with Israel. Israel's government had even begun to worry about the costs of opening embassies in all the countries with which it was establishing or rekindling diplomatic relations.[2] The era of "Israel at risk" seemed to have passed.

Unfortunately, the optimism of the 1990s was premature. In September 2000, at the beginning of the second Intifada, after Yassir Arafat's rejection of the American-led peace negotiations, I, like most American Jews, was shocked at the sudden rebirth of anti-Israelism, which was quickly followed by overt anti-Semitism.[3] While Palestinian terrorists were being glorified by radical Islamists for murdering civilian men, women and children, individuals all over Europe and in hard left-wing circles in the U.S. justified and rationalized terrorist attacks as legitimate forms of resistance against Zionist aggression.[4] Most significantly, the media in Europe and the Arab world, as well as the far left publications in the U.S., also reinforced an anti-Israeli and often anti-Semitic message through skewed reporting which relied predominantly on Palestinian sources for information about events in the disputed territories of the West Bank and the Gaza

Strip.[5] The false reports about the Jenin incursion against an embedded terrorist infrastructure, which Palestinian sympathizers and some media outlets still refer to as "the Jenin massacre," are the best known example of this phenomenon.[6] Other examples of the persistence of anti-Israeli misinformation could be cited.[7] Since the second Intifada, the future of Israel is once again being brought into question and anti-Semitism is on the rise. Some individuals and organizations in Europe and America went a step further and called for boycotts of Israeli products and divestment resolutions in support of Palestinian rights while ignoring overt anti-Semitism and anti-Americanism among Palestinians and Muslim fundamentalists across the globe.[8]

American Jews are Failing to Respond Appropriately to Rising Anti-Israelism

Faced with these new and unexpected sources of anti-Semitism which put the existence of Israel in question, Jewish defense and anti-defamation organizations not only failed to mount a rapid response of truth-telling, they failed to reiterate the basic case for the existence of Israel. They failed to remind Jews and the world that the State of Israel was created by UN authorization, that every war Israel has fought has been defensive, that the State of Israel endorses a Palestinian state, and that Israel was prepared to make broad concessions in the past. Indeed, whereas Ehud Barak offered to divide Jerusalem, return Israel to an area close to that encircled by the 1967 borders and compensate Palestinian refugees in return for peace, Yassir Arafat refused and launched the second Intifada. Jewish anti-defamation organizations have also failed to communicate the commonality of the Palestinian Authority's (PA's), Al Fatah's and Islamic fundamentalists' political objectives. Although these organizations differ in their explicit goals, all bring the existence of the state of Israel into question in some way. The PA's goal is to create a Palestinian state in Gaza and the West Bank. However, since they want the right of return for all so-called refugees from the 1948 war and their descendents to land now located in Israel, including Israeli citizenship for these "refugees," they *de facto* hope to create a Palestinian majority in Israel and thereby take over all of the territory once known as Palestine. Islamic fundamentalists, whether Palestinian terrorist groups such as Hamas or other groups across the world such as Hezbollah, Al-Qaeda and Islamic Jihad openly call for a *jihad* – a holy war of conquest – in order to take over all of Israeli land, and to "push all Israelis into the sea." Because we have not consistently made the case for Israel's existence, the media has continued to question Israel's right to self-defense.

American Promoters and Enablers of Anti-Israelism: The Media, Human Rights Organizations, and The Universities

The media and the left have consistently presented a grossly skewed picture of the Israeli-Palestinian conflict. They have focused on the suffering of Palestinians living in Gaza and the West Bank, while ignoring the terrible conditions that Palestinians endure in neighboring Arab countries, which have refused to grant them citizenship. They refuse to acknowledge the terrible suffering of victims of terror and the need for Israelis to defend themselves. They ignore the abysmal human rights record in the entire Arab world, where women are routinely murdered for being raped and where "collaborators" and moderate Muslims are shot.[9] They have also failed to publicize the endemic corruption among Palestinian politicians who siphon off billions of dollars for their personal benefit.[10] The left also conveniently forgets that Israel was created in the shadow of the greatest threat to the existence of the Jewish people in its entire history, and that the approximately 700,000 Jews who lived in Arab lands before the creation of the State of Israel have almost all left these countries, and in so doing, for the most part, left their assets behind as well.[11]

The perspective of so-called mainstream human rights organizations in the U.S., such as Human Rights Watch and Amnesty International, are often no less skewed than that of the media and the left. Despite the international scope of their operations, Israel has been the subject of more reports per million people by Amnesty International than any other country.[12] The fact that Israel permits researchers free access simply increases the amount of negative information these groups put forward. Meanwhile, the incredibly bad human rights conditions in Arab states and the Palestinian territories are reported and forgotten, as if there can be no expectation of decent human rights practices there.[13] This double standard is very hard to comprehend for an organization that advocates improving human rights across the globe.

The radical left, the media and human rights organizations receive much of their practical and ideological support from our university system. Although Jewish students are flourishing on most American campuses – the quotas for Jewish students that existed 50 or 60 years ago are gone – and large numbers of faculty, and even many college presidents, are Jews. Faculty members, especially professors of Middle Eastern Studies (MES), have been disseminating polemical, false and even deliberately malicious information about Israel under the veneer of scholarship. One of the key agents of false information about Israel is the Middle Eastern Studies department at many, though not all, universities. Since the 1970s many MES departments have come to resemble a "popular front" of left wing, pro-Arab and anti-Israel views, more than centers of critical scholarship.[14] Over the past twenty five years these experts missed or overlooked virtually all of the trends which drove Middle Eastern developments, namely the rise of Muslim fundamentalism, the brutal totalitarianism of secular regimes in Iraq and Syria, the failure of oil states like Saudi Arabia to create stable societies through equitable distribution of resources, and the massive growth of terrorism.[15] And when confronted with these troubling developments across the Arab world, those same MES academics claim that the Arab-Israeli conflict causes all of the Middle East's problems and that there will only be peace in the region once Palestinian demands are met.[16] The anti-Israel bias in many Middle Eastern Studies departments is often all too apparent and is making Jewish life on campus more and more difficult.

While most university campuses are welcoming to Jews, there are also campuses across the U.S. where academic anti-Israelism has made Jews feel unwelcome and, on occasion, unsafe. Across the U.S. students have complained about classes where only the pro-Palestinian side of the argument was considered valid. In some cases, students are intellectually intimidated and in other cases they toe the party line so as to not receive a bad grade.[17] In an English class at Berkeley entitled, "The Politics and Poetics of Palestinian Resistance," students not willing to tow the party line were explicitly told to drop the class in the course description.[18] At Columbia University a student was ordered to leave a classroom by a professor when she refused to "admit" to Israeli "atrocities." The number of incidents at Columbia prompted the Boston-based David Project to film a documentary about Columbia that led to an internal university investigation. Unfortunately, the investigating committee, which was comprised of university insiders, cleared the faculty without addressing the charges of Jewish students.[19] As one University of Illinois at Champagne-Urbana student wrote regarding the prevalence of pro-Palestinian views on her campus, the message is "if you are with us, you're for freedom; if you're against us, you're for oppression."[20]

On more and more campuses, anti-Israelism is now quickly turning into anti-Semitism. At San Francisco State University, a pro-Palestinian rally had signs directed at Jews reading, "Go back to Russia," "Get out or we will kill you" and "Hitler did not finish the job." The faculty and administration of SFSU closed their eyes to the event simply because the protestors were from the left and Muslims.[21] Carnegie Mellon hosted a series of speakers on Palestinian issues. One such speaker, after proclaiming the perfidy of the Jews, Israel's nature as a terrorist state and other such slanders, asked the Jews in the audience to identify themselves.

The event quickly degenerated. Examples of overt anti-Semitism in American universities abound.[22]

Attacks on Israel at American universities are not limited to the classrooms. Some faculty members and students have called for their universities to divest from Israeli companies and companies that do business with Israel. Columbia University's faculty has been active in this regard and there have also been campaigns at Harvard and NYU, although none have succeeded.[23] Faculty members have even led divestment drives at smaller universities such as the University of Wisconsin at Whitewater. At other universities, Muslim student groups have initiated divestment drives.[24] In addition to the inherent anti-Israelism of these drives, they have been promoted with malicious rhetoric that compares Israeli administration of the West Bank and Gaza to apartheid-era South Africa. Unfortunately, the support of prominent academics gives this disingenuous comparison the veneer of validity. It is not an exaggeration to say that contemporary American anti-Semites are beginning to openly mimic tactics used by anti-Semites in the 1930s. The far left's calls for universities to divest from Israel may lead to "don't buy in Jewish shops" movements. A trend in England today suggests that this development is not implausible. In 2006, one academic union tried to boycott Israeli academics and another has now proposed that individual members boycott Israel.[25] Even more disconcerting is the conspiratorial content of a paper written by two previously well-regarded professors from The University of Chicago and Harvard University respectively, John Mearshwimer and Stephen Walt. Like much of the anti-Semitic literature of nineteenth- and twentieth-century Europe, Mearsheimer and Walt's paper "The Israel Lobby and U.S. Foreign Policy" blames all of America's current problems in Iraq, the Middle East and much of the rest of the world on Israel, American Jews and their allies,[26] and completely ignores the most important American reason for being in the Middle East: oil. The growth of anti-Semitism in the universities and across America unfortunately masks the real threat to American society, namely, radical Islam.

Radical Islam in America Today

The arrival of radical Islamic fundamentalists who advocate terrorism in America has not taken place overnight. Some commentators such as Steve Emerson[27] and Daniel Pipes[28] have been warning Americans since the 1990s that radical Islam was finding a home in America by making use of American hospitality and naiveté, and co-opting local Muslims in an effort to lay the groundwork for future terrorist attacks. During the 1990s Islamic radicals plotted and executed a variety of terrorist acts, from the murder of CIA employees to the first attempts on the World Trade center, most of which were thankfully less lethal than their potential death toll.[29] Organized terrorist groups have also targeted America. Hezbollah and Hamas have been carrying out terrorist attacks in America for decades and, contrary to many people's perception, Al-Qaeda also attempted to attack America during the 1990s.[30] In addition to terrorist attacks on Americans in America, there have also been numerous attacks against Americans outside of the U.S. In 1995, five American soldiers were killed in Saudi Arabia by a truck bomb, in 1998 over 200 people were killed when the U.S. embassies in Kenya and Tanzania were blown up and in 2000 over seventeen U.S. sailors were killed when a boat blew a hole in the side of the destroyer U.S.S. Cole in Yemen.[31] There is no doubt that Islamic fundamentalists are increasingly targeting Americans.

Unfortunately, despite the evidence, American government officials have been afraid to call attacks on Americans, especially Jews, terrorism, preferring to see them as "isolated incidents."[32] Even attacks that follow an Islamic fundamentalist pattern of assault, such as the August 6, 2003 beheading of Ariel Sellouk by Mohammad Ali Alayed in Houston, were ascribed to individual motives.[33]The result of this type of misleading reporting is that few people recognize that radical Muslims are attacking Americans

both on American soil and abroad. The media is also not inform-
ing Americans adequately about the enormous potential for violence created by the ever-growing number of American Muslims
who have traveled to the Middle East, received terrorist training
in Afghanistan and elsewhere, and returned to the U.S. for the
purpose fighting a *jihad* against America. These sleeper cells, such
as the "Lackawana Seven," are barely known to the American
public, yet they are a real threat.

In addition to misleading reporting on the part of the American media, since the 1990s, a network of Muslim organizations
dedicated to advancing the public image of Islam in the U.S. have
pressured the media and the government to misreport events.
During the 1990s a number of organizations such as the Muslim
Arab Youth Association, the Council on American-Islamic Relations, the Islamic Circle of North America, the American Muslim
Alliance, and the Council on American Islamic Relations (CAIR)
were founded or substantially expanded to improve the image of
Islam in the U.S.[34] At first glance, these organizations, especially
CAIR, seem to operate like a traditional American civil rights
organization. Muslim and non-Muslim alike, have openly supported the efforts of these Muslim groups. Yet, upon closer scru-
tiny, there is evidence that these organizations do not exclusively
lobby for Muslim civil rights; but rather, indirectly support the
extension of Islamic fundamentalist ideologies in America. At
CAIR gatherings, speakers lead the crowd in a song, "No to the
Jews, descendants of the apes."[35] Numerous CAIR officials are also
members of organizations associated with Hamas, Al-Qaeda and
the Taliban and have refused to denounce suicide bombings and
have called for the destruction of Israel and the submission of the
United States to Islam.[36]

Other Muslim organizations operating in the U.S. openly
disseminate anti-American, Anti-Western and Anti-Semitic material. The American Muslim Council (AMC) is one such group.
One of its members is known to have proclaimed at a national
convention, "Let us damn America, let us damn Israel, and let us

damn their allies until death." Such rhetoric is hard to justify for an organization chartered to "educate" [the] public about Muslims.[37] The number of such organizations is growing and includes: The Islamic Circle of North America,[38] and The Islamic Society of North America, the main Wahhabi lobbying group in the U.S., the umbrella group for 300 organizations and possibly up to one-third of American mosques, is also blatantly anti-American.[39] Still other groups are out-and-out fronts for the Saudi government and the Saudi-led Organization of the Islamic Conference. One such organization, the Muslim Arab Youth Organization, seems at first like a wholesome group, until one notes that its basic tenet is that the U.S. is morally corrupt, debased and evil. Its exhibit booths tout books and brochures with such titles as "America's Greatest Enemy: The Jew!" and "U.S. War on Islam and Its Scholars." Other materials it disseminates compare the U.S. to Rome before its fall. At their assemblies speakers espouse the virtues of suicide bombers and the killing of children who will be future enemies of Islam.[40]

The above mentioned organizations and others are not only taking advantage of American civil liberties, they are using our democratic and philanthropic tradition to operate. The American Muslim Alliance (AMA) began to operate as a political action committee by making contributions to candidates. Although many politicians initially accepted the AMA's donations, its endorsement of Hamas suicide bombings, anti-Semitism and Holocaust denial has led politicians such as Senator Hillary Clinton to return AMA campaign contributions.[41] Other groups operate undercover by aligning with a variety of "charitable" organizations, such as the now closed Holy Land Foundation of Texas, or the Kind Hearts for Charitable Humanitarian Development of Ohio, whose goal was to collect and funnel money for terrorist activities abroad.[42] American Jews must look beyond the legitimate veneer of Islamic groups operating in America to the evidence that some of these groups are using American democratic traditions to eliminate moderate Islam, attack American political and social values, and disseminate hate propaganda against Jews.

Recognizing and Addressing The Real External Threat to Jews in America

Despite the growth of left-wing and Islamic fundamentalist anti-Semitism in America since the 1990s, the mainstream media's general sympathy for the Palestinian point of view and its misleading reporting on the growth of Islamic fundamentalism in America, Jews have still not come to terms with the threat these factors pose. Some Jews who are accustomed to speaking out for oppressed communities around the world have accepted Palestinian and left-wing rhetoric because of its omni-presence in the media and the universities, and the failure of the Jewish community to fight back, and have come to believe that Israel is an embarrassment to the Jewish people. They too have forgotten the basic case for Israel. Other Jews generously believe the claims of Muslim advocacy groups that America is infringing on the human rights of American Muslims, without taking heed of the evidence that some of these groups aid and abet terrorism whether directly or indirectly. This cannot safely continue. American Jews and mainstream Jewish organizations must recognize that radical Islam and the left are the principal sources of anti-Semitism in America today. They must re-evaluate their approach to information dissemination and reorient their operations to combat these threats accordingly.

More importantly, Jewish Organizations cannot afford to squander precious resources on campaigns that do not address these threats. We must stop misguided campaigns against the "Christianization" of America. We need dialogue, not demonization. In "The Baptizing of America,"[43] a former senior leader of the American Jewish Committee, Rabbi James Rudin, decries the risks of more Christian influence on America. In his view, Jews would benefit from a more secular society and a sharper division between Church and State. Although some of Rabbi Rudin's concerns, like those of the ADL, such as the eagerness some Christians display towards converting Jews, have validity, they are misleading, since Muslim fundamentalists and the far left constitute a much greater threat to Jews in America than do evangelical Christians. Jews should bear in mind that no evangelical Christian group calls for the U.S. government to force American citizens to become Christian or discriminate against non-Christians. Evangelical Christians may want to convert Jews, but they do not espouse anti-Semitism. In Saudi Arabia, on the other hand, other religions are officially banned; Christians have their Bibles confiscated at the airport and Jews are officially forbidden to enter the country. And unlike Muslim fundamentalists, no Christian group advocates the death penalty for individuals who convert to another religion from Christianity. There is absolutely no comparison between the attitude of radical Muslims and even the most extreme American Christians towards people of other religions and Jews. We must cease this campaign immediately and address the real threats to American Jewry.

We American Jews must also bear in mind that our fight against rising anti-Semitism is also a fight against anti-Americanism and will benefit American society as a whole. In truth, anti-Semitism is typically a symptom of deeper, unhealthy societal woes that can threaten the whole world. Historically, outbreaks of rampant anti-Semitism have unleashed negative forces that affect non-Jews as well. Although anti-Semitism was at the core of Nazism, the Nazis also victimized millions of non-Jews such as Poles, Russians, and the handicapped, as well as German enemies of the regime. Likewise, brutal regimes are almost always anti-Semitic. Stalin was a fanatical anti-Semite, and persecuted Jews, despite Communism's supposed tolerance for all peoples. Radical Islamic anti-Israelism and anti-Semitism is no different. Radical Islamic ideology, especially though not exclusively Wahhabism, is not simply hostile to Jews, it is also profoundly hostile to America, Christianity, women, secularism, democracy, the West, and moderate forms of Islam, and openly advocates armed struggle or *jihad* and suicidal terrorism in order to reconquer all former Muslim lands. Indeed, radical Islamists are a threat to peace across the globe. In the Middle East, terrorist cells have perpetrated attacks

in Lebanon, Kuwait, Jordan, Turkey, Saudi Arabia and Lebanon.
In North Africa, radical Islamists are responsible for civil war in
Algeria, and terrorists groups have been active in Morocco and
Egypt. In sub-Saharan Africa, Islamic radicals are perpetrating
genocide in Sudan and creating civil strife between Muslims and
Christians in Nigeria. In Central Asia, Islamic fundamentalists are
trying to take over the governments of former Soviet Republics
and are responsible for the war in Chechnya. In Southeast Asia,
Islamic fundamentalists are committing acts of terrorism in the
Philippines, Indonesia, Thailand and Singapore and on the Indian
subcontinent; Islamic fundamentalists are exacerbating tensions
between Muslims and other groups in Pakistan, India and Ban-
gladesh. Islamic fundamentalists also control the government in
Iran and Sudan. American Jews who are concerned about human
rights, democracy and the civil liberties, as well as the future of
the Jewish community must focus their attention on combating
radical Islam and its left-wing apologists.[44]

Although I strongly believe that the greatest threat to the
survival of American Jewry today is our internal demographic and
identity crisis and not external attacks, the latter are nonetheless
a very serious cause for concern. If we continue to ignore these
threats or invest our resources on ineffective, un-focused and
misdirected measures to combat them, we will waste precious
time and money. Moreover, those American Jews who continue
to be skeptical about the power of radical Islam, or believe that
tolerance alone will bring peace and moderation to Islamic communities in America, should look to Europe, where young European Muslim men have built a network of domestic terrorist cells
and are openly flouting European laws and democracy, to see the
consequences of refusing to take appropriate action.

Practical Solutions for the Future

There is no simple solution to the external threats that we are
facing. However, individual American Jews can take a number of
concrete steps to defend Israel and American democracy. These

include seeking out unbiased media sources, building coalitions with friendly non-Jewish American groups, reducing our consumption of foreign oil, and speaking out for other threatened minorities in Muslim lands. With these initiatives, American Jews can do a lot to combat America and world Jewry's largest contemporary external threat.

The Information Wars

It is imperative that both American Jews and Americans in general become better informed about current events. This task will require some effort because the information presented by the mainstream media is so often biased or piecemeal that readers miss the pattern of terrorist activity taking place in America and around the world today. Relying on the mainstream media is woefully insufficient. Therefore it is necessary to get alternative information on Internet sites. Since most American Jews today get some, if not all of their news from the Internet, and have a daily routine of visiting websites, adding a couple of the websites listed below that deal with threats in a more unbiased manner will not significantly change most people's routines and will make them much better informed in a short period of time. Another important source of information is the Daily Alert from the Conference of Presidents of Major American Jewish Organizations, prepared by the Jerusalem Center for Public Affairs. The web site is http://www.dailyalert.org/ and there is a link at the bottom of the page to sign up for email delivery. We can also make a difference by sending friends particularly important stories via e-mail. Most of us are used to forwarding jokes or video clips or being part of an organization's list serve for announcements, and we should do the same with news stories about terrorism and *jihad*. If one individual sends a story to just three friends, and they send it on, the information will quickly spread. For fast moving stories, which sometimes require quick responses from the Jewish community, email is perhaps the only answer.

The following websites cover stories on radical Islam that don't usually appear elsewhere. Some also allow you to sign up for email alerts.

http://jihadwatch.org/
http://jihadwatch.org/dhimmiwatch/
http://www.danielpipes.org/
http://www.campus-watch.org/
http://martinkramer.org/pages
http://camera.org/
http://www.littlegreenfootballs.com/weblog/

For American Jews who wish to know more about the growth of Anti-Semitism and radical Islam in America I would recommend a number of carefully documented studies. I would also recommend that American Jews look at the literature on radical Islam in Europe, where after thirty years of ineffective policies, media bias, and tolerance, the growth of domestic radical Islam is threatening the basis of European society. Finally, in addition to the above-mentioned web-sites American Jews can also look at some recent studies that describe the history of media and university bias against Israel.

Steven Emerson. *American Jihad: The Terrorists Living Among Us* (New York: Free Press, 2002).

Pipes, Daniel. Militant Islam Reaches America (New York: W. W. Norton & Company, 2002).

Bat Ye'or. *Eurabia: The Euro-Arab Axis* (Madison: Fairleigh Dickinson University Press, 2005).

Bawer, Bruce. *While Europe Slept* (New York: Doubleday, 2006).

Gutmann, Stephanie. *The Other War: Israelis, Palestinians and the Struggle for Media Supremacy* (San Francisco: Encounter Books, 2005).

Kramer, Martin. *Ivory Towers on Sand* (Washington: The Washington Institute for Near East Policy, 2001).

New and Old Alliances

Because Jews are not the only people threatened by radical Islam, it is important that we build coalitions with other targeted communities in America such as Christians, Hindus, atheists, and moderate Muslims. These new alliances will enable us to increase the number of voices and voters mobilized against their threats. We should begin by building coalitions with some American Christians on issues of foreign policy and anti-terrorism. These groups should include the various Evangelical churches, the Roman Catholic Church and the Orthodox Churches. The Evangelicals are generally more friendly towards Israel and the Roman Catholic and Orthodox Churches have members living in Muslim lands where they have *dhimmi* status. It will be more challenging to dialogue with mainstream Protestant churches right away, as those such as the Presbyterians, United Church of Christ and the Episcopalians, have been open critics of Israel, although as of 2006, the Presbyterians have become more open to useful dialogue. It may be very difficult for us to approach the Sabeel Ecumenical Center for Liberation Theology (Sabeel), a Jerusalem-based Ecumenical Christian group dedicated to demonstrating Palestinian Christians' solidarity with Muslim Palestinians and to encouraging foreign Christians to adopting a Pro-Palestinian stance. Nevertheless, we should approach even hostile Christian groups to let them know that regardless of their intent to improve Muslim Christian relations, they should not be fooled: they too are targets of Islamic fundamentalism. Recent Vatican and official Anglican pronouncements on the issue of radical Islam suggest that this is the time for making alliances with denominations opposed to *jihad*.[45]

In order to build bridges with American Christians, American Jews should engage in open dialogue with Christian groups and organize joint trips to Israel and the West Bank. Engaging in an open dialogue that enables both sides to speak honestly about their differences rather than force them to focus on similarities can help American Christians appreciate the Jewish perspective on the Israeli-Palestinian conflict, rather than forced "feel good" encounters, and can help American Christians appreciate the Jewish perspective on the Israeli-Palestinian conflict. General "feel good" interfaith dialogue tends to lead to a general call for social justice, which usually translates into a condemnation of Israel. Encouraging Christians to visit Israel and the West Bank also helps them to acquire a more balanced view of the Israeli-Palestinian conflict.

American Jews must also engage in dialogue with patriotic American moderate Muslims. Despite the evidence that a growing number of American Muslims are involved in terrorism, the majority of American Muslims are moderate. These Muslims need a safe space to express their theology and create a network of mosques that can withstand the onslaught of Muslim fundamentalists. Though Jews and Christians cannot be involved in this project they can express their willingness to dialogue with the emerging leaders of these moderate groups and can support moderates who are attacked by reactionary forces within their own communities.

The Universities

The best way to combat anti-Israelism on campus is to confront misinformation head on. Students, parents, and alumni can stay informed about universities through groups such as Campus Watch (http://www.campus-watch.org/) and No Indoctrination (http://www.noindoctrination.org/). Jews should also make the effort to confront scholars who use neo-Nazi and Communist sources in their writing. We should publicize any funding that Middle East Studies departments receive from Saudi Arabia and other Arab governments. And, although scholars should continue to criticize Israeli government policy if they see fit to do so, critical scholarship must remain within the bounds of academic propriety. American Jews must denounce smear campaigns against Israel and Jews. It is also important that prospective Jewish donors make sure that the environment on the campus to which they wish to donate is not slanted against Israel and Jews. They should insist that their dollars be used for objective academic research. It is sad, unfortunate and ironic that Professor Walt's chair is funded from an endowment by a Jewish philanthropist who also gives to many worthwhile Jewish causes. Donors should consider withholding donations if universities do not address anti-Semitism and anti-Israelism on their campuses. The current university environment will not change right away, but we must not allow it to continue on its current course.

Oil and Jihad

We must stop the spread of Islamic fundamentalism through our own oil expenditures. It is well known that a portion of the money Americans spend on oil from Islamic regimes is used to build Wahhabist mosques and to fund terrorists, and to spread hatred of Jews around the world. Since oil is a fungible commodity, even when we do not buy oil from Iran or other Islamic fundamentalist regimes, we are still indirectly supporting these regimes by raising the price of oil through our consumption habits. Therefore, the first step we can take is to reduce our consumption of oil. We must make an effort to buy more fuel-efficient cars instead of giant suvs, keep the heat down two or three degrees in the winter and turn off the lights when we leave a room. We should also actively support research into alternative energy sources and hybrid cars through investments, and back politicians who recognize this problem.

American Jewry should take the lead in championing the construction of a new energy SuperGrid to replace our increasingly fragile and outmoded North American electric grid. A new SuperGrid could both transmit many times the power of the existing grid through super conducting cables as well its ability to carry plasma or liquid hydrogen as fuel. Because the SuperGrid's design will greatly reduce current energy loss due to the transmission of energy over great distances, we could also build nuclear power plants in remote locations, which would make them politically feasible. The SuperGrid could also accept input from all manner of non-fossil fuel sources such as solar panel farms and wind turbines. The SuperGrid could thus enable us to increase and diversify domestic sources of energy.

Building a SuperGrid is not a fantasy: it is both practically and financially feasible. Although the SuperGrid will be engineering challenge to construct, current scientific research has advanced to such a degree that it is certainly technologically feasible. In addition, while it will cost, an estimated $1 trillion dollars, at the current value of the dollar, over a 25- year period, the cost, which amounts to $40 billion a year, it is not beyond our means.[46] The yearly cost of the SuperGrid is actually less than what the U.S. spends on imported oil *alone* during many two-month periods. Nevertheless, during the initial years of construction, the Government will have to subsidize or otherwise encourage the development of the SuperGrid. However, by the middle years of its construction, the cost of the SuperGrid should be entirely borne by the private sector. Building a SuperGrid is financially realistic. Similarly, although the full conversion to the SuperGrid would require a change in almost every part of the power infrastructure, scientists project that enough components can be in place just ten years after construction begins that we should see a marked decrease in the use of fossil fuels in electricity generation at that time.

If American Jewry can diligently apply itself to overcoming America's dependence on foreign oil, "the ultimate benefits: a carbonless, ecologically gentle domestic energy infrastructure yielding economic and physical security,"[47] would be enormous. American Jewry can make lobbying for SuperGrid funding and other alternative energy technologies a central objective.

New Jewish Priorities

The organized Jewish community must also redirect its priorities. Because the American Jewish community has been slow to react to the new fusion of threats described above, it continues to misdirect the bulk of its efforts in fighting external threats to areas which do not pose a substantial threat to the Jewish community, such as imagined governmental discrimination against Jews through the public display of Christian and religious symbols like nativity scenes or the Ten Commandments[48] and illegal immigration, where there is little to be gained from Jewish participation except a sense of self-satisfaction. These efforts are draining our resources needlessly. Instead, our defense and anti-defamation organizations need to become more efficient and more focused. Older anti-defamation organizations should emulate groups such as the David Project, FLAME, CAMERA, MEMRI, the Israel Project and others, which have shown themselves capable of recognizing today's problems and reacting quickly. The role of the Conference of Presidents of Major American Jewish Organizations as a coordinating body should also be expanded. It is imperative that groups like the American Jewish Committee and the ADL work in conjunction with newer groups and address the external threats that face us today.

Although there are clearly social issues that deeply divide Christians and Jews, American Jews should recognize that Muslim fundamentalism threatens both Christians and Jews, and that we should therefore make common cause with Christians to protect free and open expression of religion for all inhabitants in America. We should also work with American Christians to help them aid Christian communities ruled by Islamic fundamentalists. Radical Islamists in the Arab world have victimized hundreds of thousands, if not millions of Christians.[49] The recent cooperation between Jews and Christians in protesting the genocide perpetuated by Muslim fundamentalists against Christians in Darfur is a good example of an effective Jewish-Christian alliance. Making coalitions with other religious groups who are under threat from Muslim fundamentalists is a concrete way for Jews to express universalism. From the Philippines to Syria, from Singapore to Sudan, radical Islam is attacking Christians. With our experience as a Diaspora community that has long reached out to Jews at risk across the world, be it in Soviet Russia, Ethiopia or Syria, American Jews can assist Christians in developing a strategy to aid their co-religionists. In so doing, we will have truly improved the world and fulfilled a part of our role in being "a light unto the nations." Jews should also consider working alongside Hindus in America and around the world in order to face the grave threat shared by India and Israel from radical Muslims. Radical Islam is a worldwide problem, and we Jews must build coalitions to face it effectively.

Jews have always faced external threats; our survival has depended on how we dealt with them. When we do not identify external threats or take them seriously, we needlessly put ourselves at great risk. American Jews must come to terms with the fact that radical Islam and its supporters on the far left are the biggest external threats to American Jewry and America today. If we do not, we betray the very freedom, wealth and privilege we enjoy in America and betray our own mission to be a light onto the nations.

* * *

American Jews are fortunate to live in a country of unprecedented freedom and wealth. The greatest challenge to our future continues to be internal, as anti-Semitism in America is confined to discrete political and religious movements. Unfortunately, these movements, which share a common hatred for Israel and Jews, are growing. We must act now in a reasoned fashion to counteract their influence. We must build coalitions with other Americans against radical Islam, based on our shared values, for the long-term benefit of the United States and American Jewry.

Notes

1. For statistics on the number of anti-Semitic attacks in the world every year see the Anti-Defamation, "Annual Audit," Anti-Defamation League Web site, http://www.adl.org/PresRele/ASUS_12/audit_2005.htm, accessed June 2006.
2. Thirty-six countries renewed or established diplomatic relations with Israel since the signing of the Israel-PLO Declaration of Principles on September 13, 1993. The Israel Department of Foreign Affairs, "Israel's Diplomatic Mission Abroad Status of Relations," The Israel Department of Foreign

Affairs Web site, http://www.mfa.gov.il/mfa/about%20the%20ministry/ diplomatic%20missions/Israel, accessed June 2005.

3. See the Stephen Roth Institute for the Study of Contemporary Anti-Semi-tism and Racism at Tel Aviv University, "Annual Report General Analysis 2002–03," The Stephen Roth Institute for the Study of Contemporary Anti-Semitism and Racism Web site, http://www.tau.ac.il/Anti-Semitism/ asw2002–3/general.htm, accessed June 2006.

4. See the Radical Left Web site, http://www.radicalleft.net, accessed June 2006, for examples of this type of argumentation.

5. Stephanie Gutmann, *The Other War: Israelis, Palestinians and the Struggle for Media Supremacy* (San Francisco: Encounter Books, 2005).

6. The Israel Defense Forces (IDF) entered Jenin with foot soldiers to root out a center of the embedded terrorist infrastructure in the West Bank, which included bomb building factories; the incursion cost the lives of thirteen IDF soldiers and fifty-two Palestinians. The decision to enter Jenin with combat soldiers was taken in order to minimize non-combatant Palestinian casu-alties, even though this presented greater risk to IDF soldiers. Yet, despite the IDF's precautions and Israel's legitimate right to defend its population, the Palestinian Authority and left-wing activists across the globe quickly branded the Jenin incursion an Israeli atrocity and spoke of the indiscrimi-nate murder of non-combatants, citing as many as five hundred casualties. This misinformation was so effective that it led to a lengthy United Nations investigation. And even after the United Nations reported that the Palestin-ians killed by the IDF were largely armed enemy combatants, the headline of "Jenin Atrocity" has remained rooted in world consciousness. A film about the events called "Jenin, Jenin" – made by an Arab citizen of Israel – per-petuated the lies about Jenin. Israel and the Jewish world's rebuttals were buried as old news. For a discussion of falsehood about Jenin see Robert N. Hochman, "Shifting Blame," *The New Republic*, April 24, 2002.

7. Guttman, *The Other War*.

8. For a list of such groups, see The U.S. Campaign to End the Israeli Occupa-tion Web site http://www.endtheoccupation.org/groups.php, accessed June 2006. As in other radical left publications, this website focuses on Palestin-ian suffering with the stated goal to end the Israeli "occupation," and makes no mention of radical Islam, terrorism or Israel's right to defend itself.

9. Jewishvirtuallibrary, "Palestinian "Collaborators" Killed, Injured, or De-tained," http://www.jewishvirtuallibrary.org/jsource/Peace/collaborators. html, accessed September 2006.

10. Yassir Arafat was a multi-millionaire.

11. Wikipedia, "Jewish exodus from Arab lands," http://en.wikipedia.org/wiki/ Jewish_exodus_from_Arab_lands, accessed September 2006.

12. Alex Svetlicinii, "*Amnesty International's Gulag Confusion*," Capital Research

Center (*May 2006*) *http://www.capitalresearch.org/pubs/pubs.asp?ID=511*, accessed June 2006.

13. See the materials collected on the NGO-Monitor Web site, http://www. ngo-monitor.org/, accessed June 2006.

14. Martin Kramer, *Ivory Towers on Sand* (Washington: The Washington Institute for Near East Policy, 2001), p. 3.

15. For a list of missed developments and trends see Chapter 3 "Islam Obscured" in Kramer, *Ivory Towers on Sand*.

16. Ibid.

17. Deborah E. Lipstadt "Strategic Responses to Anti-Israelism and Anti-Semitism on the North American Campus" in *American Jewry and the College Campus* (American Jewish Committee), p. 16, The American Jewish Committee Web site, http://www.ajc.org/site/c.ijITI2PHKoG/b.851479/apps/nl/content3.asp?content_id=%7BB42A429E-41-72-432E-90C9−0A8364F4E285%7D&notoc=1, accessed June 2006.

18. Ibid.

19. Noah Liben, The Columbia University Report on its Middle Eastern Department's Problems: A Methodological Paradigm for Obscuring Structural Flaws, *Jerusalem Center for Public Affairs*. April 13, 2005. http://www.jcpa. org/phas/phas-liben-05.htm, accessed June 2006.

20. Rebecca Kahn, "What we are facing in Campus Wars" *The Jewish Week*, March 21, 2005.

21. Lipstadt, p. 9.

22. Lipstadt, p. 11.

23. Wikipedia,"Divestment," http://en.wikipedia.org/wiki/Disinvestmentaccessed September 2006.

24. The U.S. Campaign to End the Israeli Occupation, "Palestine Solidarity Movement Conference," The U.S. Campaign to End The Occupation Web site, http://www.endtheoccupation.org/calendar.php?calid=98, accessed September 2006.

25. Benjamin Joffe-Walt, "Lecturers back boycott of Israeli academics," *Guardian Unlimited,* Tuesday May 30, 2006, http://education.guardian.co.uk/higher/news/story/0,,1785633,00.html, accessed September 2006.

26. John J. Mearsheimer and Stehen M. Walt, "The Israel lobby and U.S. Foreign Policy," *London Review of Books* 28/6 (March 23, 2006) also available on the Internet, http://ksgnotes1.harvard.edu/Research/wpaper.nsf/rwp/RWP06-011/$File/rwp_06_011_walt.pdf, accessed June 2006.

27. Steven Emerson. *American Jihad: The Terrorists Living Among Us* (New York: Free Press, 2002).

28. Daniel Pipes, *Militant Islam Reaches America* (New York: W.W. Norton & Company, 2002).

29. Ibid.

30. Emerson, pp. 29–30.
31. "Al-Qaida timeline: Plots and attacks," MSNBC and NBC News, 2006, http://www.msnbc.msn.com/id/4677978/, accessed June 2006.
32. Boaz Ganor, "The LAX Shooting, Isolated Criminal Incident or Terror Attack?" *Institute for Counter-Terrorism*, July 4, 2002, http://www.ict.org.il/articles/articledet.cfm?articleid=442/, accessed June 2006.
33. Robert Spencer, "Terror Denial," *FrontPageMagazine.com* | May 6, 2005, http://www.www.frontpagemag.com/Articles/ReadArticle.asp?ID=17959, accessed September 2006.
34. Emerson, pp. 203–204.
35. Ibid., p. 219.
36. *Daniel Pipes and Sharon Chadha, "Islamists Fooling the Establishment,"* Middle East Quarterly *(Spring 2006) Interview with Reed Rubenstein,* Frontpage Magazine, *May 8, 2006. and Emerson, p. 219.*
37. Emerson, pp. 223–225.
38. Emerson, pp. 228 and 231.
39. Sherrie Gossett, "Federal Money Goes to Controversial Muslim Group," *Accuracy in Media*, March 15, 2005, http://www.aim.org/aim_column/2778_0_3_0_C/, accessed June 2006.
40. Emerson, pp. 205–210.
41. Emerson, pp. 233–234.
42. Joe Kaufman, "The Black Hearts of KindHearts," FrontPage Magazine, March 14, 2006, http://www.frontpagemag.com/Articles/ReadArticle.asp?ID=21619, accessed June 2006.
43. Rabbi James Rudin, *"The Baptizing of America": The Religious Right's Plans for the Rest of Us* (New York: Thunder's Mouth Press, 2006).
44. Interview with Stephen Schwartz, "The Good & The Bad." *National Review Online*, November 18, 2002, http://www.nationalreview.com/interrogatory/interrogatory111802.asp, accessed June 2006.
45. Patrick Goodenough, "Catholic Leader Ponders Violence in Koran," *Cybercast News Service*, May 08, 2006. http://www.cnsnews.com/news/viewstory.asp?Page=%5CForeignBureaus%5Carchive%5C200605%5CINT20060508b.html, accessed June 2006.
46. Paul M. Grant, Chauncey Starr and Thomas J. Overbye," A Power Grid for the Hydrogen Economy," *Scientific American* (July 2006).
47. Ibid, p.83.
48. ADL, "ADL Urges U.S. Supreme Court to Reject Government Display of the Ten Commandments as Unconstitutional," ADL Web site, http://www.adl.org/PresRele/SupremeCourt_33/4601_33.htm, accessed June 2006.
49. Erich Isaac, "A Rich History – No Future Jews and Christians in Iraq," *Mideast Outpost*, May 31, 2005, http://mideastoutpost.com/archives/2005_05.html.

Chapter XII

Social Action, Ethical Behavior and Tzedakah

"Justice justice you shall pursue..."
Deuteronomy 16:20

Plank #10: The explicit mission of the Jewish people is to provide "a light unto the nations" by being a shining ethical example to all people and by being actively involved in repairing the world. Tikkun olam, the Hebrew expression for repairing the world, has three essential components that Jews across all movements should put at the forefront of their practice. The first is the willingness to be involved in social action in order to promote justice and equity based on Jewish principles. American Jewry needs to harness the Jewish impulse for social action in a way that enhances the unity of American Jewry and provides an entry point for Jews on the periphery of Jewish communal life so that they can become part of the core. The second is a personal commitment to ethical behavior both between Jews and between Jews and non-Jews. The third is tzedakah. American Jewry and tzedakah need to be so closely intertwined that it would be hard to think of the one without thinking of the other. If American Jewry is unprepared or unable to sustain its role in repairing the world, all the effort to revitalize our community would be for naught.

I SOCIAL ACTION
Judaism and Human Life

The most radical idea in Judaism is that man is created in the image of God (*b'tzelem Elokim*). As the Mishnah explains, we learn from the Torah that all of humanity has a common ancestor in order "to teach us that the Torah condemns whoever destroys a single soul, as though he/she had destroyed the entire world; and the Torah honors whoever saves a single soul as though that person had saved the entire world."[1]

In Judaism, the value of human life is paramount: it affects every aspect of Jewish law, culture, and thinking. In Jewish law it is clearly stated that almost any rule can be broken to save a life. Culturally, Jews have always valued physical health, and have been disproportionately represented among doctors throughout history. Philosophically, Jews believe that valuing human life requires us to emulate God in our everyday life and to treat other people with the dignity appropriate to a being who was created in the image of God. The value of human life is thus central to how Jews live and treat others.

> *"Follow the Lord your God"(Deuteronomy 13:5). What does this mean? Is it possible to follows God's presence?...We should follow the attributes of the Holy One...As God clothes the naked, so you should clothe the naked. As the Torah teaches that the Holy One visited the sick, you should visit the sick. The Holy One comforted those who mourn, you should comfort those who mourn. The Holy One buried the dead, you should bury the dead.* (Babylonian Talmud, Sotah 14a.)

Although Jews are called on to emulate all of God's qualities, we also learn in the Torah that we were given a special mission to do justice. God gave Abraham, the father of the Jewish people, the command "to do righteousness and justice" (Genesis 18:3).

The Jewish Origins of Social Justice

Not only have Jews since Abraham been commanded to do justice, the central story of the Jewish people is the struggle against oppression by others and unjust rulers. The story of the Jews' enslavement in Egypt and miraculous Exodus from slavery to freedom is retold every Passover and referred to as part of weekly Shabbat services and in the daily *tefilot*. Over and over again Jews are admonished to behave in a righteous manner "because you were slaves in the land of Egypt. You shall not subvert the rights of the stranger or the fatherless; you shall not take a widow's garment as collateral. Remember that you were a slave in Egypt and that the Eternal your God redeemed you from there. When you reap the harvest in your field and overlook a sheaf in the field, do not turn back to get it; it shall go to the stranger, the fatherless, and the widow...Always remember that you were a slave in the land of Egypt." (Deuteronomy 24:17–21.) If repetition and reminders of our slavery experience were not enough, in each Passover Seder Jews recite and internalize a key sentence from the Haggadah, "In each and every generation one must feel as if he/she personally had been redeemed from Egypt." [2]

The Exodus story and the Jewish experience of emerging from slavery to freedom is the ultimate wellspring of energy for Jews involved in fighting injustice and oppression. Michael Lerner describes this internalized wellspring as follows:

> Every ruling elite of the ancient and medieval world, and many in the modern world, justified their rule by ideologies whose central message was that the world cannot be changed...Along came the Jews with a very different message; the world can be fundamentally changed. Every system of oppression, no matter how powerful it appears to be, can be overthrown...We know it, because we did it ourselves." [3]

David Elcott aptly reviewed the inherent reason for Jewish optimism in social justice causes.

> The Maccabees fought against Antiochus, who claimed he was like a god. Later Jewish rebels resisted the omnipotence of Roman power and world domination. In Europe, Jews rejected the divine rights of kings even as they denied the supremacy of the Catholic Church and of Islam. The mere existence of Jews repudiated the…truths by which Nazism attempted to control the world. And when Marxism was translated into a totalitarian absolute in the Soviet Union (which instituted an assault on all things Jewish), Jewish resistance helped bring about Communism's collapse there.[4]

The Jewish Form of Social Justice

Jews were not simply brought out of Egypt to enjoy unrestricted freedom; the redemption was followed by a clear message of how they were to build a just society in the Promised Land. At Mount Sinai the Jews were called on to be partners with God in repairing the world. As Rabbi Sidney Schwartz puts it, the Jewish experience at Sinai communicated seven core principles to Jewish existence, through which Jews repair the world. These are:

> *Compassion (chesed); respect for the dignity of all of God's creation and creatures (tzelem elohim); pursuing peace (bakesh shalom v'rodfeihu); attention to the suffering of others (lo ta-amod al dam re'echa); seeking harmonious relationships with people who are not Jewish (darchei shalom); loving the stranger in our midst (ahavat ger); and pursuing truth (emet).[5]*

Thus, the three pivotal events of Jewish history – creation, the exodus from Egypt and the giving of the Torah – are all calls to social action. The creation story taught us that man is made in the image of God and has a duty to emulate him. Our experience of slavery and redemption enables us to feel the empathy for the oppressed and the faith to communicate to them that they too can be redeemed. Finally, the Torah and Jewish tradition have given us clear and explicit guidelines for repairing the world. These values continue to form the core of the Jewish view of social action.

Though modernity has weakened the ties many Jews have to their heritage, many still exhibit attitudes and behaviors towards others and towards injustices that implicitly draw from the creation story, the story of the Exodus and the guidelines of the Torah. Jews and non-Jews perceive respect for other human beings, pursuing justice, and being kind to others as a Jewish ethnic ethos. These ingrained values also explain why secular Jews were so prominent in the civil rights struggle, why Jews continue to vote liberal despite socio-economic trends that would otherwise suggest growing conservatism, and why Jews are leaders in so many organizations that are devoted to the welfare of society and the world.[6]

Social Action Cannot Be Divorced From Jewish Values

Unfortunately, as more and more Jews today are growing up with little knowledge of Jewish tradition, their impulse for social action has been passed on and internalized without the underlying link to Judaism. This decoupling is dangerous. Without a Jewish grounding for social action, these Jews will search for other value systems or ideas to ground their deeply felt desires for social justice, leading many further and further astray from Judaism. Just as worryingly, these substitute values for social justice, be they ideologies or personal philosophies, are highly unlikely to be as potent and persistent as Judaism and may potentially lead to injustice. Children of these Jews will be unlikely to understand social action as a Jewish imperative.

Historically, when non-Jewish ideologies have informed Jewish social action, the result has been disastrous for Jews and others. From 1900 to 1930, many Jewish immigrants to the U.S. were tightly linked to a relatively radical leftist social agenda. The shared social link of those within this movement was not Judaism but Yiddish. Without a Jewish moral basis, this left-wing group veered toward Communism. Moral relativism replaced a sense of absolute, or even clear-headed, right and wrong. By 1929, *Frayhayt*, then the dominant socialist/communist Yiddish newspaper, decided to follow the Soviet Union's line and sympathize with the Arabs after the brutal murder of the majority Jewish population of Hebron. Frayhayt later endorsed the Soviet Union's 1939 pact with Germany, which all clear-headed Jews realized was against Jewish interests. By the post-war period the same Yiddish newspaper had so parted ways with the Jewish people that it endorsed the imprisonment and execution of Jewish intellectuals by the Communists. What started out as a social action movement by Jews ultimately became anti-Jewish.[7]

In recent years, far left social action groups have become increasingly anti-Israel and anti-Semitic. Without reliance on a divine compass for social justice, the perspective for social action today has largely devolved into anti-imperialist/anti-globalization ideologies and relative or self-defined moral standards, all of which are fundamentally hostile to Jewish values. The results are disastrous.

Because current social action movements lack a divine perspective to social justice, many advocate moral relativism and take ideas and actions to their logical extremes. In contrast, Judaism requires both the means and the ends to conform to divinely commanded absolute values. Although both Jews and environmentalists value nature, Judaism does not condone harming people or property in order to protect the environment. In contrast, extreme environmentalists advocate sabotage, arson, and harassment to protect forests and ecosystems.[8] Likewise, although Judaism admonishes us to be kind to animals, it also considers it morally wrong to equate animal farming with the Holocaust,[9] and does not condone threatening the lives of laboratory workers and company executives in order to stop animal testing.[10] In Judaism, morality is absolute; no person can commit a criminal or immoral act in the name of a greater good.

Americans on the far left not only justify the means by the ends, but also ignore the morally repugnant acts of people they perceive as victims. As noted in the previous plank, the far left believes that the Palestinians are the innocent victims of "Zionist aggression" and American Imperialism." As a result, they rationalize morally reprehensible acts, such as suicide and homicide bombings, as justifiable acts of resistance. Moreover, the far left also turns a blind eye to the violence Palestinian men perpetrate against other Palestinians, such as the honor killings of women who are accused of infidelity or flirting or who are victims of rape, and the murder of "collaborators" or Palestinian moderates.[11] Although the far left is focused on Israeli attacks against Palestinians,[12] Palestinians are also frequently the victims of Palestinians and other Arabs, and violence within the Arab world far exceed Israeli attacks against Palestinians. The UN estimates that there are 5,000 documented so-called "honor killings" per year in Arab lands including the Palestinian Authority, and possibly 150,000 total cases per year. According to the UN Report on Arab Human Development in 2004, most political regimes in the Arab world do not respect the basic human rights either of their citizens or of the thousands of so-called Palestinian refugees and other non-citizen groups that live within their borders.[13] Yet, because of the tenets of anti-imperialism, far left activists do not condemn inter-Palestinian and inter-Arab violence as much as they condemn Israel and the United States.

Anti-American ideology also blinds far left activists to other injustices around the world and to the violent movements led by "oppressed peoples." The National Islamic Front and the Janjaweed have brutally slaughtered an estimated 400,000 people in Darfur, are raping and murdering non-Muslim black Africans as well as black African Muslims who refuse to accept the *Sharia*, and are also deliberately destroying crop lands and water access points.[14] Yet, despite the fact that these militants are committing genocidal violence in the name of radical Islam against non-Muslim and Muslim black Africans, the far left continues to single out the

West as the world's primary villain. Some journalists have also pointed out that the the the far left has failed to speak out against the endemic violence in Africa since the late 1990s, despite their pretense to fight against all oppression.[15] Hard left activists also speak out more against Israel than against the modern-day slavery of workers in China, India and Pakistan, boy slave camel jockeys in the United Arab Emirates, sugar plantation slaves in Haiti and sex slaves in Southeast Asia. In Mauritania and Sudan, slaves are chattel, as they and their offspring and their offspring's offspring are expected to perpetually serve their owners.[16] The far left is focusing its fight against the U.S., not the true fight for human rights worldwide.

In contrast to the far left, Judaism condemns all immoral behavior regardless of skin color, religion or allegiance. Whereas the Jewish conception of Godliness requires Jews to combat all sorts of evil wherever they are, and committed by whomever, leftist social action invariably imposes an ideological agenda that distinguishes between the violence committed by perceived "oppressors" and by "victims." Thus, current far left social action goes against basic Jewish values. Simply put: far left groups lead Jews away from Judaism. Many Jews unfortunately do not recognize the danger of Jews focusing exclusively on left wing social action. Indeed, a Reform rabbi gave a sermon in which she explicitly said that it was okay for a Jew not to attend religious services if he/she were instead involved in social action. Yet, if one never "does Jewish," there will be no next generation of Jews to accomplish the Jewish social action that is our role in this world.

The challenge for American Jewry is to harness the heritage and impulse that all Jews have for social action and direct it within a Jewish context. Social responsibility must be part of our identity as Jews, with our particularistic impulse and universalistic impulse balanced in an ever-shifting duality determined by the needs of the times. However, one side can never be to the exclusion of the other. While social action has served as an exit lane for Jews, there is no reason it can also not serve as an entry lane. Many

Jews, certainly young adult Jews on campus and in the early post-college years, are seeking social action opportunities. American Jewry needs to provide a Jewish context for these opportunities. Our heritage makes this a natural opportunity for Jewish engagement. Jewish social action must be linked with Jewish learning. As such, opportunities for social action should be an entry point for a deeper commitment to Judaism.

Social Action: a Focus on Israel

The state of Israel is an excellent place for Jews to take social action. While it has often been the case in the Diaspora that the Jewish perspective provides another take on truth and morality apart from the dominant power, we Jews cannot exclude ourselves from criticism. This is particularly so now that our fellow Jews live in the sovereign State of Israel. After 2000 years, Jews do hold the reigns of power in one country in the world. American Jews can and should feel free to disagree with and protest issues regarding Israeli society while at the same time providing unqualified support for the existence and security of the State of Israel. Too often, I have heard Jews say that they cannot support Israel because they disagree with a policy, a set of policies or a negotiating position of the government of Israel. This is a confusion that must be overcome. It is also a tactic used by anti-Israel propagandists. I almost always disagree with some positions of the American government, sometimes passionately so, but I always consider myself a patriot of the U.S. If I were to feel strongly about an issue, I would feel free to protest it. Criticism of government policy is a form of patriotism in a free society.

There are important social issues in Israel that are appropriate subjects of social action efforts by Jews, such as poverty, racism between Jews, rising crime and the treatment of non-Jews in Israel. Today, a total of 18% of all families in Israel live below the poverty line.[17] Israel is also struggling to absorb different Jewish immigrant groups, particularly Ethiopian Jews, who often feel discriminated against because of their color.[18] There is also growing concern about crime in Israel. In 2004 the Israeli press began reporting on foreign women who were fraudulently or forcibly brought to Israel as "sex industry workers." Israel is also grappling with its national conduct toward its Arab minority citizens. Israeli Arabs are legally entitled to the same civil rights as Israeli Jews – although they are exempt from the three-year obligatory army service borne by Israeli Jews and Druze – yet most Israeli Arabs consider themselves Palestinians and not Israelis. American Jews who are concerned about these and other issues that affect Israeli society should get involved.

American Jews should also address the question of Israel's treatment of non-citizen Arabs in the West Bank, which has been administered by Israel since the Six Day War. There are fundamental questions that remain open – what responsibility does Israel have toward the Palestinians? Is there ever justification for collective punishment? How does having a government controlled by Hamas, which is sworn to destroy Israel, affect these responsibilities? What is appropriate self defense? These questions are being vigorously debated in Israel today. In fact, during the height of the Intifada uprisings, when one would have expected little sympathy for Arabs in occupied territories from any Israeli Jews, some Israeli groups, such as B'Tselem, were protesting and litigating against the government for better treatment of these non-citizens, while others called on Israel to take stronger security measures. So social action and the quest for social justice can be a place where Jews with very different views on the policies of the government of Israel can come together, as long as we all endorse Israel's right to exist and defend itself as a state for the Jewish people without reservation.

Social Action: Coming Together for the Rest of the World

Jews of all theological positions can meet to take authentic Jewish action on issues relating to oppression in the world and conditions in Israel. One Jewish group focusing on the world outside of Israel is the American Jewish World Services (AJWS), which has arranged for groups of rabbinical students from across the movements to work and serve together in El Salvador. AJWS offers a variety of programs to college and post-college Jewish students and young adults to offer personal volunteer assistance in impoverished countries. Even more broadly, the Jewish Coalition for Service (JCS) offers more than forty programs that give Jews the opportunity to do, as JCS calls it, "full time hands-on volunteer work": from a week to a year, from age fifteen to post-retirement. The goal of JCS is to inspire each Jew to devote some portion of his/her life to making the world a better place.[19] In essence, JCS is an organic Jewish Peace Corps. The challenge is for this to become a place where all Jews can feel free to "do Jewish" by doing social action with an authentic Jewish perspective. Ruth Messenger, the executive director of AJWS, believes that one goal of AJWS's program in helping non-Jewish impoverished communities is to help the world to "come to see Jews in the way we want to be seen, as caring about social justice."[20] So enlarging our Jewish Peace Corp will bind all segments of Jews closer, provide an entry point for Jews and let us actualize our mission to be a light unto the nations – as long as the programs are grounded in Jewishness. Yet, as previously noted, the ever present danger of social action efforts done by Jews without authentic Jewish grounding, is that these efforts can go off on tangents that not only do not sustain the Jewish impulse for social action, but make that impulse become counter-productive.

Programs

We need to place particular emphasis on engaging college youth in Jewish social action. Only 30% or so of Jewish college students walk through the doors of Hillel. (As a former Hillel of New York volunteer president, and in my current, less formal capacity, I have rarely heard a higher figure quoted by a Hillel director or rabbi.) More than 30% of Jewish college students are attracted to social action, social justice or community activist activities. In this age of great social ferment, Hillel and the rest of the Jewish community must be open and ready with a panoply of social action opportunities.

As few programs as possible should be geared to one movement. The stereotype that social action is the purview of Reform and secular Jews must be overcome. *Tikkun olam* is part of every Jew's mission, as much as bar/bat mitzvah or High Holiday service attendance. As one JCS volunteer put it, "serving the community by protecting the earth and striving to end suffering makes me feel like a practicing Jew."[21] For Jews, social action is part of the duality between Jewish universalism and Jewish particularism. This plank of social action reaches deep into the soul of American Jewry and is a core engine for Jewish renewal.

Hillels and Jewish campus groups should also offer lectures about Jewish views on contemporary ideologies and issues such as anti-globalization, Marxism, democracy, and our consumer culture, to name but a few. Jewish students at American universities are trying to discover their own core values. Some are exposed to major non-Jewish and secular Jewish thinkers of the modern era; few however, have any exposure to Reform, Conservative or Orthodox responses to these thinkers, or Jewish views on the topics they address. Lectures by prominent contemporary Jewish thinkers on current political and social topics may attract Jews to Jewish events that they would not otherwise attend. Such lectures will also help young Jews to think critically, as many university professors present current social theories as unquestionable truth.

Social Action and the Fervently Orthodox

Social action is an excellent way for the Chareidim to build bridges with other Jews and promote positive examples of Judaism to the rest of America. Because Chareidim and fervently Orthodox Jews are the most visibly Jewish members of the American Jewish community, when they participate in social action they can have an immeasurably positive impact on American Jews and on American society as a whole. The relief efforts that Lubavitcher *chasidim* organized in New Orleans were astounding. Not only did they go out of their way to help the Jewish communities across Louisiana, but they also dedicated an enormous amount of time and energy to helping all Americans caught in the hurricane. Lubavitcher *chasidim* also made American Jews proud with their valiant efforts for victims of the 2004 Tsunami in Thailand. The efforts of Lubavitcher *chasidim* to reach out to all Jews and to all Americans have had a positive impact on American society as a whole. The former Lubavitcher Rebbe, Menachem Mendel Schneerson, was well known and liked by such diverse American personalities as Bill Cosby and Jon Voight. This positive impact of the Lubavitch movement's effort for all Americans in times of crisis has reflected well on all Jews. Similarly, those Orthodox Jews who rallied against the genocide in Darfur from an explicitly and exclusively Jewish perspective brought honor to Jews in America and gave a visible and positive example to non-affiliated Jews.

II ETHICAL BEHAVIOR

Just as important as social action to *tikkun olam* is our everyday behavior in interacting with individuals and issues in our lives. Judaism emphasizes the importance of ethical behavior in all areas of life, from the larger questions to the smaller details, as a Jewish activist noted:

> *"Jews are used to believing and behaving as if small actions reflect great issues. How we pick our crops, for example, hints at our commitment to hunger and social action...How else could we integrate lofty ideals into our daily regimen if not by small, concrete acts? This is the brilliance and challenge of Judaism: Kideshanu b'mitzvotav – we are holy because of our actions."*[22]

Moreover, small actions not only affect the world we live in, but our actions as individuals reflect on the Jewish community as a whole. In the following section I have selected both positive and negative examples of Jewish behavior to illustrate the impact of unethical behavior on the world and on the world's perception of the Jewish community. To avoid *lashon hara* (evil language, including discussing people behind their backs), I have chosen examples that have been previously well publicized. These examples also illustrate how easily the unethical behavior of self-identified Jews can be used to tarnish Jewry as a whole.

Negative Examples

For much of 2005, the Jack Abramoff scandal captivated the national press. The scandal had aspects to keep everyone interested. There were fantastic junkets to exotic locations, lots of money changing hands, famous political names, a goodly amount of score settling, casinos, controversial figures, and the outsized personality of Mr. Abramoff. All of this is, of course, clearly fair game for the media; however, the media also focused on Abramoff's self-identification as an Orthodox Jew. Frank Rich, the *New York Times* columnist, could not get enough of the "Orthodox Jew" angle, and used this aspect of the scandal as a blunt bludgeoning instrument in most, if not all, of the columns he wrote on the scandal. In one column, Frank Rich wrote that:

> *"Abramoff…is now being investigated by as many federal agencies as there are nights of Passover, [he] is an Orthodox Jew who in his salad days wore a yarmulke to press interviews…Mr. Abramoff's own moral constellation can be found in e-mail messages in which he referred to his Indian clients as "idiots" and "monkeys" even as he squeezed them for every last million. A previous client was Zaire's dictator…who actually was a practitioner of torture and mass murder. In 1992 Mr. Abramoff, eager to prove that he was unlike secular show-business Democrats, told The Hollywood Reporter that he was starting a Committee for Traditional Jewish Values in Entertainment to emulate Christian anti-indecency campaigns. (He didn't.) But "Red Scorpion," on which Mr. Abramoff shares the writing credit, has many more four-letter words than "Meet the Fockers," as*

well as violence, bloodied beefcake (Dolph Lundgren's) and cru-
cifixion imagery anticipating 'The Passion of the Christ.'"[23]

While Frank Rich should know better than to use Jack Abramoff
as a paintbrush to cover "these people," whoever they may be, in
addition to those specifically referred to, Mr. Abramoff clearly
asked for it. Prior to his crash, Mr. Abramoff openly touted his
religiosity and used it as sort of a shield.[24] Mr. Abramoff compounded his other sins by besmirching all Jews and particularly
Orthodox Jews. There is nothing religious about that.

The irony is that, although Mr. Abramoff considered himself
Orthodox, he certainly is not. He could better be characterized as
a ritually observant Jew. In no stream of Judaism is it permissible
to be a practicing member if one prays to God in the morning
and then spends the rest of the day preying on people. The Torah
and the sages put interpersonal ethics first. The great sage Hillel
summed up the entire written Torah and oral law by saying "Do
not do unto other as you would not want done unto you. The rest
is commentary. Go learn it."[25] In Orthodox rabbinical ordination,
there are two levels. In order to pass judgment on interpersonal
relationships or business ethics, an Orthodox rabbi needs to have
the second, higher level, ordination (*yadin, yadin*). Yet, by virtue
of the publicity of his crimes and self-identification, Abramoff
tarnished Judaism for non-Jewish Americans and many American Jews.

A second negative example arises from the massive Enron
scandal. Andrew Fastow, who served as Enron's Chief Financial
Officer and a principal architect of the fraud, has already pleaded
guilty to two federal felonies in connection with the case. Prior
to his plea bargain, some articles made reference to Mr. Fastow's
involvement in Jewish communal activities. Shortly thereafter, Mr.
Fastow began to use these activities as an explicit shield. He en-
listed Rabbi Shaul Osadchey of his synagogue as a public character
witness.[26] As one columnist noted, "Mr. Fastow himself has been
playing the religion card by directing calls to his rabbi, who has

vouched for his moral character."[27] Although Mr. Fastow did not describe his personal observance, he did ask his rabbi to speak on his behalf. Luckily the rabbi admitted that while the Fastows have "been members, they're not overly active."[28] Thus, despite any long-term and sincere commitment to Judaism, when it came to his self-interest, Mr. Fastow, like Mr. Abramoff, did not hesitate to bring shame to Judaism.

Like with the Abramoff scandal, the press was more than happy to focus on Mr. Fastow's Jewishness. It was also interesting to note the less frequent references in the press to Mr. Fastow's receipt of an MBA from Northwestern University's Kellogg Graduate School of Management. As it happens, like Mr. Fastow, I am also a graduate of Kellogg as well as a Jew. I have yet to hear from any fellow graduate or anyone within the larger business community that Kellogg bears some responsibility for the way Fastow behaved. I agree with that assessment. Yet Kellogg nevertheless inserted an ethics segment into the core curriculum that every student is required to take.[29]

There are unfortunately other public examples that could be cited of the Jewish people and Judaism being sullied by unethical Jews of all stripes including, of course, Reform, secular and just-Jewish Jews. Even though collective blame for these types of acts is clearly not warranted, we need to acknowledge that the media is often more than willing to emphasize a person's Jewishness, therefore acts of individual Jews clearly color the perception of Jews by the world. Thus, every negative action we take has the risk of being compounded many times over for the Jewish community. The irony is that ethical behavior has always been part of Judaism's core curriculum.

Positive Examples

Fortunately, everyday actions by Jews can be a source of great inspiration as well. In 1996, a fire destroyed the plant of Malden Mills, based in Massachusetts. The owner, Aaron Feuerstein, made the unusually generous decision to pay 2,400 workers their full salary while the plant was being rebuilt. The decision received wide, but unsolicited, press coverage thrusting Feuerstein into the spotlight. Through it all, he remained modest. Feuerstein, a real Orthodox Jew, summed up his decision with three quotes from Jewish texts. "In a place where there is no righteous person, be a righteous person,"[30] "not all who increase their wealth are wise,"[31] and "let the rich man not glory in his riches…, justice and equity in the world: For in these I (God) delight."[32] As a postscript, by 2001, mounting debt, some of which was brought on by Feuerstein's generosity, forced Malden Mills into bankruptcy. Feuerstein still consistently maintained that even if he had known how things would turn out, he would have done the same thing.[33]

Another example is brought down by a great American in his own right, Stephen Carter. In his book *Civility*, Stephen Carter, distinguished Professor of Law at Yale, recalls a small act of kindness that was transformative for him and the rest of his African-American family. Carter calls his story "A Dark, Skinny Stranger in Cleveland Park." The emphasis on the stranger is uncanny for the Jewish reader.

In the summer of 1966, my parents moved with their five children to…Cleveland Park…in those days, a lily white enclave…My two brothers and two sisters and I sat on the front steps, missing our playmates, as the movers carried in our furniture. Cars passed what is now our house, slowing for a look, as did people on foot. We waited for someone to say hello, to welcome us. Nobody did…I felt as if we had moved to the fearsome Virginia…which, in my child's mind, captured all the horror of what I know of how white people treated black people. I watched strange new people passing us and wordlessly watching back, and I knew we were not welcome here. I knew we would not be liked here. I knew we would have no friends here. I knew we should not have moved here. I knew…all at once, a white woman arriving home from work at the house across the street from ours turned and smiled with obvious delight and waved and called out, "Welcome!" in a booming, confident voice I would come to love. She bustled into her house, only to emerge, minutes later, with a huge tray of cream cheese and jelly sandwiches, which she carried to our porch and offered around with her ready smile, simultaneously feeding and greeting the children of a family she had never met – and a black family at that – with nothing to gain for herself except perhaps the knowledge that she had done the right thing. We were strangers, black strangers, and she went out of her way to make us feel welcome. This woman's name was Sara Kestenbaum, and she died much too soon, but she remains, in my experience, one of the great exemplars of all that is best about civility. Sara Kestenbaum's special contribution to civility back in 1966 was to create for us a sense of belonging where none had existed before. And she did so even though she had never seen any of us in her life. She managed, in the course of a single day, to turn us from strangers into friends, a remarkable gift that few share.

Sara Kestenbaum had no idea that one of the five "strangers" would one day become a leading American public intellectual. She did what she did out of a deep groundedness in the Judaism that was so central to her being. Her act of *chesed* now influences not only Stephen Carter but countless readers of his books.

The third positive example is Rabbi Abraham Joshua Heschel's decision to march with the Rev. Dr. Martin Luther King from Selma to Montgomery Alabama. At the time, Rabbi Heschel's involvement in the civil rights movement held risk for him and arguably for the entire Jewish community. Overt anti-Semitism was still very much alive for many Jews in the U.S. Whole neighborhoods, industries and, of course, clubs had blatant "no Jews allowed" policies. As a high profile Jew, linking himself (literally) to the civil rights movement was even personally dangerous. Yet the photograph of Rabbi Heschel joined arm in arm with Dr. King and other leaders during the great march will remain in the minds of a generation of Jews for a lifetime. Of his experience marching, Rabbi Heschel at the time famously said "For many of us the march from Selma to Montgomery was both protest and prayer. Legs are not lips and walking is not kneeling. And yet our legs uttered songs. Even without words, our march was worship. I felt my legs were praying."[34] This moral high ground also led Heschel to be part of the beginning of American Jewry's focus on the plight of Soviet Jewry. In 1963, he declared that Soviet Jewry must become the number one concern of American Jews.[35] Heschel also aligned himself with the anti-Vietnam War movement.[36] Rabbi Heschel's social action agenda emerged from his Jewishness. He gave meaning to the reinforcement of Jewish particularism and universalism. Heschel's universalist concerns clearly flowed from his particularistic Jewish values. As Heschel put it, "we are messengers; let us not forget our message."[37]

These three positive stories have much in common. Each Jew acted in an unself-conscious manner, fully recognizing the costs involved in their actions. Each reacted to situations placed before them in a way that reflected back upon the Jewish people as a blessing. In Aaron Feuerstein's case, his cost was quantifiable. In Sara Kestenbaum's case, she surely knew she was potentially alienating herself from her other neighbors who may have still carried latent anti-Semitic tendencies. In Rabbi Heschel's case, the Conservative movement concedes that his social activism cost him much of his influence on the movement and JTS at the time. Of course, his long-term influence was probably far greater than anticipated because of his principled stance.[38]

But whatever the price these three individuals paid for their actions, their legacy is clear. The contrast between their actions and those of Jack Abramoff and Andrew Fastow, who tried to use Judaism as a shield, could not be brighter. We cannot know when we will be thrust into a situation in which our actions have the potential to bring honor or shame to the Jewish people and our heritage. It could be bringing sandwiches to a new neighbor, visiting a sick person or acting ethically when no one is looking. As quoted above, "we are holy because of our actions."[39]

How we treat our neighbors and day-to-day business ethics are areas that Judaism has traditionally emphasized greatly. The ancient sages recognized that money was where nice sounding theory came up against real life economic considerations and temptations. Rabbi Yishmael said, "one who wants to acquire wisdom should work on the laws of money…it is like an ever flowing stream."[40] Rabbi Yishmael foresaw that commerce is always progressing. He could have never dreamed of the complex derivative securities, partnership transactions, securities regulations and tax laws at the heart of the Enron fraud. Yet he knew that this is the area on which to focus. Comparing the difference between Andrew Fastow's and Aaron Feuerstein's attitude to business puts the ethical implications of everyday transactions into focus. Judaism also values modesty: the contrast between Jack Abramoff's influence peddling and Rabbi Heschel's willingness to diminish his influence could not be starker. Finally, we can each compare the day-to-day chances we miss to bring honor to Jews and Judaism to Sara Kestenbaum's cheerful but costly act of *chesed*. If we can each live up to the three examples of bringing honor to Judaism then the world will be a tangibly better place, and younger generations of American Jews will have great opportunities to live up to.

Ethical Behavior Among Ultra-Orthodox and Fervently Orthodox Jews

Because the fervently Orthodox are among the most visibly Jewish members of our community, it is very important that they observe the highest standards of ethical behavior. By choosing to wear a *kippah* or *sheitel* (wig) to work, Orthodox Jews are signaling their identity to the rest of the world, and therefore must be constantly aware that their actions will often be used to judge all Jews. Orthodox Jews must therefore be especially vigilant in observing the highest level of ethical behavior in their business affairs. The visibility of the Orthodox also makes it all the more important that Orthodox communities maintain amicable relations with one another. Non-Jewish newspapers are extremely fond of pointing to infighting within tight-knit Ultra-Orthodox communities in order to disparage Orthodox Jewry as a whole. Any conflict among prominent Orthodox groups is not only contrary to the command to love a fellow Jew, but it also reflects badly on all Clal Yisrael, since it brings disgrace to all Jews. Orthodox Jews must therefore be extra careful to observe the highest standards of ethical behavior.

Personal Tzedakah

The final part of the final plank, *tzedakah*, is about an action that encompasses both social action and ethical behavior. The term *tzedakah* is usually translated as charity because it typically refers to making donations. But *tzedakah's* better translation is righteousness, as previously noted. While Judaism positively values wealth and Jews view it as a blessing to be wealthy, Judaism also places a moral obligation on Jews to use their wealth wisely. Jews are required by Judaism to give *tzedakah* not simply because it feels good, but because it is the just thing to do. In Plank #5 we discussed funding the platform, which was essentially also about *tzedakah*. *Tzedakah* is not simply a voluntary act of kindness; it is a responsibility and an obligation.

Although at first blush it seems counterintuitive, Judaism ascribes a higher value to fulfilling an obligation than to doing something nice voluntarily. To understand the meaning of *tzedakah*, it is necessary to understand this reasoning. Consider a childless woman visiting her sister who has two children in diapers, one of which is a newborn who wakes up twice a night. The visiting sister kindly offers to and actually changes the dirty diapers of the babies while patiently singing and playing with them so that the mother can take a short nap. This is truly a very nice act and the visiting sister can and should feel happy with herself. But that night and every night the mother (and father) will bear the responsibility of caring for their babies while being sleep-deprived and juggling a host of other responsibilities. They may not feel like singing and playing at that time, but these parents do not avoid their responsibility. The mother and father have also made economic and career sacrifices to bring their children into the world. Judaism judges that the mother's deeds are on a far higher level than the sister's voluntary kindness. *Tzedakah* is obligatory because it is the logical outcome of viewing ourselves and every other person as carrying some reflection of God. Each person is expected to emulate God by providing for the needy and to think of providing for the needy as a form of worship in and of itself. After grasping this relationship, everything else follows. Plank #5 was about the macro/societal feel-good reasons for giving *tzedakah*. This part of this plank is about the micro/self-obligatory reasons for giving. American Jews need to give *tzedakah* not just until it feels good, but also until it feels right.

Giving to the local Federation should be an obligation for every American Jew. Indeed, if Federations did not exist, it would be crucial for us to create them. For some this is a controversial statement. However, in my 25-year experience with New York's UJA-Jewish Federation, I have learned that almost every Jew, whatever his/her background or movement affiliation, can strongly support about 90% of the allocations that the UJA-Federation makes. Most people support money spent to feed the hungry, take care of the elderly, support poor Jews abroad, help oppressed Jews escape to their homes and assist Jews to resettle in Israel. Other grants which maintain the basics of local Jewish infrastructures which are actualized through Federation support, including Hebrew Homes for the Aged, the Joint Distribution Committee, food supply programs, JCCS, Hillel, and the like, also have almost unanimous support. Only the final 10% of Federation programs are the subject of debate. These include programs such as support for day schools, Jewish culture, local Jewish newspapers or particular social action programs in Israel. Though support for controversial programs has led different groups from all three major movements to discuss boycotts of the Federation, these boycotts have never occurred. However, they have created excuses for Jews not to contribute individually. Despite protests most Jews agree that the Federation is the one place where all of the community's aspirations are mediated and everyone can sit at one table. I have seen programs pushed by a few members of a committee that others simply did not comprehend; yet not infrequently these programs are funded out of respect for the deeply felt beliefs of others at the table. Sometimes these programs are a success, sometimes not. For all of these reasons, American Jews must support the Federation, because it is the one *tzedakah* that really embraces all of Clal Yisrael in the U.S. We should also each give donations to more specific organizations commensurate with our means. But if one only has the means to make one donation, the Federation is the place to make it. It should be a part of the core charitable portfolio of every Jew. In Plank #2, I assumed that national Federation fundraising would increase by 1.5% per year. I did this for the sake of conservatism. Of course, Federations are under-funded and should grow by at least 5–10% annually for years.

Whether to Federations or any other Jewish agency, American Jews must give *tzedakah*. At this particular time in the history of the Jews in America we need to specialize in *tzedakah* toward causes that teach, preserve and advance the Jewish people. Without the Jewish people, our concept of *tikkun olam* will only be words on paper. We must give and give generously. Never before has there been such a wealthy Jewish community as today in America. We have the opportunity to use our wealth to give in a way that reflects the Godliness within others and ourselves and preserves the Jewish community in America. This is our test!

* * *

Our purpose as a people will be for naught if we fail to be "a light unto the nations." To justify all the work on the previous nine platforms, American Jewry must have a vision of *tikkun olam* that goes much farther than just preserving the Jewish people in isolation. This vision can be actualized both on the communal and the personal levels. As a community we must build on our nascent Jewish Peace Corps. The Jewish Peace Corps should be open and accessible to all Jews. It should be built on authentic Jewish values and serve both as an entry point and a binding mechanism for American Jewry. By making a volunteer experience part of the life of every Jew, the world will "come to see Jews in the way that we want to be seen, as caring about social justice." We must also promote ethical behavior within the Jewish community. Whether we like it or not, the behavior of each Jew reflects on all of us. Therefore, our good and bad actions are magnified tenfold. Using Judaism as a shield for bad actions is a major offense to the Jewish people. When taking any action that will reflect in any way upon the Jewish people, we need to think about how it would read as an article in the newspaper. Finally, we must give more *tzedakah*. Giving *tzedakah* offers us a tangible way to combine our agenda for social justice and preserve the Jewish people. In America we have been blessed with wealth; we must use it to bring blessing on all Jews, America and the world.

Notes

1. Mishnah Sanhedrin 4:5.
2. David M. Elcott, *A Sacred Journey: The Quest for a Perfect World* (Lanham: Jason Aronson Publishers, 1995), pp. 35–36.
3. Michael Lerner, *Jewish Renewal: A Path to Healing and Transformation* (New York: G.P. Putnams's Sons, 1994), p. 127.
4. Elcott, p. 42.
5. Sidney Schwartz, "Exodus and Sinai: New Thoughts on Jewish Identity" *Sh'ma* (October 2005), p. 36.
6. Ibid, p. 36.
7. Jeremy Dauber,"When Yiddish was Edgy," *The Jerusalem Report*, (February 2006), pp. 36–38.
8. The FBI estimates that radical environmentalist groups have committed over 1,100 acts of eco-terrorism since 1976. See article "Bounty Placed on Eco-terrorism in Washington State," *ABCNews*, September 21, 2005, http://abcnews.go.com/US/story?id=1145285&page=1, accessed June 2006.

9. In 2003, the animal rights groups PETA launched their "Holocaust on Your Plate" campaign, which compared the slaughter of cattle to the Holocaust of European Jews. "Group blasts PETA 'Holocaust' project," CNN, February 28, 2003. http://www.cnn.com/2003/US/Northeast/02/28/peta.holocaust/, accessed June 2006.

10. Nicola Wilcock, "Animal rights activists convicted in the US of terrorising British lab," *Timesonline*, March 4, 2006, http://www.timesonline.co.uk/article/0,,11069-2068837,00.html, accessed June 2006.

11. In 1991, the Israelis killed fewer Palestinians – about 100 – than the Palestinians did themselves Wikpedia "Intifada," http://en.wikipedia.org/wiki/First_Intifada, accessed June 2006.

12. One of the far left groups to focus on Israel is The Public Committee Against Torture in Israel. For an example of their views see The Public Committee Against Torture in Israel, "Violence Against Palestinian Women," http://www.omct.org/pdf/vaw/2005/israel_cedaw33rd.pdf, accessed June 2006.

13. UNDP, *The Time Has Come: A Call for Good Governance in the Arab World: Arab Human Development Report 2004* (New York: UNDP, 2004). http://www.rbas.undp.org/ahdr_2004/1PR_AHDR04_E.pdf, accessed June 2006.

14. See The Abolishslavery.com Web site, www.abolishslavery.com, accessed June 2006.

15. Bienart, "No Answer."

16. For a much more detailed, frightening depiction of the modern slavery, I strongly suggest reading the article Charles Jacobs, "Slavery: Worldwide Evil," iAbolish American Anti-Slavery group Web site, http://www.iabolish.com.

17. "Poverty level very high in Israel," *The Washington Times*, June 11, 2006, http://washingtontimes.com/upi/20060611-043653-5433r.htm, June 2006.

18. Guy Leshem, "Poverty and Crime Rates Reveal Israel's Failure To Absorb Ethiopian Immigrants," *Forward*, October 21, 2005, http://www.forward.com/articles/5160, June 2006.

19. See Jewish Coalition for Social Sevice Web site, www.jewishservice.org.

20. Sandra Brawavsky, "Repair One Corner of Our World," *Jewish Week*, December 30, 2005.

21. Quote from a participant in the 2005 Jewish Coalition for Service promotional brochure.

22. Andrea Cohen-Kiener, "The Sh'ma and Ecology," *Genesis 2* (Spring 1989) in *Jews, Money and Social Responsibility* eds. Lawrence Bush and Jeffrey Dekro (Philidelphia: The Shefa Fund, 1993), p. 29.

23. Frank Rich, "Get Tom DeLay to the Church on Time," *The New York Times*, April 17, 2005.

24. David Rosenbaum, "At $500 an Hour, Lobbyist's Influence Rises with GOP." *The New York Times*, April 3, 2002.
25. Babylonian Talmud, Shabbat 31a.
26. Rachel Donadio, "Houston Jews Quaking Over Enron Scandal" *Forward*, February 22, 2002.
27. Ibid.
28. Ibid.
29. See Paul Singer "Business schools add ethics in wake of corporate scandals," August 16, 2002, Kellog School of Management Web site, www.kellogg. northwestern.edu, accessed June2006.
30. Article on Aaron Feuerstein, Aish Web site, http://www.aish.com/ societyWork/work/Aaron_Feuerstein_Bankrupt_and__Wealthy.asp, accessed June 2006.
31. Ibid.
32. Jeremiah 9:22–23.
33. Dassi Zeidel "Do the Right Thing," *Jewish Action* 66/2 (Winter 2005), p. 25.
34. Quoted from Reuven Kimmelman, "Abraham Joshua Heschel: Our Generation's Teacher," *Melton Journal* No. 15 (Winter 1984).
35. Ibid.
36. Ibid.
37. From Herschel's address to the 28th World Zionist Congress in Jerusalem in 1957 as quoted in Kimmelman, "Our Generation's Teacher."
38. See article on Conservative Judaism, "Abraham Joshua Heschel" Jewish Theological Seminary Web site, http://learn@jtsa.edu.
39. Cohen-Kiener, "*the Sh'ma and Ecology.*"
40. Babylonian Talmud, Babba Batra 175b.

Chapter XIII

The "To Do List" for American Jewry

T his chapter compiles the concrete steps from the 10 planks into a "To Do List" for revitalizing American Jewry. None of the items on this list – as large as each task might be – is out of our reach. If we put our minds to it, we can accomplish the revitalization of American Jewry in a generation. We must simply remember what Moses said to the Jewish people regarding the commandments in the Torah: "[It] is not too complicated for you, nor is it beyond reach. It is not in the heavens…nor is it beyond the sea…this teaching is very close to you."[1] If we keep our mission to revitalize American Jewry in mind, remain confident that this goal is within our reach, and undertake the following concrete projects, we will succeed.

This list is designed to help readers identify those tasks they can or should undertake. Many of us can use this list to choose how to get involved. Others, who already have clear roles in the community as parents or rabbis or board members, can use this list to identify the main issues that they face and help to prioritize those issues they should address first. This list can also help Jews who are involved in specific community institutions identify how and where their time could be spent more effectively. If we belong to a Jewish organization that is inefficient or simply no longer serving the future of Jewry, we should urgently try to fix it, and if it cannot be fixed, we should quit and devote our time, efforts, and funds to more useful projects and let our co-supporters know our reasons for quitting so that they too can think about using their time more efficiently. This list will serve to help us think carefully about being as effective with our time and resources as possible.

The *To Do List* is also not uniform: some of the items, while ambitious, are readily definable and can be implemented quickly but need some cooperation; these include the Israel voucher and the ETP. Other items are less time-consuming but require a great deal of political will and courage to put into place, such as the urgently needed change in the policy of patrilineal descent. Indeed, changing Reform's policy on patrilineal descent is a simple matter operationally, but requires the consent of the majority of Reform rabbis. Reform leaders may have difficulty at first in mustering the political will to effect change; yet since Reform is now the largest American Jewish movement, Reform leaders need to take responsibility for the future of all American Jews. Thus, Reform must change its focus from being like the party of the opposition to being like the party in power. Reform must now do what is best for American Jewry as a whole and not simply what is best for the movement, by thinking of Clal Yisrael (unified Judaism) and *tircha detsibura* (an unacceptable burden on the community) when making all of its decisions.

Many of the programs on the *To Do list* require American Jews to re-direct a substantial amount of money to programs that fund the future of Clal Yisrael. These items will also require more political will than practical effort. The infrastructure for the establishment of the $2,000 voucher for all American Jews 16–25 to travel to Israel on an educational program already exists through the "Gift of Israel" program. To make this item a reality, Federation leaders, philanthropists, and the government of Israel need *only* make a difficult but eminently achievable appropriations decision.

Other *To Do List* items require further conceptual elaboration before they can be implemented. For example, directing the Jewish impulse for social change across all movements in an authentic Jewish form is a huge undertaking. Jews across all movements must get together and think critically about how and where this can be achieved. There have been hopeful signs that a lot of Jews are already moving in this direction: Jews all across the spectrum were active collaborators for the rally in Washington DC on April 30, 2006 to protest the world's lack of action in combating the genocide in Darfur. Social justice opportunities within a Jewish framework are expanding, and Jewish activists on the left are beginning to confront the irrational anti-Semitism of the far left.[2] Yet these are all baby steps in the Jewish mission to perfect the world. We must also elaborate further on the plank of encouraging young Jewish adults to marry at a younger age and have more children. While I have outlined some possible approaches, this plank invites all Jews to think about how we can build happy, healthy Jewish families.

This *To Do List* also has items that each of us can pursue immediately. Each of us can have a Friday night dinner with Kiddush and challah and song this week. We can each decide to make this a family-only event or to invite friends. We can reach out to intermarried couples and their children as soon as we can pick up a phone. We can get more involved in our children or grandchildren's Jewish educational experiences at any time. We can make this summer a year for a Jewish camping experience or an Israel experience. For those of us approaching a bar/bat mitzvah renewal age, we can start working on the appropriate Jewish learning, social action and ritual experience that we want to take up. As members of Jewish organizations, we can put the appropriate planks on the next meeting agenda. We can each subscribe to *The Daily Alert* and become more knowledgeable about external issues affecting Israel and Jews worldwide.

Getting Our Groove Back – How to Energize American Jewry

This *To Do List* is arranged by individual and organization, and as a result many items are deliberately repeated, since they involve the participation of many individuals. As you read the *To Do List* below, make your own personal *To Do List*. Together, we can re-make the future of American Jewry.

TO DO LIST FOR AMERICAN JEWRY

Parents

- Take Hebrew schooling seriously – get involved:
  Send children to youth groups;
  Send children to Jewish camps;
  Make Shabbat dinners for the entire family.

- Encourage trips to Israel for young adults such as birthright israel.

- Promote longer trips to and programs in Israel for teens and young adults.

- Help children find a mate:
  Talk to teenage boys and girls about marriage and raising a family;
  Encourage men, in particular, to marry earlier.

- Encourage children to start families earlier and to have larger families:
  Discuss with daughters the risks of pregnancy after 35;
  Support and encourage women who have children and careers;
  Acknowledge and validate stay-at-home mothers;
  Accept single mothers who wish to adopt or bear children alone.

- Reorient wedding preparations from a focus on party planning to planning a family and a meaningful future.

- Keep informed about anti-Israelism on university campuses through organizations such as Campus Watch.

Rabbis
- Get involved in making your Hebrew schools better by using an outside facilitator and putting in your own efforts:
  Tell parents that Hebrew school alone, no matter how good, is not enough without camping and youth groups.

- Encourage families to enroll their children in day schools.

With communities, synagogues, rabbis and parents:

- Promote longer trips to and programs in Israel for young adults;
- Speak personally and from the pulpit about marriage and family issues:
  Promote early marriage and larger families;
  Expand pre-marriage counseling sessions dramatically;
  Discuss raising a family during pre-marriage counseling.

With parents and community:
- Reorient wedding preparations from preparing the wedding itself to new family counseling.

Synagogues and communities
With Teachers, Parents, Congregants, Clergy and Students:

- Custom redesign Hebrew schools with an outside facilitator;
- Create youth groups;
- Encourage day school attendance;
- Sponsor Jewish camp open houses.

With Movements:
- Elevate the status of teachers and raise their pay to improve the quality of Hebrew school teaching;
- Sponsor engaging social events for singles.

With Parents:
- Encourage children to start families early and to have larger families:
  Discuss with daughters the risks of pregnancy after 35;
  Support and encourage women who have children and careers;
  Acknowledge and validate stay-at-home mothers;
  Accept single mothers who wish to adopt or bear children alone.

With Members:
- Embrace bar/bat mitzvah renewal learning, social action and rituals as a point of re-engagement for members and as a source of new members.

With Parent and Rabbis:
- Reorient wedding preparations from preparing the wedding itself to planning a family and a future in the Jewish community.

With Federations and Movements:
- Encourage American Jews to invest in projects essential for the future of American Jewish communities.

Day Schools
- Act as a resource for local Hebrew schools

- Improve current day school funding:
  Implement Egalitarian Tuition Plan (EPT);
  Allocate the net tuition budget to each family based on income;
  Find new sources of funding with a focus on community-wide responsibility.

- Attract more students:

Offer high-level secular and Jewish studies;
Reach out to Jewish students in secular private schools;
Provide more entry points for children who wish to attend day schools.

With Hebrew Schools and Synagogues:
- Offer discounts for multiple children.

Day Camps
- Add one overnight Shabbat experience to the summer;
- Hire Israeli teenagers as counselors.

Movements
- Invest in Hebrew school leadership (principals);
- Encourage more choice in supplemental day schools.

With Synagogues:
- Elevate the status of teachers and raise their pay to improve the quality of Hebrew school teaching.

With Federations:
- Measure the quality of Hebrew schools and make the results known.

Reform Movement:
- Establish clear boundaries for intermarriage;
    - Encourage conversion of the non-Jewish spouse;
    - Establish a clear conversion procedure;
    - Modify patrilineal descent:
    Offer provisional membership to the Jewish people to children of Jewish fathers until bar/bat mitzvah; if the child then wishes to be called to the Torah as a full member of the Jewish people, he/she should then be converted.
- Unify the worldwide Reform definition of "who is a Jew";

- Accept responsibility for all American Jews as the largest American Jewish Movement.

Conservative Movement:
- *Reinvent the Conservative Movement as an association of mini-Movements:*
    Abandon a fixed theology to bind all members;
    Abolish the single Law Committee;
    Accept divergence in theology: establish separate law committees for component mini-movements;
    Commit to day school education;
    Establish and declare boundary principles guided by practice: Shabbat, kashrut, synagogue attendance, tzedakah, Torah learning, matrilineal descent, halachic conversions, commitment to Israel, and support for day schools.

Orthodox
- Recognize that no part of the Jewish community can stand apart from the rest;
- Acknowledge that as the most visible part of the Jewish community, personal ethical behavior on the part of Orthodox Jews is crucial to the image of all Jews;
- Embrace the social justice aspect of Torah Judaism.

Federations and Jewish Organizations

- Create a $2,000 Israel voucher as a birthright for all American Jews.

With Jewish Cultural Groups:
- Offer child care options at the same time as meetings for adults;
- Redirect funding to institutions critical for the future of American Jewish communities;

- Develop a clear vision of how to advance the American Jewish Community:
  Convince wealthy donors to contribute proportionally more to essential Jewish institutions than to universities, symphonies, hospitals or non-essential Jewish institutions;
  Cut surplus bureaucracy;
  Cut funding for inefficient agencies.

With Movements and Synagogues:
- Encourage American Jews to invest in projects essential to the future of American Jewish communities.

With Jewish Organizations:
- Put the future of the Jewish community ahead of the survival of the organization.

With Hillel and Jewish Social Justice Groups:
- Promote Jewish social action opportunities for college and post-college age students.

Anti-Defamation Organizations
- Stop directing efforts towards governmental discrimination;
- Stop the campaign against the Christianization of America;
- Focus on the external threats that endanger Jews today;
- Focus on a constructive dialogue with our Christian neighbors.

Each American Jew
- Work toward making the egalitarian tuition plan (ETP) for day schools a reality:
- Contribute to Jewish educational institutions.
- Promote the efficient use of resources:
  Advocate merging overlapping institutions.
- Make significant donations to causes essential to the future of American and world Jewish communities:

> *Redirect the missions of historic organizations to better tackle today's most urgent problems;*
> *Speak out against and cut non-essential mega-projects.*

- Encourage mega-donations for causes essential to the future of American and world Jewish communities:
  > *Advocate creating a society of Chaverim to honor mega-donors and promote future funding.*
- Become better informed about current events:
  > *Get alternative news information on Intenet sites;*
  > *Subscribe to the Daily Alert;*
  > *Sign up for e-mail lists.*
- Denounce smear campaigns about Israel in the media or at universities.
- Confront scholars who use neo-Nazi and or Communist sources in their writings.
- Reduce our oil consumption:
  > *Buy more fuel-efficient cars;*
  > *Keep the heat down in the winter;*
  > *Turn off the lights when leaving a room;*
  > *Support alternative energy sources;*
  > *Back politicians who advocate saving energy and finding energy alternatives to oil. In particular, back policies that support the construction of a SuperGrid.*

As Members of Movements
- Discourage intermarriage:
- *Forbid clergy from performing mixed marriages.*
- Promote Jewish identity among intermarried couples:
  > *Reach out to intermarried couples;*
  > *Encourage the non-Jewish spouse of intermarriage to convert;*
  > *Encourage intermarried Jewish dads to raise their children Jewishly;*
  > *Invite less affiliated families to your home for Shabbat dinner.*

- Celebrate bar/bat mitzvah renewal every 18 years.

- Encourage adult Jewish learning:
  Integrate adult Jewish learning into the bar/bat mitzvah milestone celebrations;
  Tailor Jewish learning for each milestone: 31, 49, 67, 85.
- Declare one year each decade as the year of the Hebrew school.

As Members of Jewish Organizations
- Harness Jewish impulse for social action:
  Direct the impulse for social actions towards causes that enhance Jewish unity;
  Ground social action in Jewish values;
  Ensure that the Jewish Coalition for Service (JCS) is grounded in Jewish values;
  Warn young Jews of the dangers to Jews of Jewish involvement in social action divorced of Jewish values.
- Allow for internal dialogue about Israel:
  Give space to critiques of Israeli society and politics that do not put the existence of the state into question;
  Clarify the difference between supporting Israel's right to exist and supporting all of the policies of the Israeli government;
  Focus on Israel as a place for Jewish social action;
  Become more knowledgeable about Israel and Jewish issues.
- Commit to personal ethical behavior both between Jews and between Jews and non-Jews:
  Celebrate Jewish models of ethical behavior.
- Promote the Jewish meaning of tzedakah as responsibility, not charity:
  Promote tzedakah that ensures the future of Jewish communities in America and around the world.

- Build coalitions with other communities targeted by Muslim fundamentalists.

- Build coalitions with American Christians:
  *Engage in open dialogue with Christian groups and organize joint trips to Israel and the West Bank;
  Encourage Christians to visit Israel and the West Bank.*

- Speak out for threatened Christian minorities:
  Assist Christians in developing strategies to help their co-religionists.

- Engage in dialogue with patriotic moderate Muslims.

As Philanthropists
- Keep informed about anti-Israelism on university campuses through organizations such as Campus Watch before you donate to a given university.
- Withhold donations to universities that do not address anti-Semitism and anti-Israelism.
- Redirect donations to causes that will enhance the Jewish future.
- Support and aspire to be a member of the society of Chaverim.

Notes
1. Dvarim 30:11–14.
2. Jewish left-wing activists recently created "The Chavurah of Allies," which seeks to cleanse the left of anti-Semitism at a recent conference on social action and anti-Semitism. For a discussion of the conference, which drew seventy participants, see Dough Chandler, "The Left Looks Inward," *The Jewish Week*, April 14, 2006.

Chapter xiv

Putting it All Together – A Theory of Everything

"Where there is no vision the people perish."
Book of Proverbs, 29:18.

In order to renew American Jewry we must put our efforts into all of the planks for renewal. We must also have courage, leadership, persistence and vision and act with a positive outlook in order to succeed.

Building a Solid Platform:

Each plank in this platform is essential for the effective renewal of American Jewry, and every plank fortifies the others. We cannot fall into the trap of believing that any one initiative alone is powerful enough to be a panacea for Jewish renewal. If we do not build a solid platform for renewal, our hopes and dreams for American Jewry will fall through the cracks. Even implementing Chapter iv – sending half of American Jewish children to day school – is no panacea. Although day schools are effective conveyers of Jewish identity to the next generation, American Jewry will continue to decline if we do not improve the net fertility rate among Jewish women, as addressed in chapter VI. At the same time, if we succeed in implementing the objective of improving day school enrollment, day school graduates will likely have more children, whom they in turn will likely also send to day school. Larger day school enrollment will likely increase our ability to fund day schools as a community. Likewise, the combination of Hebrew schools, youth groups, camping and home-based Jewish experiences will likely lead to more demand for teen multi-week travel to Israel. In turn, teen Israel trips will lead to more Jewishly active college students who will be able to direct their impulse for social action in an authentic Jewish direction, which will also enable students to combat anti-Israelism on campus more effectively. Thus, no plank can succeed alone, and together they form a solid platform, each reinforcing the other even when they seem unrelated.

In short, we must do everything in our power to revitalize American Jewry and make it great. Our platform must address both the urgent problem of the dramatic demographic decline of American Jewry and implement our fundamental purpose on this planet. In order to achieve this goal we must act with creativity, courage, persistence, leadership, passion, and with a clear vision of how to successfully revitalize American Jewry.

Creativity

Now is the time to be creative. As a community, we American Jews too often get stuck in a rut. We go through the motions in our rituals. We sustain organizations long after they have outlived their usefulness. We get locked into choosing sides in battles that no longer make sense. We determine that one movement is too lax and another is too fanatical. Our opinions on Israeli politics divide us even if we have no vote there. These and other examples of tired thinking must stop. We must re-examine the issues that currently challenge American Jewry with a wider lens and come up with solutions by thinking outside the box. Bringing Jews together from across the spectrum, as well as inviting Jews from

outside current institutions to adapt rather than create new organizations *de novo* will also help us to be more creative. We can no
longer afford to do the same old thing, since the same old results
will be devastating. These planks are one set of solutions; they are
also an invitation to be more creative.

Courage

In previous generations we needed courage just to survive in a
hostile world. Thankfully, in America today, we need the courage to thrive. In order to build a solid platform for the renewal
of American Jewry, we need personal, familial, congregational,
institutional and leadership courage to make difficult decisions
and willpower to implement bold changes. We need the personal
courage to make changes in our lives and redirect our resources
in a way that will build a renewed Jewish future. We also need
willpower to renew our bar/bat mitzvah commitments, to make
a volunteer commitment, and to arrange soccer around Hebrew
school and not vice versa. Our Federation and philanthropic leaders need courage to shift funding from legacy agencies that are no
longer enhancing the Jewish future to those that are. Our rabbis
need the courage to talk about family planning with couples who
are about to be married and tell parents that any Hebrew school,
as good as it might become after being re-invented, will fail their
children if they do not ensure that their children are also exposed
to Jewish experiences such as camping, youth groups, and most
importantly, Shabbat dinner at home. The Conservative Movement needs courage to reinvent itself in a post-denominational
mode, and the Reform Movement needs courage to recognize
its responsibility to all Jewry and therefore modify its stance on
patrilineal descent. It will also take courage for various streams
of Orthodoxy to join with the other movements in the universal
Jewish quest for social justice. Facing the brutal truth is a classic
Jewish strength. This too takes courage. If we can confront the
truth about the current direction that American Jewry is headed
in, we can finally begin to imagine a better future.

Persistence

In order to renew American Jewry we must be persistent; we must think long-term – starting with a twenty year perspective – and follow through with the changes we implement. Few of our efforts will bear fruit overnight, including those initiatives we can begin immediately. The beauty of a Shabbat dinner becomes most apparent if we persist in making it a weekly tradition. The result of changing our educational paradigms will only be clear when our children become adults, start to have their own families and begin to decide where their children will go to school and so on. We also need to create milestones over the next fifty years in order to ensure that our efforts are leading us on the right path. Monitoring a program's success will ensure that it is a long-term success. There is no doubt that we can create an overall change to the environment as we described in Chapter 1. However, this requires us to cool the environment consistently over the long term. Luckily, we have a long history of being persistent: you do not get to be a 3,500 year old people without being persistent, and yes, a little stubborn too.

Leadership

American Jewry sorely needs leaders who are visionary, creative, courageous, intelligent, persistent, charismatic and most of all, leaders who will place the needs of Clal Yisrael ahead of the parochial needs of their own particular organizations. Our greatest Jewish leaders had the ability to envision a radically different future from the condition of Jewish life during their life-time. They were also persistent and understood that they would not see the full results of their efforts during their lifetime. There have been such leaders throughout Jewish history, but Moses, Ezra, Mordechai, Rabbi Yochanan ben Zakai and Theodor Herzl stand out. Each of these heroes had the personal courage to confront both internal and external threats. Each had the vision to see beyond the conventional wisdom of his day. Each exhibited the highest level of personal integrity. At the same time, each of these heroes was a realist and recognized the limits of his abilities to effect change in the short term. But most importantly, these leaders thought about the long-term good of all of Clal Yisrael, not just their community, or as is the case today, organization, even when implementing local policies. We must look to our past great leaders as role models in order to become the visionary leaders of tomorrow.

Passion

The greatest Jewish leaders have been passionate people who inspired a passionate following. As these leaders raised the consciousness of their followers, the followers understood and internalized the passion needed to reach a new era. We need widespread passion to make the platform successful. We need more individuals who feel passionate enough about Jewish education to make teaching a career. We need donors who care more about the Jewish future than having their names on a college campus building. We need families who feel passionate enough to invite an unaffiliated family to their home to experience a Shabbat dinner. Passion creates the positive energy to transform American Jewry and make the world a better place. As we say in the Sh'ma: you shall you shall love your God with *all* your heart, *all* your soul and *all* of your resources. Passion is a deeply cherished Jewish value; we need more of it.

Vision

We cannot renew American Jewry without a clear vision of the American Jewish future we desire. As Mark Twain said, "You can't depend on your eyes when your imagination is out of focus." Each and every one of us should make the effort to imagine a brighter American Jewish future. We should also share our vision so that we multiply our inspiration and our readiness for the tasks that lie ahead. The following chapter describes my own vision of the American Jewish future. Take from it what you wish and use it as a springboard for your own imagination.

Chapter xv

The Future Can Be Bright

On a cool Friday night in Autumn circa 2030, two older gentlemen sit at a table chatting. Each has owned and operated fashionable restaurants on the Upper East Side of Manhattan for decades, and observed the changes in their customers' habits. One of the gentlemen notes, while opening a bottle of seltzer, that Friday night used to be the busiest night of the week twenty-five years ago, but no more. Now, just about all the Jews are home for Shabbat dinner. His friend sips his glass of gin and responds, with the hint of a grimace, that the idea of a family dinner once a week has even caught on with non-Jews. He adds with a full scowl that his children and grandchildren want to begin this tradition in their own homes. They are talking about designating Friday night, since it is grandpa's slowest night. After another drink, they both comment about the growing popularity of vegetarian, non-shellfish items on their menus.

Although these two gentlemen might prefer a busier Friday night at their respective restaurants rather than the slowdown they have observed, by 2030 the revival of American Jewry has had remarkable benefits for the U.S. America's Jewish population well exceeds 6 million, a level last reached in 1980. All of the focus on pre-marital counseling, earlier marriages, and larger families has begun to bear fruit: divorce rates are down, Jews are marrying other born and converted Jews and the American Jewish population is increasing at a brisk rate. Jewish day schools continue to grow in number, size, and quality, serving as centers of learning, community and caring. Half of all American Jewish children are getting high quality Jewish day school educations. Supplemental Hebrew schools are housed in day schools and share teachers who make a decent salary. Day schools and synagogues are also more concerned about the lives of their member families and the larger Jewish community. American Jews in turn have become more community-oriented: most people stop at the home of an elderly or infirm individual who is homebound on Shabbat and other holidays on their way to the synagogue. Jewish communities all over America are thriving.

By 2030 parents, educators and the community have been nourishing the Jewish identity and education of our children for over twenty years. The quality of Jewish and secular education at day schools and Hebrew schools is superb. Other educational networks study our schools. The best colleges and universities vie for day school graduates. Children also go to college with the experience of enriching and fun Jewish camping and youth group adventures. Virtually every young Jew has visited Israel on an organized tour before or during college. Young American Jews have become more involved in Israeli politics and society. Interestingly, the American Jewish experience has ignited a full-fledged and diverse Israeli Jewish renewal movement.

Greater commitment among American Jews to the future of American and world Jewry has brought American Jews and Israelis closer together. Though many American Jews sometimes disagree with our Israeli brothers and sisters, we work together on humanitarian projects in Israel, America and the rest of the world. We have also learned from each other: Israeli Jews have carefully examined the American experience with minority groups as Israel works toward creating an environment of civil equality for its Israeli-Arab minority. Israel has also taken the best of the American work ethic and is increasingly affluent as a result. Israelis now encourage American Jews to direct more of their dollars to domestic American Jewish educational causes and the aliyah of Jewish communities around the world that have lost their critical mass. By 2030 American Jewish children have a high comfort level with their Jewish identity and continue to work for the future of American Jewry and Jews across the world as adults.

By 2030, all the Jewish movements in America are blossoming again. The Conservative Movement of 2030 has its groove back. A burgeoning number of mini-movements have transformed the architecture of Conservative synagogues. It is now common to find three *minyanim* conducted simultaneously on a Shabbat morning in separate areas. From monolithic frontal services conducted by the clergy, Conservative services have become participatory in the extreme. The movement is also much more responsive to laity. A variety of law committees have emerged, each much closer to the congregant level and more willing to adjudicate cases actually affecting the day-to-day lives of Conservative Jews. Theology no longer divides the movement. Instead, the mini-movements of Conservative Jews across America are united by the observance of Shabbat, kashrut, tzedakah and furtherance of Jewish education. All three major movements exhibit decisive growth in synagogue membership. From decade to decade the identity of the largest movement may change as a result of growth, yet each movement comes to think of itself as the leading movement. As a result, all of the movements consider the implications of their actions on the rest of the Jews in America and the world, rather than thinking solely about their own narrow interests. Virtually all streams of Jewry accept one definition of a Jew. With all of its warts, something akin to the Denver experiment on conversion has become normative in the United States. American Jewry is diverse, but it is also united by a common commitment to Clal Yisrael.

By 2030 Jewish values permeate the lives of every American Jewish adult. Jews look forward to the bar/bat mitzvah renewal, which has proven to be a key ingredient of the self-sustaining renewal of American Jewry. With the motivation created by these celebrations, adult Jewish literacy has reached new heights. The success of these celebrations has led our American brethren, of all religious persuasions, to consider rededication milestones of their own. Our neighbors have also noted a high level of personal ethics among Jews. In business, most Americans take it for granted that a handshake on a deal with most Jewish businessmen is as good as a written contract. This high standard of personal ethics is the hallmark of American Jewry in all professional and personal relations.

The caring exhibited by American Jews extends far beyond the borders of the American Jewish community and world Jewry. By 2030, Jews are known as leading hearts when it comes to humanitarian causes and social justice. Most American Jews commit to a full-time volunteer experience at some point during their lifetimes. American Jews are the first to respond to humanitarian outrages and attempted genocides across the globe. A partnership of American Jewish and Christian groups has successfully worked to improve the lives of minority Christians in lands of oppression. Social action by Jews and Christians stopped major genocidal attempts in real time. Other joint initiatives halted genocidal plans before they could be implemented. The far left no longer equates all that is good with anti-Israelism, as the practice of genuine good deeds has trumped theology. American Jews are a light in this nation.

The American Jewish experience as seen from 2030 embodies Moses' desire that Torah and a Jewish way of life should ignite a virtuous competition among the various peoples of the globe to improve our world. The Jewish way of life "will be proof of your wisdom and discernment to other peoples who upon hearing of all these laws will say 'surely [the Jewish people] is a wise and discerning people.'"[1] The American Jews of 2030 know that there is no contradiction between ensuring the survival of the Jewish people and the success of our universalist mission on this planet.

Even the renewal of our community in less than 25 years is itself an example for others. Our personal behavior allows us to be "a light unto the nations" each and every day for the other Americans we meet and do business with. American Jews are a proud link in the 3,500 year history of the Jewish people and a cornerstone of American life.

The world I imagine in 2030 is a world that I would like to be privileged to live in, and if we implement the platform with courage and persistence, this vision is an achievable goal. Abraham Lincoln said "You cannot escape the responsibility of tomorrow by evading it today." He could not have been more correct. We American Jews have not adequately prepared for our future. This platform is designed to put active planning for the future at the top of today's agenda. Our sages gave us some guidance in this endeavor when they said:

> *The day is short*
> *The task is great.*
> *It is not up to you*
> *To complete the work.*
> *Yet you cannot concede it.*[2]
> *All beginnings are hard.*[3]
> *If not now, when?*[4]

Notes

1. Deuteronomy 4:6.
2. Pirke Avot 2:20–21.
3. Midrash Mechilta, Parshat Yitro.
4. Pirke Avot 1:14.

Acknowledgments

W hen I gently told my wife, Susan, and my children, Benjamin, Ariel, Alison, and Abigail that I was seriously thinking about writing a book that reflected my thinking on where American Jewry was headed and how to alter its current course, they were – to say the least – surprised. The fact that I had thought a lot about the state of American Jewry and had many strong (and reasoned) opinions on the subject was not a surprise to Susan and my older children, Benjamin and Ariel. But that I intended to formulate these opinions into a book was, to say the least, unexpected. Nevertheless, Susan immediately encouraged me to go forward with my plan, although she probably mustered all of her self-control to do so, considering my demanding day job and my many commitments to various Jewish communal organizations. She has continued to support this endeavor ever since. Benjamin also encouraged me and even accepted the occasional conscription to track down particularly elusive facts for the book. Ariel, Alison and Abigail each let me know that they were sure I would finish the book even when I had my doubts. This book is dedicated to my family.

While I have been involved in Jewish organizations, whether as an active volunteer, officer, or director, since I was elected treasurer of my local USY chapter at age 15, I could not imagine writing this book without five particularly formative Jewish communal experiences. They are: the two years I spent at Ida Crown Jewish Academy, after transferring from public school at the start of 11th grade; my junior year abroad at the Hebrew University; my term as President of the Hillels of New York; my participation in the Wexner Heritage Foundation's Jewish Learning and Leadership program; and my term as Chair of UJA-Jewish Federation of New York's Commission on Jewish Identity and Renewal. During each of these experiences, I benefited from the generosity of visionary philanthropists, the creativity and kindness of colleagues/fellow students, and the wisdom and experience of teachers, rabbis, and staff professionals. To list each and everyone of these people would require at least another volume. Therefore, to all the people who should be on this list, I want to convey my deepest thanks.

A number of people have provided me with invaluable assistance during the writing of this book. I would like to extend a special thanks to Chaya Kirschbaum who greatly assisted me during the home stretch of completing this book. Chaya challenged me to sharpen arguments by articulating imaginative counter-arguments and by pointing out needless diversions in the text. Her editorial suggestions were invariably spot on. I could not have met my deadline without Chaya's assistance. I would also like to extend a special thanks to my long-time administrative assistant, Nancy Leo. Nancy tirelessly deciphered all of my hand written drafts, some of which I wrote while on planes, trains, and other moving vehicles. She also made specific editing suggestions that I incorporated in the book. I would like to thank Andrea Meiseles, Alexander Joffe, Sarah Wunder and Jay Klotz who provided research assistance on specific sections of the book.

I also benefited greatly from the comments, advice, insight, and encouragement of friends and colleagues who read most or all of the manuscript. Thank you to Harvey Arfa, Alan Barnett, Moti Bar-Or, Saul Berman, Calanit Dovere-Valfer, Benjamin Egnatz, Haskel Lookstein, Bruce Ruben, Steve Salinger, and Ron Scheinberg. My friends and colleagues, David Ebstein, Josh Elkin and Charles Jacobs read specific chapters that I asked them to consider carefully. I also want to express my heartfelt thanks to my friend Tobi Kahn who gave me crucial guidance at specific times during this project.

I would also like to extend my thanks to my publisher Yaacov Peterseil, the CEO of Devora Publishing and my editor Ari Goldman. Yaacov read an early draft of the manuscript for this book and quickly embraced the project. He gently, but nonetheless effectively, prodded me toward completing the manuscript. Yaacov's enthusiasm and tireless efforts were of great assistance to me. I also greatly appreciate Ari Goldman's suggestions. As a first time author, I felt some trepidation delivering my manuscript to such a talented editor and author. However, Ari made me feel very comfortable and gave me truly thoughtful suggestions about my ideas and choice of words.

I would also like to acknowledge my debt to a number of Jewish scholars and Jewish community leaders. I would like to thank Steven M. Cohen whose amazing contribution to the entire study of American Jewry was an essential source throughout this project. I have had the privilege to enjoy challenging conversations with Steve over the years. I have also learned a great deal from my lay colleagues and the staff at the Commission on Jewish Identity and Renewal. My debt to them is unquantifiable. In particular, my conversations with Deborah Joselow, the chief professional of CoJIR, have deepened my appreciation for thinking through the long-term consequences of funding decisions.

Although, this book has been a personal project, I would be remiss not to note and thank my close business associates, partners and friends Lew Ranieri, Joe DePaolo, Bob Perro, and John Tamberlane who have all inspired me with their ability to turn vision into reality.

Even with all the people to whom I owe a debt of gratitude, I should still note that I am entirely responsible for the contents of this book. I am solely to blame for any fault, error or mischaracterization found herein.

Finally, I would like to mention my father of blessed memory,

George Shay, z"l, who was liberated from a concentration camp by the U.S. Army. He was then nursed back to health by Americans in a U.S.-run hospital in occupied Germany, and re-built his life in the U.S. After arriving in Chicago, he married my mother Helene neé Forman who also had a tremendous influence on me. My father conveyed to me his deep felt sense of American patriotism and his view that one should always be optimistic and persistent. My father's fifth yarhtzeit approaches as I complete these words. This book is a testament to many of his values.

I conclude by reciting the *Shehechiyanu* blessing. I thank the Almighty for giving me the life that I have, for preserving me, and for bringing me to this point in my life so that I could write and complete this book.

New York, New York
July 9, 2006
13 Tammuz, 5766

Bibliography

Demographic studies

United Jewish Communities in cooperation with The Mandell L. Berman Institute – North American Jewish Data Bank. *The National Jewish Population Survey 2000-2001: Strength, Challenge, and Diversity in the American Jewish Population* (New York: United Jewish Communities, 2002), http://www.ujc.org/content_display.html?ArticleID=60346, accessed June 2006.

United Jewish Communities. *National Jewish Population Survey 2000–01 Orthodox Jews: A United Jewish Communities Presentation of Findings* (New York: United Jewish Communities, February 2004), http://www.ujc.org/content_display. html?ArticleID=155417, accessed June 2006.

United Jewish Communities. *National Jewish Population Survey 2000–01 Conservative Jews: A United Jewish Communities Presentation of Findings* (New York: United Jewish Communities, February 2004), http://www.ujc.org/content_display. html?ArticleID=155417, accessed June 2006.

Ament, Jonathon. "American Jewish Religious Denominations,"

United Jewish Communities Report Series on the National Jewish Population Survey 10 (February, 2005).

Sheskin, Ira M. "Geographic Differences among American Jews," United Jewish Communities Report Series on the National Jewish Population Survey 8 (October 2004), http://www.ujc.org/content_display.html?ArticleID=155417, accessed June 2006.

Cohen, Steven M., and Laurence Kotler-Berkowitz. "The Impact of Childhood Jewish Education on Adults' Jewish Identity: Schooling, Israel Travel, Camping and Youth Groups," *United Jewish Communities Report Series on the National Jewish Population Survey* 3 (July, 2004), http://www.ujc.org/content_display.html?ArticleID=155417, accessed June 2006.

Cohen, Steven M., and Laurence Kotler-Berkowitz, "*The Impact of Childhood Jewish Education on Adults' Jewish Identity: Schooling, Israel Travel, Camping and Youth Groups,*" United Jewish Communities Report Series on the National Jewish Population Survey 2000–01 3 (July 2004), http://acaje.org/content/teen-Education/articles/articles.shtml, accessed June 2006.

DellaPergola, Sergio, and Brig. Gen (Res) Amos Gilboa. *The Jewish People Policy Planning Institute Annual Assessment 2004–2005: Between Thriving and Decline* (Jerusalem: The Jewish People Policy Planning Institute, 2005).

Federation of Jewish Philanthropies of New York. *The Jewish Population of Greater New York: A Profile* (New York: Federation of Jewish Philanthropies of New York, 1984).

Beck, Pearl, Jacob B. Ukeles, and Ron Miller. *The Jewish Community Study of New York: 2002 Geographic Profile* (New York: UJA, June 2004).

Studies

Horowitz, Bethamie. *Connections and Journeys: Assessing Critical Opportunities for Enhancing Jewish Identity* (New York: Commission of Jewish Identity and Renewal – UJA-Federation, June 2000), pp. 100 and 176, http://www.jewishdatabank. org/CJ2003.pdf, accessed June 2006.

Lunz, Frank. *Israel in the Age of 'Eminem* (New York: The Andrea and Charles Bronfman Philanthropies, The Alan B. Slifka Foundation and The Michael and Judy Steinhart Foundation, 2004), http:// www.shalomdc.org/getfile.asp?id=11162 accessed June 2006.

Goodman, Robert Louis, and Eli Schapp. *What are the Numbers of Jewish Educators and Students in Formal Jewish Educational Settings?* (New York: Council for the Advancement of Jewish Education, 2002).

Cohen, Steven M. *A Tale of Two Jewries: The "Inconvenient Truth" for American Jews* (New York: HUC-JIR, June 2006).

Cohen, Steven M., and Judith Schor, *The Alumni of Five Year Israel Experience Programs and their Distinctive Jewish Identity Profiles* (New York: Alliance for Educational Programs in Israel, October 2004), http://alliancedata.org.il/alliance/ downloads/survey2004.pdf.

Cohen, Steven M., and Alan Ganapol, *The 1998 Young Judea Jewish Continuity Study* (New York: Young Judea, March 1999), http://www.youngjudaea.org/html/full_study.html, accessed June 2006.

Diamond, Jack J. "A Reader in Demography," in *American Jewish Year Book* 1977 Volume 77, ed. Morris Fine and Milton Himmelfarb (New York: The American Jewish Committee; Philidelphia: The Jewish Publication Society of America, 1976), http://www.ajcarchives.org/AJC_DATA/Files/Vol_77_1977. pdf, accessed June 2006.

Goodman, Robert Louis, and Eli Schaap. *What are the Numbers of Jewish Educators and Students in Formal Jewish Educational settings?* (New York: CAJE, 2002), http://www.caje-cbank. org/research-njps2.pdf, accessed June 2006.

JESNA, *A Vision for Excellence Report of the Task Force on Congregational and Communal Jewish Education* (New York: JESNA, 2000), http://archive.jesna.org/pdfs/cc_visexc.pdf, accessed June 2006.

JESNA/UJC, *Day school Tuition Subvention, Reduction and Scholarship Programs Affordability Working Group Project* (New York: JESNA/UJC, June 2003), http://archive.jesna.org/pdfs/affordabilityreport.pdf, accessed June 2006.

Sax, Linda J. *America's Jewish Freshman, Current Characteristics and Recent Trends Among Students Entering College* (New York: Hillel, 2002).

Schick, Marvin. *A Census of Jewish Day Schools in the United States 2003–2004* (New York: The AVI CHAI Foundation, 2004), p. 17. http://www.avichai.org/Static/Binaries/Publications/Second%20Census%202003-04_0.pdf, accessed June 2006.

Wertheimer, Jack. *Talking Dollars and Sense about Jewish Education* (New York; Jerusalem: The AVI CHAI Foundation, 2001), http://www.avi- chai.org/Static/Binaries/Publications/ACO50.dollars&sense.print_0.pdf, accessed May 2006.

Saxe, Leonard. Charles Kedushin, Shahar Hecht, Mark I. Rosen, Benjamin Phillips, and Shaul Kelner. *Evaluating birthright israel: Long Term Impact and Recent Findings* (Waltham: The Cohen Center for Modern Jewish Studies, 2004), http://www.cmjs.org/files/evaluatingbri.04.pdf, accessed June 2006.

Tobin, Gary A. Jeffrey R. Solomon, and Alexandra C. Karp, *Mega-Gifts in American Philanthropy: General & Jewish Giving Patterns between 1995–2000.* (San Francisco: Institute for Jewish & Community Research, 2003), p. 1, http://www.jewishresearch.org/PDFs/MegaGift_03_web.pdf, accessed June 2006.

Newspaper articles

Birkner, Gabriella. "Conservative Call for Openness," *The Jewish Week*, December 9, 2005.

Bowley, Graham. "Out of his league," *The Financial Times*, May 12, 2006.

Brawavsky, Sandra. "Repair One Corner of Our World," *The Jewish Week*, December 30, 2005.

Bright, Beckey. "In a Year of Disasters, Americans Continue to Give, Polls Find," *The Wall Street Journal Online*, November 25, 2005.

Cohen, Steven M. "Non Denominational and Post Denominational: Two Tendencies in American Jewry" *Contact Magazine* (Summer 2005).

Donadio, Rachel. "Houston Jews Quaking Over Enron Scandal" *Forward*, February 22, 2002.

Goldman, Ari. "Suzuki Judaism," *The Jewish Week*, September 16, 2005.

Harmon, Amy. "First Comes Baby Carriage," *The New York Times*, October 13, 2005.

Hechinger, John. "When $26 Billion Isn't Enough," *The Wall Street Journal*, December 17–18, 2005.

Hochman, Robert N. "Shifting Blame," *The New Republic*, April 24, 2002.

Interview with Reed Rubenstein, Frontpage Magazine, May 8, 2006.

Kahn, Rebecca. "What we are facing in Campus Wars" *The Jewish Week*, March 21, 2005.

Kaufman, Joe. "The Black Hearts of KindHearts," *FrontPage Magazine*, March 14, 2006, http://www.frontpagemag.com/Articles/ReadArticle.asp?ID=21619, accessed June 2006.

Lerner, Rabbi David. "Toward a Passionate Conservative Judaism," *The Jewish Week*, December 30, 2005.

Leshem, Guy. "Poverty and Crime Rates Reveal Israel's Failure To Absorb Ethiopian Immigrants," *Forward*, October 21, 2005, http://www.forward.com/articles/5160, June 2006.

Mearsheimer, John J., and Stehen M. Walt, "The Israel lobby and U.S. Foreign Policy," *London Review of Books* 28/6 (March 23, 2006) also available on the Internet, http://ksgnotes1.harvard. edu/Research/wpaper.nsf/rwp/RWPO-011/$File/rwp_06_011_ walt.pdf, accessed June 2006.

Pipes, Daniel, and Sharon Chadha, "Islamists Fooling the Establishment," Middle East Quarterly (Spring 2006).

"Poverty level very high in Israel," *The Washington Times*, June 11, 2006, http://washingtontimes.com/upi/20060611-043653-5433r. htm, June 2006.

Rosenbaum, David. "At $500 an Hour, Lobbyist's Influence Rises with G.O.P." *The New York Times*, April 3, 2002.

Rosenblatt, Gary. "'Eminem' Jews Rap Establishment," *The Jewish Week*, May 2, 2003.

Rosenblatt, Gary. "All Eyes on Rabbi Leicher at Povel," *The Jewish Week*, January 20, 2006.

Schick, Marvin. "The Message from Lawrence," *The Jewish* Week, September 16, 2005.

Shapiro, Mendel. "Qeri'at ha-Torah by Women, A Halakhic Analysis," *The Edah Journal* 1:2 (Spring 2001).

Silverman, Jerry. "Where Jewish Leaders are Bred," *Jerusalem Post*, December 9, 2004.

Spencer, Robert "Terror Denial," *FrontPage Magazine*, May 6, 2005, http://www.frontpagemag.com/Articles/ReadArticle. asp?ID=17959, accessed June 2006.

Story, Louise. "Many Women at Elite Colleges Set Career Path to Motherhood," *New York Times*, September 20, 2005.

Wilcock, Nicola. "Animal rights activists convicted in the U.S. of terrorising British lab," *Timesonline,* March 4, 2006, http://www.timesonline.co.uk/article/0,,11069- 2068837,00.html, accessed June 2006.

Wolpe, Rabbi David. "What is Conservative Judaism," *The Jewish Week*, December 16, 2005.

Online Newspaper articles

"Al-Qaida timeline: Plots and attacks," MSNBC *and* NBC *News,* 2006, http://www.msnbc.msn.com/id/4677978/, accessed June 2006.

Beinart, Peter. "No Answer," The New Republic, July 11 2003, http://www.tnr.com/doc.mhtml?i=20030721&s=trb072103S, accessed June 2006.

"Bounty Placed on Eco-terrorism in Washington State," ABC-*News,* 21 September 2005. http://abcnews.go.com/US story?id=1145285&page=1, accessed June 2006.

Ganor, Boaz. "The LAX Shooting, Isolated Criminal Incident or Terror Attack?" *Institute for Counter-Terrorism*, July 4, 2002, http://www.ict.org.il/articles/articledet.cfm?articleid=442/, accessed June 2006.

Goodenough, Patrick. "Catholic Leader Ponders Violence in Koran," *Cybercast News Service*, May 08, 2006. http://www.cnsnews.com/news/viewstory.asp?Page 5CForeignBureaus%5Carchive%5C200605%5CINT20060508b.html, accessed June 2006.

Gossett, Sherrie. "Federal Money Goes to Controversial Muslim Group," *Accuracy in Media*, March 15, 2005, http://www.aim.org/aim_column/2778_0_3_0_C/, accessed June 2006.

"Holocaust on Your Plate," Campaign, which compared the

slaughter of cattle to the Holocaust of European Jews. "Group blasts PETA 'Holocaust' project," CNN, February 28, 2003. http://www.cnn.com/2003/US/Northeast/02/28/peta. holocaust/, accessed June 2006.

Interview with Stephen Schwartz, "The Good & The Bad." *National Review Online*, November 18, 2002, http://www. nationalreview.com/interrogatory/interrogatory111802.asp, accessed June 2006.

Jacobs, Charles. "Slavery: Worldwide Evil," iAbolish American Anti-Slavery group Web site, http://www.iabolish.com, accessed June 2006.

The Public Committee Against Torture in Israel, "Violence Against Palestinian Women," http://www.omct.org/pdf/vaw/2005/ israel_cedaw33rd.pdf, accessed June 2006.

UNDP, *The Time Has Come: A Call for Good Governance in the Arab World: Arab Human Development Report 2004* (New York: UNDP, 2004). http://www.rbas.undp.org/ahdr_2004/1PR_ AHDR04_E.pdf, accessed June 2006.

Books

Adler, Elkan Nathan. *Jewish Travelers; a Treasury of Travelogues from 9 Centuries* (New York: Hermon Press, 1966).

Aron, Isa. *Becoming a Congregation of Learners* (New York: Jewish Lights Publishing, 2000).

Ball, Philip. *Critical Mass: How One Thing Leads to Another* (London: Arrow, 2005).

Bat Ye'or. *Eurabia: The Euro-Arab Axis* (Madison: Fairleigh Dickinson University Press, 2005).

Bawer, Bruce. *While Europe Slept* (New York: Doubleday, 2006).

Brisk, Maria Estela. *Bilingual Education: From Compensatory to Quality Schooling* (Mahwah: Lawrence Erlbaum Associates, 2006).

Cahill, Thomas. *The Gifts of the Jews: How a Tribe of Desert Nomads Changed The Way Everyone Thinks and Feels* (New York: Nan A. Talese, 1998).

Chertak, Fern, Leonard Saxe, and Rebecca Silvera-Sasson, *Exploring the Impact of the Wexner Heritage Program on a Development of Leadership capital in the Jewish Community* (New Albany: Wexner Foundations, November 2005).

Cohen, Steven M., Arnold M. Eisen, *The Jew Within: Self, Family and Community in America* (Bloomington, Indiana University Press, 2000).

Dimont, Max I. *The Indestructible Jews: Is There a Manifest Destiny in Jewish History?* (New York: Signet, 1973).

Ehrlich, M. Avrum. The Messiah of Brooklyn: Understanding Lubavitch Hasidism Past and Present (Jersey City: KTAV Publishing House, 2004).

Elcott, David M. *A Sacred Journey: The Quest for a Perfect World* (Lanham: Jason Aronson Publishers, 1995).

Emerson, Steven. *American Jihad: The Terrorists Living Among Us* (New York: Free Press, 2002).

Fackenheim, Emil L. *The Jewish Return into History: Reflection in the Age of Auschwitz and a New Jerusalem* (New York: Shocken Books, 1978).

Gladwell, Malcolm. *The Tipping Point: How Little Things Can Make a Big Difference* (Boston: Little, Brown, 2000).

Glazer, Nathan. *American Judaism* (Chicago: University of Chicago Press, 1989).

Gleick, James. *Chaos: Making a New Science* (New York: Viking, 1987).

Gordis, Daniel. *Does the World Need the Jews?: Rethinking Chosenness and American Jewish Identity* (New York: Scribner, 1997).

Greenberg, Anna. *OMG! How Generation Y is Redefining Faith in the iPod Era*, (Washington: Greenberg Quinlan Rosner Research, April 2005),, http://www.greenbergresearch.com/index.php?ID=1218, accessed June 2006.

Grundin Denholtz, Elaine. *Balancing Work and Love – Jewish Women Facing the Family-Career Challenge* (Waltham: Brandeis University Press, 2000).

Grzelakowski, Moe. *Mother Leads Best: 50 Women who are Changing the Way Organizations Define Leadership* (Chicago: Dearborn Trade Pub., 2005).

Gutmann, Stephanie. *The Other War: Israelis, Palestinians and the Struggle for Media Supremacy* (San Francisco: Encounter Books, 2005).

Huntington, Samuel P. *Who Are We? The Challenges to America's Identity* (New York: Simon & Schuster, 2004).

Johnson, Spencer. *Who moved my Cheese: An Amazing Way to Deal with Change in Your Work and in Your Life* (New York: G.P. Putnams Sons, 1998).

Katz, Nathan. *Who are the Jews of India?* (Berkeley: University of California Press, 2000).

Katz, Nathan. "The Judaisms of Kaifeng and Cochin" in *Jews in China from Kaifeng to Shanghai*, ed. Roman Malek (Sankt Augustin: Steyler, 2000).

Katz, Eliyahu, and Mordichai Rimor. *Jewish Involvement of the Baby Boom Generation: Interrogating the 1990 National Jewish Population Survey* (Jerusalem; New York: Louis Guttman Israel Institute of Applied Social Research, 1993).

Keynes, John Maynard. *A Tract on Monetary Reform* (London: Macmillan and Co., 1923).

Kind, Desmond. *The Liberty of Strangers: Making the American Nation* (New York: Oxford University Press, 2005).

Kotler, Philip and Eduardo L. Roberto. *Social Marketing: Strategies for Changing Public Behavior* (New York: Free Press, 1989).

Kramer, Martin. *Ivory Towers on Sand* (Washington: The Washington Institute for Near East Policy, 2001).

Lerner, Michael. *Jewish Renewal: A Path to Healing and Transformation* (New York: G.P. Putnams's Sons, 1994).

Lookstein, Haskel. *Were We Our Brothers' Keepers: The Public Response of American Jews to the Holocaust, 1938–1944* (New York: Hartmore House, 1985).

Marcus, Jacob R. Marcus. *To Count a People: American Jewish Population Data 1585–1984* (Lanham: University Press of American 1990).

Martin, Anne. *The Baby Sitters Club – Abby's Lucky Thirteen* (New York: Scholastic Inc., 1996).

Mencken, H.L. "The Divine Afflatus," in *A Mencken Chrestomathy* (New York: Alfred A. Knopf Inc., 1949).

Peers, Robert. *Adult Education* (London: Routledge & Kegan,1958).

Pipes, Daniel. *Militant Islam Reaches America* (New York: W.W. Norton & Company, 2002).

Raphael, Marc Lee. *Judaism In America* (New York: Columbia University Press, 2003).

Roof, Wade Clark, Bruce Greer, Mary Johnson, Andrea Leibson. *A Generation of Seekers: The Spiritual Journeys of the Baby Boom Generation* (New York: HarperCollins, 1993).

Rudin, Rabbi James. *The Baptizing of America: The Religious Right's Plans for the Rest of Us* (New York: Thunder's Mouth Press, 2006).

Sachar, Howard. *A History of the Jews in America* (New York: Knopf, 1992).

Sachar, Howard. *A History of Israel From the Rise of Zionism to Our Time* (New York: Alfred A Knopf Inc. 1976).

Sacks, Jonathan. *A Letter in the Scroll: Understanding Our Jewish Identity and Exploring the Legacy of the World's Oldest Religion* (New York: The Free Press, 2000).

Sales, Amy L. and Leonard Saxe. *"How Goodly are Thy Tents": Summer Camps as Jewish Socializing Experiences* (Lebanon: Brandeis University Press, 2004).

Sarna, Jonathan D. *American Judaism: a History* (New Haven: Yale University Press, 2004).

Shehan, Constance L. *Marriages and Families*, (Boston: Allyn and Bacon, 2003).

Sklare, Marshall, and Joseph Greenblum. *Jewish Identity on the Suburban Frontier* (New York: Basic Books, 1967).

Tocqueville, Alexis de. *Democracy in America,* trans. Henry Reeve (New York: A.A. Knopf, 1980).

Wein, Berel. *Faith & Fate: the Story of the Jewish People in the Twentieth Century* (Brooklyn: Shaar Press, 2001).

Weinstein, Miriam. *The Surprising Power of Family Meals* (Hanover: Steerforth Press, 2005).

Government Documents

Mark, Clyde. *Israel: US Foreign Assistance,* Washington DC: Congressional Research Service, 1997–2003 JTA, February 27, 2003. www.jewishvirtuallibrary.org/ jsource/US-Israel/foreign_aid.html, accessed June 2006.

US Census Data, 2030 Population projections, http://www.census.gov/population/projections/PressTab1.xls.

Journal Articles

Kimmelman, Reuven. "Abraham Joshua Heschel: Our Generation's Teacher," *Melton Journal* No. 15 (Winter 1984).

Liben, Noah. The Columbia University Report on its Middle Eastern Department's Problems: A Methodological Paradigm for Obscuring Structural Flaws, *Jerusalem Center for Public Affairs* April 13, 2005. http://www.jcpa.org/phas/phas-liben-05.htm, accessed June 2006.

Sklare, Marshall, et al. "Forms and Expressions of Jewish Identification," *Jewish Social Studies* 27 (1955).

Weinberg, Rob. "Creating and Enacting Shared Visions for Congregational Education" *Jewish Education News* (Winter, 2006).

Magazine Articles

Cohen, Steven M. "Change in a Very Conservative Movement," *Sh'ma* (February 2006).

Dauber, Jeremy. "When Yiddish was Edgy," *The Jerusalem Report* (February 2006).

Epstein, Rabbi Jerome. "Defining a Conservative Jew," *Sh'ma* (February 2006).

Freedman, James O. "Ghosts of the Past: Anti-Semitism at Elite Colleges," *The Chronicle Review* (December 1, 2000), http://chronicle.com/free/v47/i14/14b00701.htm, accessed June 2006.

Freud, Sigmund. "On Being of the B'nai Brith," *Commentary* (March 1946).

Grant, Paul M. and Chauncey Starr and Thomas J. Overbye,"A Power Grid for the Hydrogen Economy," *Scientific American* (July 2006).

Hodge, Susan E. "To the new Chancellor," *Sh'ma* (February 2006).

Katz, Nathan, and Ellen S. Goldberg, "The Last Jews of India and Burma," *Jerusalem Letter* 101 (April 1988), http://www.jcpa.org, accessed June 2006.

Lerner, Rabbi David. "Toward a Passionate Conservative Judaism," *The Jewish Week*, December 30, 2005.

"Persons of the Year," *Time Magazine*, December 26, 2005.

Pullout section, *Lifestyles Magazine*, (Summer 2005).

"The Richest People in America." Forbes Magazine, October 10, 2005.

Rabbi Shlomo Riskin, "Zalman Bernstein: An Unorthodox Orthodox Baal Teshuvah," *Jewish Action* (Summer 1998), http://www.ou.org/publications/ja/5759summer/bernsteinprofile.pdf, accessed June 2006.

Schwartz, Jeffrey E., "To the new Chancellor," *Sh'ma* (February 2006).

Schwartz, Sidney. "Exodus and Sinai: New Thoughts on Jewish Identity" *Sh'ma* (October 2005).

Twain, Mark. "Concerning The Jews," *Harper's Magazine*, March 1898.

Ukeles, Jacob. "Reinventing the Conservative Movement" *Sh'ma* (2006).

Zeidel, Dassi. "Do the Right Thing," *Jewish Action* 66/2 (Winter 2005).

Pamphlets
Sarna, Jonathan D. *A Great Awakening: The Transformation that Shaped Twentieth century American Judaism and Its Implications For Today* (New York: Council for Initiatives in Jewish Education).

Articles

Cohen-Kiener, Andrea. "The Sh'ma and Ecology," *Genesis 2* (Spring 1989) in *Jews, Money and Social Responsibility* eds. Lawrence Bush and Jeffrey Dekro (Philidelphia: The Shefa Fund, 1993).

Strassfield, Sharon, and Kathy Green. "In Praise of Jewish Day Schools," in *The Jewish Family Book: A Creative Approach to Raising Kids*, eds. Sharon Strassfield and Kathy Green (New York: Bantam Books, 1981).

Speeches

Professor Jonathan Sarna's address to the Rabbinical Assembly, March 6, 2005.

Unpublished articles

Weinberg, Rob. "Programmatic Innovation in Religious Schools of ECE Congregations – Two Examples," (Unpublished article, 2005).

Unpublished paper

Sales, Amy. unpublished paper, (New York, Synergy Conference on Synagogues, January 9, 2006) sponsored by UJA-Federation of New York's Commission on Jewish Identity and Renewal.

Articles on Websites

ADL, "Anti-Israel Protest Calendar", ADL Web site, http://www.adl.org/Israel/israel_protest_calendar_archive.asp, accessed June 2006.

ADL, "ADL Urges U.S. Supreme Court to Reject Government Display of the Ten Commandments as Unconstitutional," ADL Web site, http://www.adl.org/PresRele/SupremeCourt_33/4601_33.htm, accessed June 2006.

Article on Conservative Judaism, "Abraham Joshua Heschel" Jewish Theological Seminary Web site, http://learn@jtsa.edu, accessed June 2006.

Article on Aaron Feuerstein, Aish Web site, http://www.aish.com/societyWork/work/Aaron_Feuerstein_Bankrupt_and_Wealthy.asp, accessed June 2006.

Joffe-Walt, Benjamin "Lecturers back boycott of Israeli academics," *Guardian Unlimited,* Tuesday May 30, 2006, http://education.guardian.co.uk/higher/news/story/0,,1785633,00.html, accessed September 2006.

Lipstadt, Deborah E. "Strategic Responses to Anti-Israelism and Anti-Semitism on the North American Campus" in *American Jewry and the College Campus* (American Jewish Committee), The American Jewish Committee Web site, http://www.ajc.org/site/c.ijITI2PHKoG/b.851479/apps/nl/content3.asp?content_id =%7BB42A429E-4172–432E-90C9–0A8364F4E285%7D&notoc=1, accessed June 2006.

Sacks, Jonathan. "The Practical Implications of Infinity," http://www.chabad.org/library/article.asp?AID=2096, accessed June 2006.

Singer, Paul. "Business schools add ethics in wake of corporate scandals," August 16, 2002, Kellog School of Management Web site, www.kellogg.northwestern.edu, accessed June2006.

Svetlicinii, Alex. "Amnesty International's Gulag Confusion," *Capital Research Center* (May 2006) http://www.capitalresearch.org/pubs/pubs.asp?ID=511, accessed June 2006.

The Anti-Defamation League, "Annual Audit," Anti-Defamation League Web site, http://www.adl.org/PresRele/ASUS_12/audit_2005.htm, accessed June 2006.

The U.S. Campaign to End the Israeli Occupation, "Palestine Solidarity Movement Conference, The U.S. Campaign to

End The Occupation Web site, http://www.endtheoccupation. org/calendar.php?calid=98, accessed September 2006.

The Israel Department of Foreign Affairs, "Israel's Diplomatic Mission Abroad Status of Relations," The Israel Department of Foreign Affairs Web site, http://www.mfa.gov.il/mfa/ about%20the%20ministry/diplomatic%20missions/Israel, accessed June 2006.

The Stephen Roth Institute for the Study of Contemporary Anti-Semitism and Racism at Tel Aviv University, "Annual Report General Analysis 2002–03," The Stephen Roth Institute for the Study of Contemporary Anti-Semitism and Racism Web site, http://www.tau.ac.il/Anti-Semitism/asw2002-3/general. htm, accessed June 2006.

Jewishvirtuallibrary, "Palestinian "Collaborators" Killed, Injured, or Detained," http://www.jewishvirtuallibrary.org/jsource/ Peace/collaborators.html, accessed September 2006.

Wikpedia "Intifada," http://en.wikipedia.org/wiki/First_Intifada, accessed June 2006.

Wikipedia, "Jewish exodus from Arab lands," http://en.wikipedia. org/wiki/Jewish_exodus_from_Arab_lands, accessed September 2006.

Wikipedia, "Leslie Wexner," http://en.wikipedia.org/wiki/Leslie_Wexner, accessed June 2006.

Wikipedia, "Private Schools." http://en.wikipedia.org/wiki/Private_ school#Types_of_private_school_in_North_ America, accessed May 2006.

Internet sites.

David Project Web site, www.davidproject.org, accessed June 2006.

Encyclopedia Britannica Almanac 2004 (Chicago: Encyclopedia

Britannica Corporation, October 2003), www.britannica.com, accessed June 2006.

Jewish Coalition for Social Sevice Web site, www.jewishservice.org, accessed June 2006.

The Manhattan County School Web site, www.manhattancountryschool.org, accessed June 2006.

NGO-Monitor Web site, http://www.ngo-monitor.org/, accessed June 2006.

The Radical Left Web site, http://www.radicalleft.net, accessed June 2006.

The U.S. Campaign to End the Israeli Occupation Web site http://www.endtheoccupation.org/groups.php, accessed June 2006.

World Organization Against Torture (OMCT) Web site, http://www.omct.org/pdf/vaw/2005/israel_cedaw 33rd.pdf, accessed June 2006.

U.S. Census Data, 2030 Population projections, http://www.census.gov/population/projections/PressTab1.xls, accessed June 2006.

Index

A

Abramoff, Jack, 242–244, 247, 248
Aliyah, 4, 275
American Jewry
  as part of general American
    society, 71, 124–126, 137, 138, 186,
    191, 205, 212, 216, 240, 241
  Renewal, 3, 6–8, 99, 121, 130, 132, 140,
    142, 182, 183, 240, 267, 269, 276, 277,
    280, 281
  wealth of, 3, 80, 83, 121, 127, 142, 225,
    245, 249, 251, 252
Anti-defamation groups, 128, 129, 130,
    215, 224
Anti-Israelism, 127, 206–211, 216, 221,
    222, 234, 237, 258, 266, 268, 276
Anti-Semitism and Anti-Semites
  in America, 20, 36, 42, 205–207,
    213–216, 219, 225, 246, 247
  in universities, 127, 210, 211, 222, 266
Assimilation, 12, 17, 24, 25, 42, 43, 124,
    138

B

B'tzelem Elokim, 150, 232
Baby boom, 102, 103, 105, 117, 118,

Bar/Bat Mitzvah
  and education, 59, 158–160, 167, 168,
    265
  and milestones, 155, 158, 159, 161, 163,
    166–168, 240, 261, 265
  Renewal ceremonies, 165, 170,
    172–175, 177–181, 183, 257, 265, 269,
    275
Bible, 91, 135–137, 151, 216
birthright israel
  attendance, 87, 92–99, 258
  impact, 92–95

C

Career/Family balance, 106, 108, 109,
    113–115, 171, 174, 175, 250
Carter, Stephen, 245, 246
CCAR, 148, 159, 193
Chabad, 21, 23
Chareidi/Fervently Orthodox
  dependence on other groups, 23
  fundraising, 23
  growth in numbers, 21
  isolationist communities, 21, 22, 23
Charity
  distribution of, 80

Jewish vs. non-Jewish causes, 122, 124
non-essential causes, 127, 128, 263, 264
overlapping causes, 129, 130, 263
"Chaverim, Society of ", 132, 133, 264, 266
Christian Evangelism, 129
Conservative Movement
    and Halacha, 185, 187–189, 193, 199, 201
    and homosexual clergy, 185, 192, 193, 199, 202
    affiliation, 194
    crisis, 41, 44, 186, 187
    egalitarianism, 192
    historically, 185, 187
    leadership, 189–191, 197–199, 202
    post-denominational, 197, 202, 269
Conversion and Converts
    and impact on Jewish People, 150, 155
    and intermarriage, 261
    and patrilineal descent, 261
    historically, 150, 151
    process, 160

D
Daily Alert, 218, 257, 264
David Project, 210, 224
Definition of a Jew
    and citizenship 152–154
    and Law of Return, 152
    Halachic, 32
Delayed Marriage, 45, 106
Demographics
    and physics, 11, 12, 18, 20, 25, 27
    figures, 31, 32, 34, 37
    New York, 22, 34, 35, 37
    population density, 18

E
Egalitarian Tuition Plan, 74, 76, 77, 79, 260, 263
Eisen, Arnold, 202
Enron, 243, 248
European-Arab Dialogue, 265

F
Far Left, 205, 206, 211, 215, 225, 234–236, 257, 276
Fastow, Andrew, 243, 244, 247, 248
Fertility rates
    and infertility, 110
    as result of delayed marriage, 40–42, 45, 101–103, 105, 106, 109, 110, 111, 268
Feuerstein, Aaron, 244, 245, 247, 248
"Five Percent Answer", 79, 80, 84
Frayhayt, 234
Freud, Sigmund, 169, 170, 202
Fundraising, 23, 74, 75, 78, 97, 128, 251

H
Heschel, Rabbi Abraham Joshua, 186, 246, 247, 248
Hillel, the sage, 20, 125, 243
Hillel on campus, 33, 43, 93, 239, 240, 250, 263, 280
Holocaust, 89, 103, 104, 128, 152, 214, 234
Honor Killings, 235

I
Immigration from FSU, 33, 34, 42, 43, 46
Intermarriage
    and freedom of choice, 17, 36, 145, 146, 149
    and informal education, 93
    and Jewish affiliation, 194, 261, 264
    and Jewish identity, 46, 147, 155, 167
    as form of tolerance, 146
    descendants of, 37, 38, 102, 145, 147, 156–158, 160, 163
    in America, 21, 145–148, 162
Islamic Fundamentalism
    in America, 128, 212, 213, 215
    in Europe, 206, 217, 219
    worldwide, 207, 208, 217, 220, 222, 224
"Israel Lobby and U.S. Foreign Policy", 211
Israel Travel Voucher, 95

J

Joint Distribution Committee, 81

Jenin, 207

Jewish Agency, 81, 97

Jewish Camping

    as positive experience 49, 59–62, 84, 90, 134, 199, 257, 259, 268, 269, 274

    cost of, 126

Jewish Education

    adult, 38, 57, 150, 168, 170, 171, 181, 182, 265

    and community, 22, 75

    benefits, 69, 78

    cost, 54, 57, 72–74, 76–78

    day school, 69, 72

    ECE, 56

    figures, 33, 38, 42, 43, 69, 147

    Hebrew school, 51, 54

    informal, 59. 60, 61, 81

    Orthodox, 22

    parental involvement, 49, 59, 175, 257

Jewish Federations, 81–83, 97

Jewish Identity, 11, 20, 22, 24, 45, 169–170

    and Bar/Bat Mitzvah (see Chapters 8 and 9)

    and cultural experiences, 26

    and education, 52, 70, 158

    and intermarriage (see Chapter 8)

    and Israel trips (see Chapter 5)

    and isolation, 22, 23, 169, 180, 252

Jewish leadership, 25, 182

Jewish mission

    as "a light unto the Nations", 225, 229, 239, 251, 277,

    as a moral compass, 135

    justice, 221, 229, 231–234, 238, 239, 245, 252, 257, 262, 269, 276

    responsibility to others, 57, 74, 75, 78, 79, 81, 82, 83, 89, 138, 142, 148, 176, 236, 238, 249, 256, 260, 262, 269, 277

    Tikkun olam, 163, 229, 240, 241, 251

Jewish Outreach Institute, 156

Jihad, 208, 213, 216, 218, 220, 222

M

Missionaries, 42

Moderate Muslims, 208, 220, 221, 266,

Muslim Organizations, 213

Oil, 209, 211, 218, 222, 223, 264

Oral Law, 187, 243

Orthodoxy

    response to existential threats, 194

    revival, 195

Palestinian Authority, 207, 235

Patrilineal Descent

    and conversion rates, 155

    and provisional Jewish Membership, 158–162

Pittsburgh Platform, 157, 195

Purim story, 7

Reform Movement

    and intermarriage 145, 147, 148, 155, 158, 162, 163, 261

    international, 192

    response to existential threats, 194

S

Shabbat, 38, 43, 44, 54, 55, 58, 61–63, 91, 150, 157, 196, 199, 201, 231, 258, 261, 262, 264, 269, 270, 271, 273–275

Shari'a, 235

Single parenthood, 115, 258, 260

Social Action, 165, 166, 174, 177, 180, 181, 199, 229, 230, 232, 233, 236–241, 247, 249, 250, 257, 260, 263, 265

T

Ten Spies, 8, 9

U

Universities

    anti-semitism on campus 127, 209, 211, 215, 221, 264, 266

    Jewish donations to, 122, 124–127, 139, 222, 263, 266

W
Wahhabism, 214, 216, 222
"Who Moved My Cheese?", 191
Women in Judaism
    Jewish women and marriage, 108–118
    Women and Jewish practice, 192, 196

Z
Zero Population Growth, 40, 44, 103